Demonic possession in the New Testament : its relations historical, medical, and theological

William Menzies Alexander

This work has been selected by scholars as being culturally important, and is part of the knowledge base of civilization as we know it. This work was reproduced from the original artifact, and remains as true to the original work as possible. Therefore, you will see the original copyright references, library stamps (as most of these works have been housed in our most important libraries around the world), and other notations in the work.

This work is in the public domain in the United States of America, and possibly other nations. Within the United States, you may freely copy and distribute this work, as no entity (individual or corporate) has a copyright on the body of the work.

As a reproduction of a historical artifact, this work may contain missing or blurred pages, poor pictures, errant marks, etc. Scholars believe, and we concur, that this work is important enough to be preserved, reproduced, and made generally available to the public. We appreciate your support of the preservation process, and thank you for being an important part of keeping this knowledge alive and relevant.

DEMONIC POSSESSION

IN THE

NEW TESTAMENT

*Its Relations
Historical, Medical, and Theological*

BY

WM. MENZIES ALEXANDER
M.A., B.Sc., B.D., C.M., M.D.

EDINBURGH
T. & T. CLARK, 38 GEORGE STREET
1902

54045

PRINTED BY
MORRISON AND GIBB LIMITED,

FOR

T. & T. CLARK, EDINBURGH.

LONDON: SIMPKIN, MARSHALL, HAMILTON, KENT, AND CO. LIMITED.
NEW YORK: CHARLES SCRIBNER'S SONS.

PREFACE

DEMONIC Possession in the New Testament is still an unsolved problem. That statement is at variance with a considerable body of opinion recently expressed on two Continents. Nevertheless, it is a correct representation of the present state of the case. Modern writers have attained a certain unanimity, only by approaching the subject from one point of view and confining attention to the more conspicuous phenomena. But any investigation which claims finality must explore the whole environment and scrutinise all residual facts. There is a comparative demonology to be studied; there are types of mental disease to be examined; there is a criterion of genuine possession to be discovered and applied. The inquiry thus broadens out and takes account of many points hitherto ignored or neglected. The whole subject thereby assumes a new complexion and has received restatement accordingly.

This work is an original research; not a compilation. Few authorities have therefore been directly quoted; but any one familiar with the vast literature concerned will readily perceive that previous writings are constantly in sight. The tactics of the controversialist have likewise been avoided as essentially unprofitable. The opinions of others have been combated where necessary; but by an array of facts rather than a war of words. This treatise is at most only a fragment. A large amount of material has been held *in retentis*, and many important questions have been left untouched. The conclusions attained have been reached independently, and are of a novel character. They confirm, in the highest degree, the claim of Christ to be considered the Good Physician and the Revealer of the Father.

WM. MENZIES ALEXANDER.

GLASGOW, *January* 1902.

CONTENTS

CHAPTER I

INTRODUCTORY

Composite relations of the subject. Views of Meyer, Farrar, Bruce, Wendt, Gould. The dilemma. The luminous background. The concrete investigation. The residual phenomenon. Application of the preceding results to the Beelzebul controversy, the Gerasene affair, the alleged continuance of possession 1–12

CHAPTER II

HISTORIC DEMONOLOGY

Demonology of the Old Testament. Shadow-figures. Degraded gods. A possessing demon. Demonology of the Septuagint. Continued iconoclasm. Spirits of the giants. Asmodæus. Rabbinic demonology. Recipe for seeing spirits. Their origin, numbers, forms, haunts, times of activity, powers, restrictions, management, redeeming features. Ethnic parallels. Christ and common demonology. Christ and common magic. Cause of Christ's superiority to superstition . . . 13–60

CHAPTER III

MEDICAL ASPECTS OF DEMONIC POSSESSION

Data of the present inquiry. Uses of a correct diagnosis. Simple epilepsy not possession. The Capernaum demoniac. The Gerasene demoniac. The epileptic idiot. *Significance of the demoniac state.* The Syro-Phœnician girl. The dumb demoniac. The blind-and-dumb demoniac. Mary Magdalene. The Philippian Pythoness. The Ephesian demoniac . 61–102

CHAPTER IV

MEDICAL ASPECTS OF DEMONIC POSSESSION—*continued*

Numbers of the possessed in the time of our Lord. Regions whence the possessed were brought. Capernaum as focus of the Eastern and Western Dispersions. Population of Palestine. Mental temperament of the people. Mental health of the people. Representations of the Gospels. Comparison of the Jews with the Greeks and the Romans. Comparison of the Jews with the peoples of the British Isles. Approximate estimate of the numbers of the possessed. Naturalness of the ethnic theory of possession. Naturalness of the terms "evil" and "unclean." Responsibility of the possessed. The treatment of the possessed among the Jews. Ethnic parallels. Comparative results. Christ and current methods of treatment. The psychological explanations of Strauss, Renan, Keim, Matthew Arnold. Their perpetual futility. Proofs of the expulsion of spirits 103–146

CHAPTER V

THE EXISTENCE OF GENUINE DEMONIC POSSESSION

Principles of investigation. Historicity of the narratives. *The criterion of genuine demonic possession.* Significance of the confession of Jesus as Messiah. Accident, clairvoyance, verbal information, genuine discrimination, as theories to explain this confession. Demonic inspiration, the only competent explanation. Classification of the possessed. Results of the same. Paucity of cases "self-attested." Their restriction to the early ministry of Christ. Proof of "the strong one" being bound. Antecedents of genuine demonic possession. Relation to moral depravity. Views of the Fathers, Lightfoot, Olshausen, Dieringer, Trench, Weiss. The fundamental error. Limits of genuine demonic possession. The moral and intellectual damage. The time-limit. Hypnotism not the true analogue of demonic action 147–175

CHAPTER VI

THE BEELZEBUL CONTROVERSY

Occasioned by the cure of idiots. Beelzebul neither Ashmedai nor Satan. The fly-gods of the ancients. The Scarab-Beetle. Baalzebub. Zeus and Hercules. Beelzebul, lord of dung or lord of the dwelling? Beelzebul as Bel-Ea-Mul-lil. Christ possessed of Beelzebul. Refutation of the Pharisaic theory. Proposal of a new alternative. The sign from hell. The parable of the last state. The sequel to this controversy. Why the Nine failed 174–193

CHAPTER VII

THE DIFFICULTIES OF THE GERASENE AFFAIR

Scene of the event. The Huxley-Gladstone controversy. Number of the demoniacs. *Folie à deux*. Alleged transmigration of the demons. Motives of the same. Failure of previous explanations. Data for a reconstruction. The facts and the theory. Not a case of manifold possession. No demonic supplication. Simple command of Jesus: Begone! The stampede of the swine. Theories of Paulus, Lange, Farrar, Rosenmüller, Lutteroth. Incompetency of the same. Fresh scrutiny of time, place, and incidents. Probable cause of the panic. Loss of the swine-owners. Possible reduction of it. Remarks of Wetstein and Heilprin. Inane criticisms of Woolston, Strauss, and Huxley 194–215

CHAPTER VIII

ALLEGED CONTINUANCE OF GENUINE DEMONIC POSSESSION

Possession in sub-apostolic times. Absence of "possession" from the Didache, the writings of Clement of Rome, Hermas, Barnabas, Ignatius, Polycarp, etc. Possession in ante-Nicene and post-Nicene times. Testimonies to theory and practice in the writings of Justin Martyr, Minucius Felix, Tertullian, Cyprian, Origen, Lactantius, Jerome, etc. Treatment of energumens. "The Bidding Prayer." Order of exorcists. Possession in mediæval and modern times. Gregory

  PAGES

the Great. The old demonism and the new diabolism.
Witchcraft. The demonomania of South-Eastern Europe.
The Dancing Manias. The convulsionnaires of France. The
demonolaters of India. The dervishes of Algiers. The
demoniacs of China. The cessation of genuine possession?
The peculiarity of the environment in the time of our Lord   216–249

APPENDICES

A.	Rabbinic Literature	250
B.	Nomenclature of the New Testament	251
C.	The Dumb Demoniac versus the Blind-and-Dumb Demoniac	253
D.	Fact-basis of the Ephesian Narrative	255
E.	The Mission of the Seventy	256
F.	Greek Demonology	259
G.	Greek Medicine	265
H.	Testimonies to the Success of Jesus	268
I.	Fallacies	269
J.	The Use of popular Language by Jesus	271
K.	The Demonising of the Heathen Gods	272
L.	Jesus out of His Senses	274
M.	Was Jesus nicknamed Beelzebul?	275
N.	Scene of the Healing of the Blind-and-Dumb Demoniac	276
O.	Did Jesus practise Accommodation?	277
P.	Ejection of Demons by Fasting	278
Q.	The popular Treatment of Epilepsy	280
R.	Witchcraft	280

INDEX 285–291

DEMONIC POSSESSION IN THE NEW TESTAMENT

CHAPTER I

INTRODUCTORY

THE anthropologist here finds himself on ground which he deems common to the races of the lower culture. The expert physician here discovers, in the phenomena of possession, indubitable evidence of mental disease. The student of Scripture, after utilising the best exegetical data, finds himself confronted by a fact to which he finds it difficult to assign any definite significance. The perplexities of the subject are really enormous, and have scarcely been realised as yet. History and medicine and theology have their separate contributions to make towards the solution of this problem; but the awkwardness of the situation lies in the fact that they persist in making these contributions separately. The result is a conflict of opinion or a suspense of judgment.

The trend of modern opinion is most easily

indicated by citing the views of a few eminent and fair-minded writers. These are set forth without prejudice to the detailed investigation of this vexed question.

According to Meyer,[1] the demoniacs of the Gospels were popularly regarded as persons possessed of demons; a view of the matter shared by the first Evangelist. The bodies of the possessed (οἱ δαιμονιζόμενοι) were thus looked upon as the seat and organ of demonic working. They were really sick persons, suffering from peculiar diseases (mania, epilepsy, delirium, hypochondria, paralysis, temporary dumbness); these being apparently inexplicable from physical causes, and believed therefore to have their foundation, not in an abnormal organisation or in natural disturbances of the physical condition, but in the actual indwelling of demonic personalities. Many of these might be counted in a single sick person. The belief is conceivable from the decay of the old theocratic consciousness and of its moral strength, which referred all misfortunes to the sending of God. This belief, however, rendered healing possible only through the acceptance of the existing view, leaving the latter untouched; but making the healing all the more certain for the Messiah, Who has power over the kingdom of devils, and Who now stood victoriously opposed to all diabolic power.

If it be assumed that Jesus Himself shared the opinion of His age and nation regarding the reality of

---

[1] *Commentary*, Matt. iv. 24.

possession by demons, then we must either set up the old doctrine on the authority of Jesus, or attribute to Him an error, not simply physiological, but essentially religious, and irreconcilable with the pure height of His divine knowledge.

Against the old view, apart from all physiological and medical objections, the following are urged as decisive:—

1. The non-occurrence of demoniacs in the Old Testament.
2. The undisputed healing of the same by many exorcists.
3. The non-occurrence of reliable instances in modern times.
4. The complete silence of the fourth Evangelist on the subject.
5. The absence from Paul's Epistles of definite references to expulsions.
6. The conduct of the demoniacs, who were not *at all* filled with godless dispositions and antichristian wickedness, which was necessarily to be expected as the result of the real indwelling of *devils*.

The opinion of Dean Farrar[1] is as follows: "So many good, able, and perfectly orthodox writers have, with the same data before them, arrived at different conclusions on this question, that any certainty respecting it appears to be impossible. My own view under these circumstances is of no particular import-

[1] *Life of Christ*, chap. xxiii.

ance, but it is this. I have shown that the Jews, like all unscientific nations in all ages, attributed many nervous disorders and physical obstructions to demoniac possession which we should attribute to natural causes; but I am not prepared to deny that in the dark and desperate age which saw the Redeemer's advent, there *may* have been forms of madness which owed their more immediate manifestation to evil powers. I should not personally find much hardship or difficulty in accepting such a belief, and have only been arguing against the uncharitable and pernicious attempt to treat it as a necessary article of faith for all. The subject is too obscure (even to science) to admit of dogmatism on either side." In connection with the cure of the Gerasene demoniac(s), Dean Farrar remarks: "If, indeed, we could be sure that Jesus directly encouraged or sanctioned in the man's mind the belief that the swine were indeed driven wild by the unclean spirits, which passed objectively from the body of the Gergesene into the bodies of those dumb beasts, then we could, without hesitation, believe as a literal truth, however incomprehensible, that so it was. But this by no means follows indisputably from what we know of the methods of the Evangelists."

The late Professor Bruce asserted[1] that in relation to the demonised "the most *certain* and, in that respect, the primary datum, was a real physical or mental disease. In every case of which we have

[1] *The Miraculous Element in the Gospels*, p. 177 ff.

details there was a disease, either madness, or epilepsy, or dumbness, or dumbness accompanied with blindness, or chronic muscular contraction. These diseases were as real as are the mental and nervous maladies with which our experience makes us familiar; and they must not be explained away because one happens to think that the notion of possession was a delusion. To those who are inclined to follow this course, these questions may be put: Were there no insane persons in Judæa in our Lord's day? were none of them cured by Him? and where is the record of them? That there were many such sufferers cannot be doubted; that many of them experienced the benefit of Christ's healing power, may also be taken for granted; and that the cure of maladies, so fitted to call forth sympathy, would be overlooked in the records, is not credible. But there is no account of any such cures, unless we find it in the narratives of the demoniacs." Our author then proceeds to compare the evidence, on this side and on that, regarding the objective reality of possession; his aim being the exhibition of the subject as one beset with difficulty on which it is excusable to be in suspense. Reference is made to the impression that the character of Christ is somehow involved, leading devout minds more than anything else to regard the reality of demoniacal possession as a matter not open to dispute. Further, it is said that if the veracity of Christ or His competency to guide men infallibly in moral and religious truth would be compromised by the denial of the reality of possession, no believer would hesitate to accept the same as an article of faith. Beyond securing or affirming the historicity of the Gospel narratives, the arguments for and against the objective reality of possession are virtually left in a state of equipoise.

The opinion of Professor Wendt[1] is that Jesus followed traditional ideas in regard to supernatural beings, whether good or bad; though He took quite a different view from that of His Jewish contemporaries regarding the significance of those spiritual agencies for the restoring or hindering of the health-giving intercourse of man with God. As far as the existence, nature, and ordinary mode of activity of these agents are concerned, Christ simply accepted the current ideas of His countrymen. The view that demoniac influences aim, not at immorality, but at the misery of man, was not original on the part of Jesus. In accordance with the vulgar conception, He specially regarded sickness as the result of demonic influence; and this mode of view was applied in a general way to all sicknesses. Thus, the woman with the spirit of infirmity is said to have been bound of Satan. In the case of certain extraordinary morbid phenomena, such as intermittent diseases, it was thought that the person was so possessed or indwelt by the demon, or in specially bad cases, by many demons, as to be made the powerless object of their pernicious dealings and the involuntary organ of their utterances. That Jesus had much to do with sick persons who passed for

[1] *The Teaching of Jesus*, i. pp. 161 ff., 296 ff.

demoniacs; that He regarded and treated them as possessed of real demons; and that He saw in their seizures a special task for Himself and His disciples, cannot be doubtful. This mode of view finds characteristic expression in the parable of the demon returning with seven others worse than himself. Not the possessed, but the malicious demons, were regarded as morally evil. Yet Jesus divested the Jewish idea of demons of its importance, which was detrimental to faith. It did not tend with Him as with them to superstitious fear and cowardice. He associated the idea of evil spirits with the absolute certainty of possessing, through God's help, such power over evil spirits that they must hearken and yield to Him and cease from injury. Jesus set aside the practical dualism of Jewish demonology. In the assurance that He was the Stronger One Who was able to conquer Satan, the strong one, and to spoil his goods, Jesus was able to aid effectively the demoniacs whom He met, and to command evil spirits with a voice of authority. The certainty of His power was but the reverse side of trust in the love and might of God.

Professor Gould thus regards the matter.[1] "The reality of demoniacal possession is a matter of doubt. The serious argument against it is that the phenomena are mostly natural, not supernatural. It was the unscientific habit of the ancient mind to account for abnormal and uncanny things, such as lunacy and

[1] International Critical Commentary, *Mark*, p. 23.

epilepsy, supernaturally. And in such cases outside of the Bible, we accept the facts, but ascribe them to natural causes. Another serious difficulty is that lunacy and epilepsy are common in the East as elsewhere, and yet, unless these are cases, we do not find Jesus healing these disorders as such, but only cases of demoniacal possession in which these were symptoms. The dilemma is very curious. Outside the New Testament, no demoniacal possession, but only lunacy and epilepsy; in the New Testament, no cases of lunacy and epilepsy proper, but only demoniacal possession."

No critique of these views is offered at this stage. Their limitations or errors reveal themselves hereafter. Nor need additional opinions be now cited.[1] The foregoing clearly prove the existence of an unsolved problem, and directly raise important apologetic issues. The subject has sometimes been discussed in the form of the dilemma: *Possession in the New Testament was either real or unreal.* Thence certain far-reaching inferences have been drawn.

A. *Possession real.*—Was this phenomenon, then, confined to Palestine and the ministry of our Lord? If so, what was peculiar in the environment? Or was this phenomenon neither local nor temporary?

---

[1] The views of Braun, Conybeare, Delitzsch, Ebrard, Edersheim, Ewald, Farmer, Geikie, Gfrörer, Gore, Lardner, Mead, Neander, Plummer, Pressensé, Row, Sanday, Schwartzkopff, Steinmeyer, Trench, Wetstein, Whitehouse, and a host of others, are implicitly in view throughout; but space forbids little more than the mention of their names.

If so, where are the instances of it to be discovered now?

B. *Possession unreal.*—Was Jesus, then, as ignorant and superstitious as His contemporaries? If so, can He still be taken as the guide of mankind in religion? Or did He accommodate Himself to the ignorance and superstition of the age? If so, what becomes of His integrity?

But this mode of approaching the subject is thoroughly vicious; because the dilemma begs the question at issue — the reality of demonic agency. It may be handled cleverly by the littérateur, but it leads to nothing. Any valid contribution to the solution of this problem must make a scientific examination of the fundamental facts, and thence work upwards towards such conclusions as are well founded. When that is done, the dilemma is seen to have no place in the discussion at all.

The narratives of possession in the New Testament have often been studied with much diligence but little profit; because their actual setting has been neglected. They have a distinct background which is capable of being made historically luminous. The current doctrine of demons among the Jewish people in the time of Christ is to be carefully set forth; not only as a separate system, but in relation to the ethnic creed. The superstitions of the period then become self-evident, and the attitude of Jesus towards them easily discovered from His Own teaching and practice.

The determination of the environment of the subject is a necessary preliminary to the question: What was possession? That is first to be considered in its medical aspects. The reports of possession are not all equally complete. Some are described with copious notes of the symptoms presented by the demoniacs; others are simply labelled "demoniac." The detailed study of the former leads to a scientific conception of the physical aspects of the "demoniac state." It is thus possible to pass from the known to the unknown. In every case a consistent and reliable diagnosis is attainable.

But medical science concerns itself also with the extent of this disorder, the areas affected, the factors of causation, the comparative condition of the Jews, and modes of treatment. It has a special interest in the method of Christ, both as regards its uniqueness and its efficiency. This science alone can gauge the worth of the psychological explanations now prevalent. In making these researches it renders a most important service to Apologetics.

But beyond the discovery of the physical significance of the "demoniac state" lies the question of "possession" being *more* than a purely pathological condition. That initiates a further inquiry whose data are the notices contained in the Gospels. These indicate the existence of a residual feature, superadded to the former. That residual factor becomes the criterion of genuine demonic possession, surviving all naturalistic explanations. It attaches itself to a few cases only, and determines two types of "possession" in the New Testament. The cases "self-attested" belong to the earlier portion of the ministry of our Lord, their absence from its later phases being proof that "the strong one" was already bound. By the application of this criterion also, the antecedents and the limits of genuine demonic possession are capable of being determined.

The preceding discussions permit a new departure in the study of three outstanding problems — the Beelzebul controversy, the Gerasene affair, and the continuance of possession. Each of these has a special interest and importance.

1. The Beelzebul controversy gives us a deep insight into the superstitions of the period. It had its natural beginning and middle and end in the cure of some of the worst forms of "possession." The appeal to "the prince of demons" introduces us to Bel-Ea of the Babylonians. The scribes and Pharisees were immersed in the pseudo-science of their times; the Nine were crippled by the same. Jesus alone is mighty in deed and in word, being in a supreme degree—Medicus et Illuminator.

2. The Huxley-Gladstone controversy brought some of the difficulties of the Gerasene affair into prominence. It contributed little or nothing to the removal of them, as the discussion ended in an obscure and trifling side-issue. The difficulties of the story are real; but a restatement of the whole case has now become possible. The reports of the Evangelists still leave a few details uncertain; but further research

shows that the chief stumbling-blocks of the story, physical, legal, moral, and spiritual, admit of a satisfactory solution.

3. The alleged continuance of possession from the time of Christ onwards to the present, can now be discussed to advantage. The illumination of the Apostolic Fathers led them to discard crude ethnic superstitions; but these returned in the writings of the Apologists and others; maintaining themselves in some sort from age to age. Genuine demonic possession, as set forth in the New Testament, contains an element that is natural, another that is supernatural. The former belongs to the category of mental disease, and still continues; the latter belongs to the category of Satanic opposition, and was summarily suppressed. In this department, the words of our Lord have a valid application: *Now is the crisis of this world: now shall the prince of this world be cast out.*

CHAPTER II

HISTORIC DEMONOLOGY

THE doctrine of demonic possession is but a fragment of the doctrine of demons in general. The latter constitutes the setting of the former, and cannot be understood apart from it. This environment, therefore, requires the most careful scrutiny first of all. From the study of it, interesting and important results immediately accrue.

DEMONOLOGY OF THE OLD TESTAMENT

The Old Testament repeatedly refers to demons; but its rigid application of the monotheistic principle placed them outside the pale of the pure religion of Israel. They were excluded from public recognition as objects of worship and adoration. There is a vague conception of them as something "between the divine and the human."[1] Some are mere "shadow-figures," others are degraded gods, one is a possessing spirit.

A. Some shadow-figures

These are mostly the relics of ancient superstitions

[1] Cf. Plato, *Symposium*, 202 D, Μέταξυ θεοῦ τε καὶ θνητοῦ.

or imaginations. In ethnic phraseology they may be called good or evil, *i.e.* helpful or harmful; for the distinction is not ethical, but economic.

1. *The good.*—By implication, these are discoverable in the Fountain of Judgment at Kadesh (Gen. xiv. 7); in the dread sanctity of the oath by the Seven Wells (Gen. xxi. 31; Amos viii. 14); in the unchallenged use of the Teraphim (1 Sam. xix. 13; Hos. iii. 4); in the animated rod of the diviner (Hos. iv. 12); in the fairy hosts and tree spirits (Can. ii. 7, iii. 5).[1] These appear to belong to the dawn of history, and may be regarded as part of the heritage of primitive races.

2. *The evil.*—These are suggestive of an antiquity equal to the former, and fall into two divisions.

(*a*) *Creatures haunting the waters.*—These recall the Creation Legend of Cutha and the Babylonian Myths of Berosus. Their importation from the East is possible. The founder of the Hebrew race came from Ur of the Khasdim (Gen. xi. 31). It was then a busy seaport near the mouth of the Euphrates; though now remote from the sea by the rapid silting of the channel. The early settlers on the site of Ur (Mugheir) must have long maintained a strenuous conflict against river floods and tidal inundations; not less than against the serpents of the marshes and the strange creatures of the deep. Reminiscences of these early struggles may have passed westwards and remained as survivals in the poetry of the Hebrews,

---

[1] Cf. Baudissin, *Studien zur Semitischen Religionsgeschichte.*

celebrating the ancient triumphs of God over elemental forces and the beasts of the sea. These are glanced at in the following and other passages:—

Rahab	Job ix. 13.
Tannin	Isa. xxvii. 1.
The Sea	Ps. lxxiv. 13.
Leviathan	Isa. xxvii. 1.
Sea Serpent	Amos ix. 3.

(*b*) *Creatures haunting the desert.*—There are two passages in Isaiah which in their present form may be post-exilic, but which are charged with ideas essentially primeval.

The oracle concerning the desolation of Babylon: Wild cats of the desert shall lie there; their houses shall be full of doleful creatures; ostriches shall dwell there, and Seirim shall dance there.[1] And wolves shall cry in their castles, and jackals in their pleasant palaces (Isa. xiii. 21, 22).

The oracle concerning the desolation of Edom: Wild cats of the desert shall meet with the wolves,[2] and the satyr shall cry to his fellow; yea, Lilith shall settle there, and shall find her a place of rest. There shall the arrow-snake make her nest, and lay, and hatch, and gather under her shadow" (Isa. xxxiv. 14, 15).

The creatures here enumerated seem to correspond to the Jinn of the Southern Semites. The primitive

---

[1] Seirim shall dance there; LXX: Δαιμόνια ἐκεῖ ὀρχηθήσονται.
[2] Wild cats of the desert shall meet with the wolves; LXX: Συναντήσουσι δαιμόνια ὀνοκενταύροις (tailless apes. Aelian, *Hist. Nat.*).

sons of the desert are always moving as in an enchanted land. The fierce glare of the sun and the unequal refraction of the atmosphere play strange tricks with the vision of the traveller; so that on the horizon, the skulking denizens of the desert assume the most paradoxical forms, even without the aid of the imagination. Then, when the daylight dies, the beasts of the wild come forth and the scene becomes a howling desert, where strange forms, in awful guise, flit hither and thither, half-concealed and half-revealed; assailing the ear with dismal voices. By day or night on the open waste, the wanderer or huntsman finds himself confronted by beings superior to himself in strength, agility, cunning, and keenness of vision. These he invests with superhuman attributes as objects of dread or veneration, to be vanquished by spells or appeased by offerings. Hence the Jinn are a numerous host; corporeal, mutable at will, assuming at times the human form, always retaining some bestial trait. Shagginess is a frequent feature; and that is the special trait of the Seirim. The name is variously applied to "goats" (Lev. iv. 24), "devils" (Lev. xvii. 7), "satyrs" (Isa. xiii. 21). The term readily includes such goat-like creatures (*cavicornia*) as the gazelle. The serpent, the ostrich, the wild cat, the wolf, the jackal, and the gazelle, belong distinctly to the Jinn of the Southern Semites.[1]

Lilith has features attaching her also to the Jinn, though a Babylonian origin has been claimed for her.

---

[1] W. R. Smith, *Religion of the Semites*, p. 121 ff.

Sayce asserts that *lil* is the dust-storm, and the name was applied to ghosts whose food was dust. When the word was borrowed by the Semites, it became *lillum* (masc.), and *lilatu* (fem.). Lilatu was the handmaid of the *lil*, and soon came to be confounded with the Semitic *lilatu*—the night. The latter was ultimately identified with Lilat, the night-demon that sucked the blood of her sleeping victims.[1] But the Babylonian extraction of Lilith is not thereby proven. Her nearest counterpart is not the vampire, but the ghul. The foregoing congeners of Lilith are dwellers in the desert; and in the Targum on Job i. 15, Lilith is the queen of Zemargad. Now Zemargad is Sheba.[2] There seems no need to postulate exilic or post-exilic influence to account for more than the name Lilith. This creature belongs apparently to a far-off age.

B. *The degraded gods*

In picturesque language the prophets had long carried on a vigorous polemic against the claims of the heathen divinities. A few instances of this rich vein of oriental scorn are subjoined. The gods are derided as—

Lies	Amos ii. 4.
Breath	Deut. xxxii. 21.
No-god	Jer. xvi. 20.

---

[1] Sayce, *Hibbert Lectures*, pp. 145, 146. Cf. Maspero, *Dawn of Civilisation*, p. 632. The vampire is the dead of either sex, that leaves the grave to suck the blood of the sleeper. Such is the *'aluqam* (עלקם) of Prov. xxx. 15, otherwise the "horse-leech."

[2] The modern Yemen in South Arabia.

Blocks	Ezek. xx. 7.
Carcases	Lev. xxvi. 30.
Emptiness	1 Sam. xii. 21.
Nothing	Ps. xcvi. 5.

The stern logic of events had demonstrated at once the utter impotence of the heathen gods as effective agents in history, and the peerlessness of Jehovah as Governor among the nations. The pretensions of those deities were completely exposed, and their worship in Israel was forthwith discountenanced. A fatal blow was struck at their supremacy. They became "lies," "emptiness," and "nothings." Deprived thus of public recognition and support, they sank to that vague position which the conventions of the East assign to demonic creatures. But their viability was not impaired. Over their pagan devotees they were still supposed to exercise authority (Judg. xi. 24). Yet for the true worshippers of Jehovah they were practically non-existent. A pure monotheism had transmuted them into an absolutely *negligible quantity*. They were but impotent Shedim, and mere nothings. In two passages this wholesale reduction of heathen gods to the rank of demons is set forth—

They sacrificed to Shedim, to no-god. Deut. xxxii. 17.
They sacrificed their sons and their daughters to Shedim. Ps. cvi. 37.

The name Shedim — once derived from the Hebrew שׁוּד—is now regarded as a Babylonian loan-word—Shidu, a genius, good or evil; represented by the bull-colossus. This demonising of the heathen gods has been ascribed to Babylonian influence. That is surely a mistake; for this process is the result of the monotheistic principle which asserted that Jehovah was the first and the last, and that beside Him there was no God.

This reduction of the heathen divinities to the rank of demons is unique in Israel in regard to monotheism, which was its motive. But the relegation of heathen gods to positions of dishonour is a process which is always going forward. Polytheism is essentially in a state of unstable equilibrium. Its deities are constantly in a state of flux. The Indian sage quaintly remarks that "many thousands of Indras have passed away in course of time, in every age of the world." Indeed, wars and revolutions have not been more fateful to earthly potentates than to pagan divinities; while barbaric caprice and unlettered philosophy have often caused them to shrivel up to the dimensions of subaltern spirits. Thus, Baal and Set, the gods of the Shepherd-Kings, became the possessing spirits of the later Egyptians. The Vedic Dævas, originally the gods in heaven, are now the demons of the Parsees. The Brahmanic deities of the ancient Cingalese survive as the demons of Buddhistic Ceylon. The classical divinities of Greece and Rome were transmuted into the demons of the early Christians. The gods of the old heathen Arabs are counted among the Jinn of Islamic Arabia.

C. *A possessing demon*

It has been repeatedly asserted that "possession" is unknown to the Old Testament. Keim declared it "a modern disease among the Jews." That is virtually the opinion of Meyer also. But the case of Saul is undoubtedly to be regarded as one of possession by an evil spirit. The terms describing the mode of action of this spirit are analogous to those which set forth the action of the Holy Spirit upon man; but the effects produced are those attributed by the ethnic creed to possessing spirits.

Of Saul it is said—

When the evil spirit of Elohim is upon (על) thee. 1 Sam. xvi. 16.
The evil spirit of Elohim came upon (אל) Saul. 1 Sam. xviii. 10.
The evil spirit of Jahveh came upon (אל) Saul. 1 Sam. xix. 9.

Of the Spirit of God it is said—

The spirit of Elohim came upon (על) him. Num. xxiv. 2.
The spirit of Jahveh came upon (על) him. Judg. iii. 10.
The spirit of Jahveh shall come upon (על) thee. 1 Sam. x. 6.
The spirit of Elohim came upon (על) Azariah. 2 Chron. xv. 1.
The spirit of Jahveh shall rest upon (על) him. Isa. xi. 2.

The evil spirit terrifies Saul (1 Sam. xvi. 14); when it leaves him, he is well (1 Sam. xvi. 23); when it returns, he is ill (1 Sam. xviii. 10); it causes him to prophesy (rave) in his house (1 Sam. xviii. 10); it incites him to murder (1 Sam. xix. 9, 10). The nomenclature and the details of the narrative fully confirm the opinion that Saul's illness was regarded as demonic in nature.

DEMONOLOGY OF THE SEPTUAGINT

The translation of the Hebrew Scriptures into Greek was undertaken in Alexandria under Ptolemy Philadelphus (284–246 B.C.), and completed somewhere about 150 B.C. The work is of very unequal merit, and the translators manifest a freedom which is variously traceable to prejudice, insight, or ignorance. It shows that the demonising of the heathen gods was still proceeding apace, as the following parallels indicate:—

1. Ps. xcvi. (xcv.) 5—

    All the gods of the heathen are nothings.
    All the gods of the heathen are demons.
    Πάντες οἱ θεοὶ τῶν ἐθνῶν δαιμόνια.

2. Isa. lxv. 3—

    Burning incense upon bricks.
    They burn incense upon bricks (to demons that are not).
    Θυμιῶσιν ἐπὶ ταῖς πλίνθοις τοῖς δαιμονίοις ἃ οὐκ ἔστιν.

3. Isa. lxv. 11—

    Ye are they that prepare a table for Fortune.
    Preparing also a table for the demon.
    Ἑτοιμάζοντες τῷ δαιμονίῳ τράπεζαν.

4. Ps. xci. (xc.) 6—

    For the destruction that wasteth at noonday.
    For mischance and the demon of noonday.
    Ἀπὸ συμπτώματος καὶ δαιμονίου μεσημβρινοῦ.

The demon of noonday is a novel figure which can hardly owe its origin to a flaw in the Hebrew text.[1] The adjacent discrepancies of the Septuagint lead to the belief that the translation is here very free. The

[1] ושד for ישוד.

idea that demons devote their attention to certain portions of the day is an ethnic one. Theocritus, who visited Alexandria shortly before the translation of the Hebrew Scriptures into Greek, warns the shepherd against playing on his pipe at noon, lest he disturb the noonday rest of Pan.[1] The same thought recurs in the literature of the Babylonians, the Persians, and other peoples.

DEMONOLOGY OF THE APOCRYPHAL AND APOCALYPTIC BOOKS

The iconoclasm which transformed the gods into demons still continues here. In the Book of Enoch reference is made to those who "worship foul spirits and demons" (xcix.); the angels being charged as they that led men thus astray (xix.). In the Sibylline Oracles, it is written: Ye shall have the reward of your evil council; because, neglecting the true and everlasting God, ye have made your sacrifices to the demons in Hades (Proem 19–22). Rome is censured for worshipping "soulless demons, ghosts of the departed dead" (viii. 47). Demons are also said to have blood poured out to them (viii. 386), and are again scorned as "dead" (viii. 393). In the Book of Baruch mention is made of sacrificing to demons and not to God (iv. 7).

The story of the fallen Bene-Elohim of Gen. vi. 2, was greatly exploited in later times, and a doctrine of

[1] *Idylls*, i. 15–18.

demons was attached to it. According to the Book of Enoch, the giants produced " from spirit and flesh will be called evil spirits upon the earth, and on earth will be their habitation. Evil spirits proceed from their bodies because they are created from above: from the Heavenly Watchers is their beginning and primal origin. They will be evil spirits upon the earth, and evil spirits will they be named. And the spirits of the giants will devour, oppress, attack, do battle, cause destruction on earth, and work affliction. They will rise up against the children of men and against the women (xv., xvi.)."

In the Book of Jubilees, demons are said to arise from the fallen angels. They harass and deceive the sons of Noah; whereupon the patriarch prays, and the good angels bind them. But Mastemah, their chief, entreated that some of them might be left to do his will. So one tenth were left; but the remainder were reserved for judgment. These demons introduced diseases, which the good angels taught Noah how to combat by the use of medicine and herbs. God rules over Israel to the good of the nation; but angels and demons lord it over the Gentiles with disastrous results (v. x.).

In the Testimony of the Twelve Patriarchs, man is said to have received seven spirits—life, sight, hearing, smell, speech, taste, procreation. With these Beliar has mingled spirits of error—fornication, greed, pugnacity, flattery, arrogance, falsehood, injustice (Reub. 2, 3). Spirits of error, spirits of fornication and pride, are also mentioned (Dan. 5). These are, however, personifications rather than specific entities.

In the Book of Tobit, Sarah the daughter of Raguel is beloved of a jealous demon (vi. 15), who has killed her seven husbands in the bridal chamber (iii. 8). This demon is not a danger to Sarah personally, but to the newly-wedded husbands. His name, Asmodæus, is not derivable from the Hebrew שמד, to destroy; though Shamdon is found in the Talmud. He is the Æshma-Dæva of the Zend-Avesta. According to Darmesteter, the davas by an accident of language became demons.[1] According to the same authority, Æshma-Dæva belongs to the group of the storm demons—the Drvants, Dvarants, Dregvants — "the running ones."[2] The leader of the onset is Æshma—"the raving"—"the fiend of the wounding spear." At first Æshma was a mere epithet of the storm fiend, but afterwards became an abstract, viz. the demon of rage and anger; finally, an expression for all moral wickedness, a mere name of Ahriman. Windischmann, Fritzsche, and others translate the name as "covetous," "lustful." Fuller has taken the attribute as Babylonian; though the name be Persian. There are certain features answering to the description of the Babylonian spirits—

> Wife they have not, son they know not,
> Prayer and supplication hear they not.
>
> They snatch the wife from the husband's embrace,
> They drive the man from the bridal chamber.

---

[1] *Zend-Avesta*, vol. i. lxxx.   [2] *Ibid.* vol. i. lxvii.

But such traits are not the monopoly of the Babylonian spirits. An incident of a similar nature, tacitly demonic, befalls Zoroaster.[1] Indeed, the demon-lover is frequently encountered in the study of anthropology. Accepting Asmodæus as undoubtedly of Persian origin, it is, nevertheless, impossible to accept the view of Kohut, who sees in this demon a triple combination of Persian attributes—

>Angro-Mainyu, the death-angel.
>Akom-mano or evil concupiscence.
>Azi-Dahaka, the triple-headed serpent.

That produces a monster of deadliness, passion, and craft which is without parallel elsewhere, and enormously in excess of the simple remedies employed under the direction of the angel Raphael, for getting rid of Asmodæus—the heart and liver of the magic fish on embers of ashes (Tob. vi. 16, viii. 2).

RABBINIC DEMONOLOGY [2]

The Rabbis had one comprehensive category for the powers of evil—the Mazziqin or Hurtful Ones. Supreme over all was Satan-Sammael, "the angel, the offender, the head of all the satans" (Debar. R. C. 11). These Mazziqin consisted of two sections: one composed of *purely spiritual beings*, the other of *half-spirits* (halbgeister). The latter are variously designated as Shedim, Seirim, Ruchin, Ruchoth, and Lilin.

[1] *Zend-Avesta*, vol. ii. p. 195.
[2] Appendix A, Rabbinic Literature.

The doctrine of demons is highly developed, and lays claim to direct verification. The following is the elegant preparation for opening the eyes:—

Whosoever desires to see the demons, let him take the after-birth of a black cat which is also the daughter of a black cat, both being firstborn. Let him burn it in the fire; then powder it. Seal the powder in an iron tube with an iron signet; then fill the eyes with it (Ber. 6*a*). It is said that Rabbi Bibi performed this experiment with complete success; but was hurt by the demons. He was, however, restored to health by the intercession of the Rabbis. Such an adventurous *séance*, with this ingenious eye salve, ought to carry conviction regarding the truth of the Rabbinic doctrine of demons to the minds of the most sceptical.

Origin.—That is variously reported. Thus, the demons were created on the eve of the first Sabbath (Pes. 54*a*). Their souls were ready: but the Sabbath drew on before their bodies were prepared. Creation was ended, and thus they remained (Pirqe Abh. 12*b*; Ber. R. 7). Again, they are the progeny of Adam and Eve, during the one hundred and thirty years which elapsed before the birth of Seth. The demons are the offspring of Adam on the one hand, with Lilith or the Lilin; or of Eve on the other, with the Shedim (Erub. 18*b*; Ber. R. 20). Another account derives them from that section of the race which was scattered abroad at the building of the tower of Babel. At "the time of scattering," those who said, We will ascend into heaven, were transformed into Shedim, Ruchin, Lilin, and monkeys" (Sanh. 109a: Yalkut Shim. Ber. 62). Some are derived from a male hyena, which in successive periods of seven years becomes a bat, a vampire, a nettle (thistle), a thorn, a demon (Baba Kamma 16a). Demons are also said to arise from the backbone of him who has not bent in worship (Baba Kamma 16a; Jer. Shab. 36). Being male and female, they propagate their kind. Mention is made of the son of a Shed (Chag. 16a). Ahriman is the son of Lilith (Baba Bathra 73a). Demons may be the souls of the wicked dead (Yalkut Shim. Is. 46b; Jos. B. J. VII. vi. 3).[1]

Numbers.—The whole world is full of the Mazziqin (Tanch. Mish. 19). Lilith, the queen of female demons, roams about with eighteen myriads in her train (Pes. 112b). Abba Benjamin says that if our eyes were permitted to see the malignant spirits that beset us, we could not rest on account of them. R. Hunna mentions one thousand at the left hand, ten thousand at the right.[2] Shedim swarm round brides: and in the Academies they cause crowding and the feeling of weariness in the knees of the Rabbis;[3] even wearing out the clothes of the sages by hustling

---

[1] Josephus here contradicts one of the tenets of his own sect; as he elsewhere asserts that the Pharisees held that "souls have an immortal vigour in them, and that under the earth there will be rewards or punishments, according as they have lived virtuously or viciously in this life; and the latter are to be retained in an everlasting prison" (*Ant.* XVIII. i. 3; cf. *B. J.* II. viii. 14).

[2] Cf. Ps. xci. 7. [3] Bruising of the legs?

against them (Ber. 6a). Three hundred species of male demons are mentioned in Gittin 68a.

Forms.—Their appearance is mostly human; but they assume other forms at will. Their reflection, however, is different from that of a man. Those associated with dirty places are themselves black (Kidd. 72a). Those that dwell in the caper bushes are blind (Pes. 111b). In three things they resemble angels—they possess wings, they can fly from one end of the earth to the other, they know the future by listening behind the veil of the Upper Sanctuary. In three things they are like men—they eat and drink, they produce their kind, they are subject to death (Chag. 16a). Demons have the feet of fowls, and by strewing the floor with fine ashes, their gallinaceous footprints may be discovered (Ber. 6a; Gittin 68b). Lilith is sometimes represented as a fair woman, but mostly covered with luxuriant hair (Nidd. 24b; Erub. 100b). A demon appeared in the school of Abaji, a dangerous seven-headed monster, injuring the men in pairs, even in the daytime. Some demons have round their faces a covering like asses driving a mill (Tanch. Mish. 19). When conjured up, the Shedim appear with head or feet uppermost, according to the mode of conjuring.

Haunts.—Demons infest all places. The atmosphere is charged with them. They invade the Upper Sanctuary itself. Abaji says that they surround us as earthed-up soil in garden beds. They are thus at the elbows of the living everywhere. They lurk in crumbs on the floor, and rest on the surface of drinking water, and on oil in vessels. They are set over all even numbers, and care must therefore be taken not to drink an even number of cups (Ber. 51b). They are found on hands that remain unwashen for religious purposes, and on water that has been thus used. The blind prefer caper bushes for their abode. These things annoy demons—turning in between a wall and a date-palm or between two date-palms, drinking borrowed water, or stepping across spilt water (Pes. 111a). Shadows cast by the moon, certain trees, and other objects may be the lurking place of demons. The places of uncleanness are highly congenial to them. Graveyards are their favourite resorts (Nidd. 17a; Chag. 3, 6). When a man spends a night there, a demon may descend upon him. "The searcher after the dead" remained fasting on a grave to get into touch with an unclean spirit.[1] Ruins should not be entered on account of these foes (Ber. 3a). Ruined baths are their beloved haunts. There they may cause injury in the daytime, even in the presence of two men (Kidd. 39b). One ought not to sleep in a house alone, for fear of Lilith (Shab. 151b). Demons invade the Academies. Samaria and Tiberias had their local Shedim.[2] The desert is, however, their special home (Ber. 3a). There one may hear them howl (Jer. Targ. I. Deut. xxxii. 10). They may be connected with certain animals, such as the mad dog;

[1] Cf. Isa. lxv. 4.
[2] The latter was built on the site of an old burying-ground.

apparently also with the fly of Egypt, the wasp of Nineveh, the scorpion of Hadabiah, the serpent of the land of Israel (Shab. 121*b*). The stubborn ass and the bull from the cane-brake are likewise associated with demons. In the case of the latter, one is warned not to face the bull; for a satan sports between his horns (Pes. 112*b*).

Times of activity.—The demons form themselves into bands (Ber. 51*a*), "the society of the angels of destruction." According to the same passage, a whole legion lies in wait for a person to fall into their hands, on the commission of some fault. Their action is thus a kind of obsession which may readily pass into possession. The demons have been arranged in four classes, according to the divisions of the day—

Tsaphririn or morning spirits (Targ. Ps. cxxi. 16; Targ. Cant. iv. 6).

Tiharin or midday spirits (Targ. Ps. Jon. Deut. xxxii. 24; Targ. Cant. iv. 6).

Telanin or evening spirits (Targ. Cant. iii. 8, iv. 6; Targ. Eccles. ii. 5).

Lilin or night spirits (Targ. Ps. Jon. Deut. xxxii. 34; Targ. Is. xxxiv. 14).

The morning and evening spirits seem least baleful. The midday demons start at noon to destroy (Targ. 2 Chron. xi. 15; Ps. xci. 7). The Lilin are the most malignant. On account of them it is particularly dangerous to drink water on the eve of Wednesday or the Sabbath. To do so is to have one's blood on one's own head. Similarly, the night-traveller has to brave great perils on these occasions also (Pes. 112a b). This is said to have been due to the imprudent generosity of Rabbi Chanina, who had once been threatened with serious harm by Agrath, the daughter of Machloth. He escaped, because his greatness was known in heaven; and he would have imposed his majesty on the demoness by banning her from all inhabited places. In the end, however, he gave her liberty for the occasions mentioned. The Lilin are specially deadly to children who venture out of the house during the hours of darkness. Even for adults the night was reckoned most unsafe without a torch: though moonlight was far safer. Under cover of darkness, demons surround the house and injure those that fall into their hands. The risk of going out to unclean places was enormous (Shab. 67a; Ber. 3a b, 62a). A company of two generally escaped the danger, but not always (Kidd. 39b). Before three persons the Shed did not even venture to appear (Ber. 43b). No one should greet a person in the dark, as he might unwittingly wish a demon Godspeed (Sanh. 44a). Shabriri was always a menace to those who drank water by night. Unless special precautions were taken, such individuals rushed into the danger of death. At cock-crow, the power of the demons of the night comes to an end, and they return to their places (Ber. R. 36).

Powers.—These have been in part adverted to: but others remain which are peculiar and varied. Demons have the gift of speech; and Rabbi Ben Zacchai knew their language as well as that of the angels (Succah 28a). They know the future and the past, so that they may be consulted in both respects; but questions about lost property had better not be directed to them on the Sabbath (Sanh. 101a). Accidents, such as an encounter with a bull, are traceable to them. Chamath, the demon of oil, causes eruptions on the face; Cardicus (Cardiacus) is a demon that rules over those who take too much wine; also causing headache (Gittin 77b). Asinam causes the birth of epileptic children on Sabbath night. Asmodæus tempted Noah, saying to the planter of the vine, Let me partake with thee.[1] Shabriri smites with blindness at night. Bath-Chorin is a demoness of sickness, resting on the hands at night. Disease in general is caused by demons. Sick women, at and after childbirth; also brides, bridegrooms, mourners, and the pupils of the Rabbis, are specially obnoxious to the demons of darkness (Ber. 54b). To demons are ascribed leprosy (Horayoth 10a), rabies (Yoma 83b), croup (Yoma 77b; Taanith 20b), asthma (Bekhoroth 44b), cardiac disease (Gittin 67b). Nervous diseases are the speciality of evil demons; such as epilepsy (Shab. Bab. 67a; Jos. *Ant.* VI. viii. 2, VIII. ii. 5). Rambanus says that the Jews held that all kinds of melancholy were due to an evil spirit.[1] Bodily distortions and mental distractions were thus produced.[1] Shibta causes convulsive ailments among children,

---

[1] Lightfoot, *Horæ Hebraicæ*. See on Luke xi. 15, xiii. 14; Matt. xviii. 15.

specially at night. Possessing spirits are always busy. Among the humbler functions of the Shedim was the sending of evil dreams (Ber. 55*b*), or compelling a man to go beyond the Sabbath boundary (Erub. 41*b*), or inducing one to eat the passover-bread (Rosh-ha-Shanah 28*a*), or causing a religious crank to afflict himself with fasting (Bab. Taanith 22*b*).

Restrictions. — Life would be intolerable if the demons had all their own way. But, like Satan-Sammael, they are under strict limitations. They are "half-spirits"; and are therefore possessed of a semi-sensuous or psycho-sarcous constitution. This imposes upon them many restrictions. They require sustenance; and that they find in certain essences, or in the elements of fire and water. Wine is a great abomination to them as to Ashmedai, their chief. Pungent odours or loathsome smells are equally detested by them. The blind may suffer death by misadventure. One such pursued a Rabbi; but tripped over a root and was killed (Pes. 111*b*). In any case, all of them are mortal. They are said to be unable to create anything. They can produce nothing, save their own kind. They have no power over what has been measured or sealed or tied up (Chullin 105*b*). According to their divisions, their activities are confined to the hours, the days, and the environments noted. On the evening of the Passover, they are bound (Pes. 109*b*–112*b*). The loss of the divine image has rendered man subject to those agents of mischief and destruction. Originally he was immune from such attacks (Ber. R. 23).

Management.—By human agency, further curtailments of the powers of demons become possible. Torchlight by night, washing of hands, ablutions against Shibta, phylacteries, and amulets, are all protective. The last might or might not contain a verse of Scripture, but magic formulæ instead, the worth of which seems to have been inversely proportional to their rationality. Along with these had to be inserted the names and numbers of the demons aimed at. To ward off danger anticipated from drinking water on the eve of Wednesday or the Sabbath, it was enough to repeat the formula: Lul, Shaphan, Anigron, Anirdaphin,—between the stars I sit, between the fat and the lean I walk (Pes. 112*b*). If alone by night and compelled to drink, one might scare away Shabriri thus. The person struck with the lid of the jug into the jug, saying: Thou N. the son of N., thy mother has warned thee and said: Beware of Shabriri, Beriri, Riri, Iri, Ri, who is in the white cups (Abod. Zara 12*b*). According to Rashi, the demon gets weaker as each syllable of his name is dropped, and at last he flees in terror. But sometimes the drinking of water was reckoned too dangerous to be attempted at all. To neutralise the danger arising from having to step over spilt water, it was necessary to spit on the water or to take the shoes off (Pes. 111*a*). The application of rouge removed "The Princess," a demoness injurious to the eyes

(Shab. 109a). The covenant salt (Lev. ii. 13; Num. xviii. 19), eaten and drunk at every meal, has great defensive virtue (Ber. 40a). Circumcision was apparently held in much esteem (Origen, C. C. v. 48). The keeping of certain ordinances, such as the Feast of Tabernacles, was likewise deemed useful (Pesiqta 187a). To jump four cubits, or to repeat the Shema: "Hear, O Israel, the Lord our God is one Lord," was reckoned potent against evil spirits. If the place were not fit for repetition, then a person might mutter: The goat at the butcher's is fatter than I (Sanh. 94a). The demon of foul places had this hurled at him: On the head of the lion and on the nose of the lioness, I found the demon, Bar-Shiriqa Panda. I cast him into a bed of cresses and beat him with the jawbone of an ass (Shab. 67a). Among the more laudable means of managing demons was the simple recitation of passages of Scripture, such as Ps. xci., before falling asleep; or Ps. xxix. 3–9, containing the "qol" or voice, seven times. Prayer also takes high rank among agencies, prophylactic and remedial. By this means, Rabbi Acha was more than a match for the seven-headed monster which infested the school of Abaji; the seven heads dropping off with the lowly genuflections of the Rabbi (Kidd. 29b). The pronunciation of the Aaronic blessing by the priest affords defence. The keeping is done by the guardian angels whom God assigns to the faithful. So long as the angel calls to the Mazziqin, "Give honour to the image of the Holy One," man remains in peace; but when he is silent, man is injured (Tanch. Mish. 19). Mention is often made of sacrifices to demons (Targ. Onk. Lev. xvii. 7). All the Shedim may be vanquished by the Ineffable Name (Ber. 5a). The management of the possessing demons receives separate treatment.

Redeeming features.—While most of the demons were said to be hostile to man, some were believed to be harmless or even helpful. These constitute the class of the good demons, whose existence added to the glory of God. Some of them were learned in the Law and were even tutors of the Rabbis; such as the Shed, Joseph (Pes. 110a), and the Shed, Jonathan (Yeb. 122a). Rabbi Papa had a young Shed to wait on him (Chullin 105b). Demons might at times be eminently reasonable. Thus, the prince of demons once detected a Rabbi distributing alms at night. This was a manifest infringement of the demon's nocturnal rights, and the latter aptly quoted the words, Thou shalt not remove thy neighbour's landmark. With equal wit and courtesy the Rabbi replied, A gift in secret pacifieth anger. Thereupon the demon fled (Ber. Peah viii. 9). To conjure up and to make use of demons, even on the Sabbath, was considered legitimate, but dangerous; unless ample precautions were taken (Sanh. 65a b). Any latent danger might be warded off by wily conjurors who knew how to render their demons innocuous (Sanh. 67b; Pes. 110b). Still, several accidents did happen. R. Isaac had a parlous experience with a wrathful demon. He was saved only by a cedar tree thoughtfully opening of its own accord to receive him; then bursting again to set him free when the danger was over (Sanh. 101a). Death is said to have overtaken certain operators; but that supposes contributory negligence. The Egyptian magicians, by demonic help, withstood Moses. In the same way, all that the prophets and great men of the past had done might be repeated or simulated (Shemoth R. 9).[1] Demons might be summoned even for the cure of disease. The following is an euphemistic appeal to them as angels: " Baz, Bazijah, Mas, Masijah, Kas, Kasijah, Sharlai, and Amarlai, ye angels that come from Sodom to heal painful boils! Let the colour not become more red! Let it not further spread! Let its seed be absorbed in the belly! As a mule does not propagate itself; so let not this evil propagate itself in the body of M., the son of M." (Shab. 67a)!

The Asmodæus of the Book of Tobit is a surly, malignant being; but the Ashmedai of Solomon is a jolly, humane, obliging, and astute demon; though crafty and unreliable. Solomon had some instructive adventures with him. When the king was about to build the Temple, as iron tools were forbidden, the king sought the services of the worm, Shamir, which was mighty in the cutting of stones. The worm was not at hand; and for its discovery, Solomon, at the advice of the Sanhedrim, conjured up a male and female demon. Though tortured, these Shedim could only

[1] Cf. Rev. xvi. 14.

refer the king to Ashmedai, their prince. He was then lodging at the bottom of a deep well, on the top of a high mountain. On leaving his lair in the morning, Ashmedai sealed the mouth of the cistern against his return. Solomon sent Benaiah, armed with his own signet-ring bearing the Ineffable Name; also a heavy iron chain, with some skins of wine and other accessories. Benaiah, arriving at his destination, set artfully to work; drained the well from beneath without touching the seal of Ashmedai; and introduced the wine instead of the water. The prince of demons returned from heaven, whither he went daily to hear the decrees of the Upper Sanhedrim; examined the seal, which he found unbroken; and descended the cistern to quench his thirst. He was surprised to find wine instead of water; but though detesting it, the drouthy demon imbibed too freely and fell asleep. Benaiah now promptly emerged from his ambush close at hand, and secured "The Prince" when "drunk and incapable." Ashmedai was thereafter led away captive to Solomon; but on the journey contrived to do several kind things. He hailed a blind man and put him on the right way; because he had heard in heaven that he was perfectly righteous, and whoso helped him, would attain to the life to come. He did the same for a drunken man; though he knew that he was a thorough villain. But he obliged him that the scoundrel might not lose all good in this world. Ashmedai beheld a wedding procession and wept over it; for he knew that in thirty days the bridegroom would die, and the bride would have to wait thirteen years (to marry an infant brother). He laughed at the man who ordered a pair of shoes to last him seven years; for he knew that he had but seven days to live. He uttered shrieks of scorn at a juggler; for with all his tricks he did not know that a king's ransom was beneath his feet. After his arrival, Solomon learned that the worm Shamir was in charge of the moor-cock,[1] to which it had been entrusted by the prince of the sea. The nest of this fowl was soon found; and over it was put a glass shade, so that the bird saw its young but could not come at them. Thereupon the moor-cock ran off to fetch Shamir to cleave the glass. On its return with the same, the messengers of Solomon shouted, when Naggar Tura dropped the worm, which was instantly carried off by the envoys of the king. But the moor-cock, unable to restore the worm to the prince of the sea, went and strangled himself. Ashmedai was long kept in custody, and the Temple was built by the aid of Shamir. But "The Prince" avenged himself on Solomon; securing his seal with the Ineffable Name, then swallowing him alive, and afterwards belching him forth, four hundred miles away. Ashmedai now reigned in his stead, and Solomon wandered about as a beggar. He came at last to the house of the Sanhedrim, where he went on repeating the words:

[1] The moor-cock, Tarnegol Bera (Targ. Ps. 1. 11), is otherwise Naggar Tura, the "mountain-splitter."

I, the preacher, was king in Jerusalem. Suspicion now fell upon Ashmedai, who was still masquerading in the palace under the guise of Solomon. The floor was then strewn with fine ashes to discover the traces of the demon's feet; but the wily Ashmedai frustrated these designs by wearing socks over his cock's toes. The signet-ring was at length found again; having been swallowed by a fish. The demon was now deforced in turn, by the might of the Ineffable Name, vanishing into thin air (Gittin 68a b). It is said that after these escapades, Solomon was afraid of the demons, and had his couch surrounded by "threescore valiant men" (Cant. iii. 7, 8). Prior to those events, he had such power over the demons that at his bidding, they danced before him (II Targ. ii. 1, 3; Pesiqta 45b).[1]

ETHNIC PARALLELS

Ethnic parallels to Jewish demonology are easily obtained from the huge mass of material now available. A limited selection only is offered. The position of Philo is not remote from that of Herbert Spencer. The former remarks that " souls, demons, and angels differ indeed in name; but by conceiving the underlying element as one and the same, you will get rid of

---

[1] The story here rests on a confusion of two similar Hebrew letters in Eccles. ii. 8—

| Men-singers, שרים. | Women-singers, שרות. |
| Male demons, שדים. | Female demons, שדות. |

a heavy burden,—superstition."[1] The latter asserts that the meaning of "ghost, spirit, demon, angel," was originally the same.[2] Neither statement merits unreserved acceptance; yet in a wide general sense appropriate to the cosmic standpoint of anthropology, the element of truth here present facilitates the production of ethnic parallels.

Rabbinic demonology is not at all alone in its claim to direct verification. The seeing of spirits is often claimed by professional men among the Australians, Karens, Zulus, Greenlanders, Indians, and others too numerous to mention. Certain fastings and vigils, or similar performances, are among the commoner methods of glimpsing spirits; but these processes are very tame compared with the Rabbinic recipe already described.

Origin.—The creation of demons by Angro-Mainyu is the nearest approach to the alleged creation of demons by God. The Rabbinic idea of alliances, human and demonic, has numerous analogues. The *Zend-Avesta* speaks, perhaps pictorially, of the female Druj with her four earthly paramours. The Tantric ritual professes to provide a ghostly mistress for the infamous Vamacharis of India. The Cabalists of the Middle Ages thought it possible and desirable to marry their sylphs. The natives of Lapland, New Zealand, and the Samoan Islands, ascribe monstrous births to such lawless unions. Classical mythology is full of the comminglings of the divine and the earthborn; thus corresponding to the tale of the love of the "sons of

[1] *De Gigantibus.*   [2] *Sociology,* i. p. 261.

God" for the daughters of men.¹ The transformation of human beings into demonic animals receives extensive credit among the races of the lower culture. The legend of the were-wolf, with its local variants, is world-wide. In Arabia, certain tribes of the Hadramaut are believed to be thus transfigured in times of drought. In Abyssinia, blacksmiths and potters are supposed to become hyenas. In India, wizards may change into tigers; one such being caught and deprived of his fangs to render him harmless. In almost all lands, the idea that demons may be the souls of the wicked dead, finds acceptance. The orthodox Chinaman of to-day is entirely at one with Josephus in his definition of a demon. In India, suicide is a recognised mode of becoming an evil spirit, in pursuit of ghostly vengeance. Drowning has the preference to poisoning. The unfortunate, the destitute, the victims of repulsive diseases, or of violent death; likewise the unburied, are popularly suspected of drifting into the ranks of evil spirits. It is not surprising, therefore, to find that a British officer mortally wounded at Travancore, and a notorious criminal hanged at Trichinopoly, equally arrived at the dignity of demonic state.

[1] The legend of the Bene-Elohim, in the Book of Enoch and the Book of the Secrets of Enoch, connects itself with Mount Hermon. That locality seems to have been the first point of contact between the Hivite aborigines of Kadesh (daughters of men?) and the tall, handsome, blue-eyed, light-haired, and pale-skinned Amorites (Bene-Elohim?). For the home of the former, see Josh. xi. 3; Judg. iii. 3; 2 Sam. xxiv. 7. The affinities of the latter are with the Cro-Magnon race of France.

Numbers.—Having regard to the manner in which ethnic spirits originate, it is clear that their numbers are constantly on the increase. The Arabs so thickly people the desert with their Jinn that they apologise to them, on throwing anything away; lest they should hit some of them. So when pouring water on the ground, or entering a bath, or letting a bucket down into a well, or entering the place of uncleanness, a well-bred son of the desert will say, Permission, ye blessed! The modern Parsee knows that round the dakhmas where the dead are exposed to vultures, demons, male and female, hover in fifties, hundreds, thousands, and myriads. The Fuegians seem to be constantly exhaling the demons of the air. The heretical Messalians religiously spat them out. So the Jewish allocation of one thousand to the left hand, and a myriad to the right, is not prodigiously extravagant.

Forms.—Demons may be anthropomorphic; but may change their shape as need or whim directs. The Vedic Yatus and the Greek Empousæ are typical in this respect; as also the Arabian Jinn. The spirits of Milton answer the ethnic ideal—

> As they please,
> They limb themselves, and colour, shape, or size
> Assume, as likes them best, condense or rare.

The grotesque form of the Rabbinic demons with their cock's feet, finds its nearest homologue in the genii of the house of Allat in the under-world. The

Chaldæan genius of the South-West Wind bears off the palm for monstrosity; with its shrivelled face, its goat's horns, its scorpion's tail, its four wings, and its arms ending in talons. The Druj Nasu of the *Zend-Avesta*, which rushes from the regions of the North (hell) to take possession of the corpse in the name of Angro-Mainyu, when expelled from the body of the dead, assumes the form of a raging fly, " with knees and tail sticking out, all stained with stains." The Arabs know of demons disguised as dogs, cats, jackals, lions, scorpions, wolves, or having human or promiscuous shape. Of these some possess the power of flight; all apparently have the capacity of appearing or disappearing at will. The ghul is practically the counterpart of Lilith; a creature of night and darkness; wandering abroad to decoy and devour her lone human victims. The Paris of the *Zend-Avesta* are analogous to the Lilin; and Azi-Dahaka corresponds in some ways to the many-headed monster which invaded the school of Abaji: " being three-headed, six-eyed, with a thousand powers, and mighty strength, a male demon of the Daevas, made by Angro-Mainyu, a most mighty Druj (Yasna ix. 8)."

Haunts.—Where the Jews contemplated the resting of demons on articles of food and drink, they find sympathisers in the Bulgarians who fumigate their flour fresh from the mill, and in the Greenlanders who dread the spirit of strange waters. The Arabs believe in Jinn haunting " baths, wells, latrines, ovens, ruined houses, market-places, the junctions of roads, the sea, and rivers"; also burial-grounds, sequestered spots, and human habitations. Rabbinic doctrine hints at an elemental origin for many of its spirits, by assigning them trees and fountains for their abodes. In this respect they are akin to other peoples; such as the Greeks, the Egyptians, the Indians, and many tribes of the Dark Continent. The genii of the Babylonians swarmed everywhere; creeping under the door, filling every nook and corner, from floor to roof-tree; hiding in lonely places; lurking behind walls and hedges; or roosting among trees. The association of demons with the places of impurity or of interment, is characteristic of a certain stage of culture. Where Jews and Babylonians believed in the howling of the Shedim of the wilderness, the modern Arab, Hindoo, and Chinaman hear the voices of evil demons in the weird sounds of the night. Even the Finnlander still listens for the call of spirits in his native forests.

Times of activity.—Special demons have their special times for business; but the degree of their organisation is often a matter of pious imagination. The Chaldæans believed in organised bands of them acting at set intervals; and the Parsees have a similar notion. Superstitious peoples so multiply their numbers that no part of the day or of the night is void of their visitations. The surprises and ambushes of evil demons are thus constantly to be feared; and countless expedients are devised in the form of charms, incantations, and such things, to fray them away.

Night is everywhere regarded as the appropriate season of demonic revelries. The neglected double of the ancient Egyptian went forth under cover of the darkness to prowl among the living, to terrify them by sudden apparitions, or to smite them with headache and madness. It were needless to multiply instances in proof of the popular belief that night is most congenial to the powers of evil. Equally common is the idea that the dawn scares them away. The Jew could appreciate the sentiment of the *Zend-Avesta:* The cock is the drum of the world, that crows in the dawn which dazzles away the fiends. That thought recurs in our Border Ballads.

Powers.—These have been partly noticed; but the following examples may be added. Demons have always been credited with foreknowledge, and therefore oracles have usually been sought from them. Their evil disposition has earned for them the reputation of causing accidents and diseases. The ancient Egyptians divided the body into thirty-six regions, with an equal number of demons associated with them. The traces of demonic action were sought in the several organs. The Babylonians believed that the inhalation or swallowing of stray demons was the cause of disease. The Parsee knows that Angro-Mainyu has one hundred thousand diseases, *less one*, wherewith to vex mankind (*Zend-Avesta*, Farg. XXIII. iii. 15). The Burman refers his fever to the demon of the jungle; the Arab, his insanity or epilepsy, to the Jinn; the New Zealander, his headache, to Tonga.

Evil dreams and nightmares are by general consent of the savage or his more cultured congener, accounted the work of hateful demons. The Neo-Platonic philosophy referred ritual excesses or mistakes to demonic influences.

Restrictions.—Life would be a burden, were not limits set to the action of demons. But uncultured man is fertile in his inventions against these foes. The semi-sensuous constitution of those creatures is in itself a restraining power. The Egyptian double, in default of better diet, might be forced to take to stable refuse; and the Babylonian demon might sometimes be driven to contend with dogs over offal. The Zoroastrian demons "take food and void filth." The Chinese spirits stand in need of the good things of their former existence; and are therefore supplied with mock-houses, mock-clothes, mock-money, and other mock-comforts. The huntsman of the Brazilian forests knows of some that are lame; and the Chinaman knows of others that are lame, and blind, and headless. The idea of a "second death" ranges among peoples whose intellectual limits are represented, on the one hand by the Fiji Islanders; and on the other, by the Neo-Platonists.[1] Plutarch relates what he believed to be an authentic instance of the death of a demon. He recounts with poetic emotion the "passing" of Pan, as announced by a voice and confirmed by lamentations, in the hearing of the voyagers,

[1] Plutarch gives a peculiar interpretation to the "second death," in his essay on "The Face in the Moon" (xvii. xxviii.).

abreast of Palodes. The mortality of this order of beings was also a tenet of the Stoics.

Management.—Where earthly relatives have neglected the soul of the departed, demonic annoyances may be expected by way of asserting spiritual rights. The remedy is the immediate satisfaction of outstanding claims. Modes of keeping evil spirits in their proper place are simply legion. Among these, fire holds a conspicuous place. The Babylonians put their trust in Gibil (Gihir), the lord of fire. The peoples of Africa, Australia, India, among many others, are vigorous upholders of the ancient rite. Lamps, lanterns, torches, and fires, have always been much in demand for such purposes. The exact significance to be attached to the lighting of consecrated candles, in the Roman Church, is that "in whatever places these candles are lit or placed, the powers of darkness may depart in trembling and flee away in terror." Ablutions, odd articles of dress, or curious amulets, have always had their advocates for the subjection of demons. Incantations and cryptic formulæ are universal among exorcists; the more meaningless, apparently the better. A most valiant sentence is that thundered against the Druj Nasu, when exorcised from the corpse. This withering denunciation is described as "fiend-smiting," and "most healing"—

Perish, O fiendish Druj! Perish, O brood of the fiend!
Perish, O world of the fiend! Perish away, O Druj!
Rush away, O Druj! Perish away, O Druj!
Perish away to the regions of the North!
Never more to give to death, the living world of the Holy Spirit!

The efficacy of this menace is enhanced by the use of Sagdid,—the look of the four-eyed dog. The Druj is supposed to become weaker at every word, and finally to flee away in confusion. In Southern India more especially, devil-dances and bloody sacrifices are often employed to pacify offended demons. The British officer of Travancore, already alluded to, was worshipped as a local demon; receiving offerings of cigars and brandy, which the thrifty devotees themselves consumed thereafter. Prayer is an obvious mode of combating the powers of evil. The *Zend-Avesta* comes near to Scripture, when it represents Zoroaster as warding off demons by chanting, The will of the Lord is the Law of Holiness. This prophet also fends them off by prayer and the keeping of the Law. The Rabbis do not seem to have contemplated such arduous methods of disposing of evil spirits, as clubbing, shooting, stabbing, or exporting them; though these practices are still honoured in many parts of the world. Ethnic methods of ejecting possessing demons receive separate consideration.

Redeeming features.—Like a few of the Jewish Shedim, some ethnic spirits are genial and helpful. The Zulus, the Chinese, the Jains of India, and many others, look to the shades of their ancestors for help and direction. They are thus like the good demons of Hesiod in the Golden Age. Some of the Jewish Shedim were learned in the Law; but they have no monopoly of such excellence. Some of the Arabic Jinn are converts to Islam; having heard the prophet

4

read the *Koran*. Hence they confess, "Verily we have heard an excellent discourse which directeth unto the right institution; wherefore we believe therein and will by no means associate any other with our Lord. We formerly attempted to pry into the transactions of heaven; but we found the same filled with a strong guard of angels and with flaming darts; and we sat on some of the thrones thereof to listen to the discourses of its inhabitants; but whoso listeneth now, findeth a flame laid in ambush for him, to guard the celestial confines. There are some among us that are upright, and there are some among us otherwise. Some of us are Moslems, and others of us swerve from righteousness."[1] Demons, in China more particularly, are resorted to for the cure of disease; sometimes promising their aid, of their own accord, through their human mediums.

CHRIST AND COMMON DEMONOLOGY

A comparison of the Rabbinic and ethnic demonologies reveals certain interesting results—

1. The preceding ethnic parallels possess a character which is really universal, both as regards time and place.

2. Between the two systems of doctrine there is substantial harmony; their salient features being in essential agreement.

3. Any slight divergences remaining are traceable

to local differences of environment. The seed is one; the soil and climate slightly diverse.

Ethnic demonology may be said to be practically timeless. It represents a phase of culture rather than a definite era; just as the Stone Age of the archaeologist represents a stage of civilisation rather than a specific period. Rabbinic demonology bears a similar stamp. It was no new creation in the time of our Lord. It drew from out the deep of primitive ages. When the people were carried into captivity, their mind was no mere *tabula rasa* awaiting the impress of Babylonian and Persian superstitions.[1]

They had their magic waters, oracular trees, divining rods, consultations of the Teraphim, interviews with the ghosts of the departed, and possessing spirits. In common with other peoples, the fathers of the Hebrew race had sought to press behind "the shows of the world," and to find in the activities of spirits their machinery of causation.

The Rabbinic doctrine of demons, as a whole, was undoubtedly prevalent in the time of Christ. Most of the preceding quotations from Rabbinic literature

[1] To trace the whole or the greater part of Jewish demonology to the influences of the Exile, is a proceeding which greatly fails to commend itself to the student of anthropology. Certain consequences are perceptible as flowing from contact with the peoples of the East; but it will require much stronger evidence than any now available, to prove extensive importations of Shedim. Lenormant, Sayce, and Geiger seem to attach undue importance to Babylonian factors; while Kohut and Schorr, who are strongly discrepant *inter se*, appear to overestimate the Zoroastrian influence. See also Cheyne, *Origin of the Psalter*, p. 391 ff.

are taken from the Mishna, which, according to Schürer, was "collected and edited towards the end of the second century after Christ." But "the final redaction had been preceded by two earlier summaries of written documents."[1] The teaching of the Mishna was therefore in circulation in the time of our Lord.

Independent proof of this is found in the narratives of the Book of Tobit and the *Antiquities* of Josephus. In point of date, the former approximates to the Book of Daniel; while the latter is almost in contact with Christ. The theory and practice underlying the demonology of these writings is identical with that embedded in Rabbinic literature. Their common presupposition is the popular animistic (poly-demonistic) philosophy which repeatedly emerges in the pages of the New Testament. *What was the attitude of Jesus to the foregoing superstitions?*

One tradition describes demons as purely spiritual beings; attributing their condition to delay or mistake on the part of the Creator. That belief was an audacious assault upon the power and wisdom of God. Christ could have had no sympathy with such a statement. But this opinion was essentially heterodox even among superstitious Jews; because it was inconsistent with the magical practices of the times; and

---

[1] *The Jewish People*, I. i. p. 129. Occasional reference has been made to writings which are somewhat late of publication; such as Bereshith Rabba, Pesiqta, Pirqe de R. Eliezer, Tanchuma, and Yalkut Shimeoni. These are, however, relevant to the issue on hand; because they go back to older traditional or written material, and are entirely homogeneous with the earlier writings.

at variance with the fundamental tenet of Rabbinic demonology which assumed the semi-sensuous nature of the Shedim. As "half-spirits," they possessed a psycho-sarcous constitution which involved them in physical needs and functions. But in two passages, Christ gave what is practically a definition of "spirit," which is wholly opposed to the Rabbinic conception—

> God is spirit. John iv. 24.
> A spirit hath not flesh and bones. Luke xxiv. 39.

According to Christ, then, *the non-material, the incorporeal*, is the specific attribute of "spirit." That in itself disposes of the greater portion of Rabbinic demonology.

Origin.—Primitive man draws a fluctuating line between animals, men, and superhuman beings, in accordance with the principles of his animistic creed. But Jesus recognised that in all worlds and amid all the changes of the future, the distinctive rank of man among intelligent beings must be maintained without faltering. Comminglings of the human and the demonic, or transmutation of the human into the demonic, must have been incredible to Him. That is the condemnation of the legends of Adam and Eve with reference to demons, and the derivation of demons from the profane. The evolution of a demon from a hyena was unthinkable to Christ, Who had a clear insight into natural processes. The loose wanderings of the souls of the wicked dead as Shedim are opposed to His doctrine of moral retribution.

Numbers. — The idea that demons hustle the Rabbis, wear out their dresses by friction, or bruise their shins by impact, implies their semi-sensuous nature, which Jesus did not credit. The assertion that demons swarm everywhere, to the incessant danger of man, is not in harmony with our Lord's teaching on divine providence. It is likewise opposed to His action on many occasions.

Forms. — Forms of spirits, animal, human, or monstrous; appendages such as cock's toes, wings, multiple heads; eating, drinking, propagation, death by misadventure or constitutional defect; all presuppose the error of the semi-sensuous nature of demons, and are therewith set aside.

Haunts. — The Rabbis crammed the earth with evil spirits, and thrust them even into heaven. But while Jesus allowed a restricted place to the demons on earth, He assigned them no place in heaven. He commanded His disciples to gather up the fragments; thus discouraging the idea that demons lurk on crumbs. He had no faith in the ceremonial washing of hands; so repelling the notion that spirits may rest on unwashen hands. He asked a draught of water from the woman of Samaria and thereafter entered the city; proving that He had no fear of drinking borrowed water and no belief in local Shedim. He retired repeatedly to desert places and fasted in the wilderness; therein rejecting the popular conception that the waste is the special haunt of evil spirits. The hiding of these beings among trees, shadows, and foul places, postulates their psycho-sarcous constitution which stands rejected with its correlates. The association of demons with animals is in conflict with Christ's assertion of God's special care over them.

Times of activity.—In opposition to current ideas, Jesus did not regard one hour of the day as more dangerous than another. The only risk of travelling by night is that of stumbling in the dark (John xi. 9, 10). That discounts the division of the day into four parts for the four classes of demons.[1] Christ refused to think of sexual distinctions as existing among spiritual beings (Luke xx. 36). That reduces Ashmedai and Lilith, with their attendant hosts, to non-existence. With the disappearance of the queen of female demons, vanish the perils of the eves of Wednesday and the Sabbath; as well as dangers to children, solitary travellers, lone sleepers, and others. To abet an evil spirit by wishing a demon a mistaken God-speed, is a puerility whose presupposition is the seeing of a Shed in human form.

Powers.—Dangers supposed to threaten sick women, brides, bridegrooms, and others; also gastric troubles ascribed to the ingestion of demons, rest upon the mistaken assumption of the psycho-sarcous constitu-

[1] The warning of Peter and the crowing of the cock have been foolishly connected with demonic activity. Satan is not a demon. The temptation is not demonic, but Satanic; the issue not physical, but ethical. The common idea was that the power of the night-demons ceased at cock-crow; whereas that was the beginning of fresh peril for Peter.

tion of the Shedim. To ascribe the causation of accident or disease to those beings, contradicts Christ's doctrine of the sovereignty of God. As a matter of fact, He did not trace accidents (Luke xiii. 4), nor special diseases such as leprosy, blindness, or cardiac disease,[1] to the foregoing agents. The conduct of the possessed was never attributed by Him to possessing spirits.

Restrictions.—The Rabbis were free to imagine the semi-sensuous nature of the Shedim as a partial restraint upon their mischievous doings. But such limitations become inconceivable with the rejection of the underlying error. Restrictions of demonic energy by measures, seals, fastenings, and similar devices, could find no favour with Him, Who steadfastly abjured the employment of all charms and counter-charms.

Management.—Many of the Rabbinic methods for controlling demons were operative only on the assumption of their being "half-spirits." Belief in their pneumatic mode of existence reduced such methods to sheer absurdities. To that category belong attempts to wash off demons from the hands with water, or to frighten Shabriri with a rattle. Other methods amounted to a chronic confusion of the physical and the ethical. The clear distinction drawn by Jesus between those two sets of phenomena, (Matt. xv. 16–20), disclosed the irrational character of the Rabbinic procedure. To this class belong the use

---

[1] The dropsical man in Luke xiv. 2 may have suffered from cardiac disease.

of the covenant salt, the practice of circumcision, and the observance of certain festivals. Other common methods involved the use of incantations, Scriptural or non-Scriptural. But Christ neither used, nor permitted the use of, magic formulæ. These were essentially "vain repetitions." The ethnic management of demons as a whole was an outstanding contradiction of His view of God and the world.

Redeeming features.—While Rabbinic demonology might contemplate good and evil demons, such beings were for Jesus all evil, always evil, and incurably evil. To attribute to spirits the gifts of divination, the healing of disease, the teaching of the Law, or the service of the saints, must have appeared to Christ pure fabrications.

CHRIST AND COMMON MAGIC

Among the Jews in the time of our Lord, the magic arts were widely diffused. Abraham is made to figure as an expert; imparting gifts to the sons of his concubines. These are "gifts of impurity" (Sanh. 91b), which Rashi explains as "exorcism and the works of the Shedim." Solomon is assigned high rank in this department, as one taught of God (Jos. *Ant.* VIII. ii. 5). Hezekiah was another patron of the occult sciences; having had a "Book of Remedies" (Pes. 56a). But magic was practised under both its forms—"white" and "black."

A new religious movement among polytheists may

result in the reduction of the gods to demonic rank, with their retention as objects of veneration or dread. The old magic ritual may continue slightly modified, according as the degraded gods are demons, good or evil. In the former case, they are virtually *dii minores*. Among them, the magician moves as among the excellent of the earth and heaven; their goodwill being a guarantee of his safety, and their power a pledge of his success. He is a theurgist whose art is properly called " white magic." Where the operator deems that he has to do with irate demons, he commands their services by force and against their will; believing himself safe in his pseudo-scientific panoply. He is a sorcerer whose art is properly called " black magic." [1]

Among theurgists might be counted R. Chaninah and R. Oshayah, who created a calf equal in size to a three-year-old, every Friday; and ate it (Sanh. 65a). The creation of such a fine calf, and its consumption by its creators, are, doubtless, complementary operations; but history does not show how far those Rabbis fattened on their spectral diet. Others of this gifted fraternity could create vegetable marrows, melons, deer, bucks, and does (Jer. Sanh. vii. 25d). Rabbi Simeon could likewise say to a valley, Be filled with gold dinars; and it was so (Jer. Ber. 13d). Sorcery was much more in evidence. Women were deeply suspected of being adepts in it (Pes. 111b; Ber. 53a; Erub. 64b; Jer. Sanh. vii. 9). The

[1] Cf. Lenormant, *Chaldæan Magic*, chap. v.

daughters of the Rabbis dabbled in it (Gittin 48a). Members of the Sanhedrim were obliged to possess a knowledge of it; so as to be able to act as judges in such cases (Sanh. 17a). The claims of rampant sorcery are well set forth in the story that R. Yannai was once presented in an inn with a magic potion by a woman. Being suspicious, he poured out some of the draught, which turned to scorpions. He then said to the woman, I have drunk of thine, now thou shalt drink of mine. So the woman drank and became an ass, on which the gallant Rabbi rode to market. But the ass was restored to womanhood by a friend who broke the spell (Sanh. 67b). Again, by intense study of the "Book of Creation," Rabba succeeded in creating a man whom he sent to R. Zira. But this recent creation was not endowed with the gift of speech; and R. Zira said to the new man, Thou art a fabrication (of the necromancers). Return to thine original dust! At once the dumb figure returned to nothing (Sanh. 65b).

Wholly remote from these magical practices are the miracles of our Lord. Their fine humanitarian tone alone thoroughly differentiates them from the vulgar glorification of the theurgist or the hateful spite of the sorcerer. "He went about continually doing good."

CAUSE OF CHRIST'S FREEDOM FROM SUPERSTITION

One large section of Jewish demonology was inconsistent with a pure monotheistic faith and morality.

The malignity, caprice, and independence allowed to demons were compatible only with a polytheistic creed; and intensely alien to Israel's prolonged experience of Jehovah's goodness, righteousness, and power. A rigid application of the monotheistic principle would have abolished those crooked superstitions which impinged upon the majesty of God and the moral freedom of man. The fuller illumination possessed by Jesus rendered these irrational beliefs unthinkable for Him.

Another large section of Jewish demonology was inconsistent with a true knowledge of Nature. The error here could only be removed by clear insight into natural processes. That has been wrongly denied to Jesus. He evinced a deep insight into the processes of health and disease on many occasions; as when He asked the Gerasene for his name, or appointed rest and diet for the daughter of Jairus, or made a physical examination of the ears and tongue of the stammerer. On these and other opportunities, He showed that He was not working in the dark. Hence His superiority to ordinary superstitions, which in others were the product of sheer ignorance of Nature.

CHAPTER III

MEDICAL ASPECTS OF DEMONIC POSSESSION

DATA OF THE PRESENT INQUIRY

THESE are primarily the narratives of the New Testament. But the descriptions often savour of the terminology of the animistic philosophy.[1] To the latter, demons and spirits are natural enough; but to modern psychological medicine, these are unknown as causes of disease. They involve a theory which is alien to the principles of scientific pathology. Investigation would thus be blocked at the outset, had not the Synoptists also furnished us with an account of the symptoms manifested by the possessed. These phenomena constitute the fundamental facts for the elucidation of the real nature of the derangement called "possession." In the case of the demoniacs of Capernaum and Gerasa, with that of the boy at the Hill of Transfiguration, these symptoms have been recorded in profusion. There are also duplicate or triplicate narratives of these three cases, which may be called "typical." The details are not identical; but they are never divergent. Their wealth of

[1] Appendix B, Nomenclature of the New Testament.

clinical material furnishes the clue to the right understanding of the physical basis of the "demoniac state." By the help of these three typical cases, we are able to explore the more obscure. The ailments of the Syro-Phœnician girl, the dumb demoniac, the blind and dumb demoniac, Mary of Magdala, and the infirm woman, are thus cleared up. The investigation of these proceeds with a great degree of confidence; for in the earlier analysis, the "demoniac state" has attained to the precision of a scientific conception. The uses of a correct diagnosis are many, some of which may be indicated here—

1. The exhibition of the physical basis of possession.
2. The testing of the value of "psychological explanations."
3. The demonstration of the historicity of the Gospel narratives.
4. The discovery of the proper criterion of genuine demonic possession.

SIMPLE EPILEPSY IS NOT POSSESSION

In the Authorised Version, we read that Christ healed "those which were possessed with devils, and those which were lunatic, and those that had the palsy" (Matt. iv. 24). The term *lunatic* (σεληνιαζό-μενοι) is a misnomer. Bruce alleges here "a certain want of strictness in the use of terms."[1] But Matthew's language is most exact. The σεληνιαζό-

[1] *Miraculous Elements in the Gospels*, p. 176.

μενοι are the *epileptic*. The evidence on this point is unimpeachable. Aretæus, in his treatise on *Chronic Diseases*, remarks that epilepsy is regarded as a disgraceful disease; for it is supposed to be inflicted on persons who have sinned against the *moon*.[1] Galen, another physician, in his work on *Critical Days*, says that the *moon* governs the periods of epileptic seizures. Lucian, in his *Philopseudes*, describes certain persons as falling to the ground by *moonlight*, rolling their eyes about, and foaming at the mouth. Alexander Trallianus, in his medical disquisitions, alludes to a cure which he had learned from a countryman in Etruria. The latter was cutting rue, when his companion, being epileptic (σεληνιακός), fell down. The σεληνιαζόμενοι of Matthew are therefore most clearly the epileptic, and are here distinguished from the possessed. *Apart from this notice, there is no reference to this class of sufferers in the New Testament.* Weiss is wrong in supposing that the boy at the Hill of Transfiguration was simply epileptic. It will be shown that he suffered from epileptic idiocy.[2]

[1] Hobart is mistaken in asserting that Aretæus admits the "possibility of this disease being produced by diabolical agency." Aretæus states that epilepsy "is reckoned a disgraceful form of disease; for it is supposed to be an infliction on persons who have sinned against the moon, and hence some have called it the Sacred Disease; and that for more reasons than one; as from the greatness of the evil, for the Greek word ἱερός also signifies 'great'; or because the cure of it is not human but divine; or from the opinion that it proceeded from the entrance of a demon into a man. From some one or all of these causes together, it has been called 'Sacred'" (*Chronic Diseases*, Bk. I. iv.).

[2] The popular idea that there is some connection between the moon

THE CAPERNAUM DEMONIAC

And they go into Capernaum; and straightway on the Sabbath day, he entered into the synagogue and taught. And they were astonished at his teaching; for he taught them as having authority, and not as the scribes. And straightway there was in the synagogue a man in an unclean spirit; and he cried out, saying, What have we to do with thee, thou Jesus of Nazareth? art thou come to destroy us? I know thee who thou art, the Holy One of God. And Jesus rebuked him, saying, Hold thy peace and come out of him. And the unclean spirit, tearing him and crying with a loud voice, came out of him. And they were all amazed, insomuch that they questioned among themselves, saying, What is this? a new teaching! With authority he commandeth even the unclean spirits, and they obey him. And the report of him went out straightway everywhere into all the region of Galilee round about. Mark i. 21–28.

And he came down to Capernaum, a city of Galilee. And he was teaching them on the Sabbath day; and they were astonished at his teaching; for his word was with authority. And in the synagogue there was a man, who had a spirit of an unclean demon; and he cried out with a loud voice, Ah! what have we to do with thee, thou Jesus of Nazareth? art thou come to destroy us? I know thee who thou art, the Holy One of God. And Jesus rebuked him, saying, Hold thy peace and come out of him. And when the demon had thrown him down in the midst, he came out of him; having done him no hurt. And amazement came upon all, and they spake together, one with another, saying,

and epilepsy is probably due to a confusion of epilepsy with epileptic insanity. The bright sunlight of the Orient has a curious stimulating effect on such creatures as cows and dogs; making them restless and noisy. It has an exciting effect on those afflicted with epileptic insanity also. In both cases, darkness acts as a sedative.

What is this word? for with authority and power he commandeth the unclean spirits, and they come out. And there went forth a rumour concerning him into every place of the region round about. Luke iv. 31-37.

The cure of this man was the beginning of miracles in this department of Christ's activity. It naturally led to a great stir in Capernaum and the regions adjacent to or depending on this flourishing commercial community. Mark's account is highly graphic, and brings us into close contact with the original eye-witness; while the little artistic touches of Luke may contain a tincturing of medical lore. But even with the aid of both Evangelists, it does not seem easy to expiscate a diagnosis from the meagre details thus provided. Keim boldly asserts that "the incident bears all the marks of invention." Holtzmann sees here "the glorification of miracle"! One bound by authority would hesitate to go further. But there is a luminous background to the story, imperceptible to those writers, providing an abiding refutation to this overweening dogmatism. The two narratives, by their suggestive hints, lead to one sure conclusion.

The word "straightway" ($εὐθὺς$) is an invaluable contribution to this investigation. It is furnished by Mark alone (i. 21). The Authorised Version weakly omits it; obviously owing to the fact that its retention seemed very superfluous to scribes and commentators. The Revised Version rightly restores it; but most exegetes are inclined to treat it with neglect. Mark, however, uses it with a purpose. It embodies an important fact. The demoniac was an intruder from without. His appearance in the synagogue took the worshippers completely by surprise. The services of the day were well advanced; and Jesus had been addressing the people so long and so impressively that they had passed into a state of extraordinary enthusiasm. At the height of this excitement—"straightway"—without pause and without warning, within the building there was "a man in an unclean spirit." How he got there, remains unexplained. Possibly, he glided in noiselessly without attracting attention; more probably he shot through the door with a bound before any one could arrest his career. Conjecture was needless. The startling fact now patent to all was that the man, with the unclean spirit, was in their midst. He was an outsider who by stealth or agility had thrust his most unwelcome presence upon the congregation. The surprise and horror caused by his sudden appearance were intensified by his loud cry, What have we to do with thee, Jesus of Nazareth? Thou didst come to destroy us! I know thee who thou art, the Holy One of God!

These phenomena were manifest at the moment of entrance into the synagogue, and were plainly maniacal in character. There is here complete loss of self-control with intense emotional excitement, evinced in wild shrieks and boisterous conduct. The demoniac is quite out of touch with his surroundings, and wholly unable to appreciate his position. The rules for decorous conduct in the synagogue are still extant;

forbidding such things as talking, laughter, and frivolity. But this man was lost to all sense of propriety; for he cried with a loud voice and interrupted the services of the hour. The bearing of this intruder towards Jesus is that of a man aggrieved and labouring under a sense of persecution. His demeanour is aggressive and menacing. He addresses Christ as an enemy bent upon his destruction. Yet in the same breath almost, he invokes Him as "the Holy One of God." The whole conduct of this demoniac proves that he is labouring under a maniacal attack of an acute and dangerous kind.

That does not however complete the diagnosis; for epileptic symptoms conclude the cycle of events. These are described in the words of the two Evangelists.

The unclean spirit, having convulsed him, and having cried with a loud voice, came out of him. Mark i. 26.

The demon, having dashed him into the midst, came out of him, having done him no harm. Luke iv. 35.

Restricting attention to the physical symptoms here present, three things emerge—

1. A loud cry.
2. A falling down.
3. A severe convulsion.

But these are the specific features of an epileptic attack, and are to be placed alongside of those features which point to acute insanity. By correlating these two groups of symptoms with each other, the final diagnosis is reached without difficulty. The case is one of epileptic insanity.

That conclusion is not only consonant with all the features here manifest; but enables us to clear up certain other things previously obscure. Judging from the absence of paralysis, imbecility, or dementia, this man's disorder is in its less advanced stages, and of an intermittent character. Probably there had been hallucinations of the senses, more specially those of hearing; so that this patient was likely to suffer from piercing noises, or warning and threatening voices. In such cases, delusions often arise spontaneously, causing the subject of them to believe that he is persecuted. Hence the frequent and powerful tendency to violence, either homicidal or suicidal; mostly the former. In those earlier stages of this disorder, there is commonly a peculiar disposition to wander abroad aimlessly; and religious monomania is not infrequent. On the eve of an attack, the temper is liable to sudden change. There is restlessness with a readiness to react violently to any stimulus, moral or physical. That seems to have been precisely the condition of this demoniac prior to his invasion of the synagogue. Apparently he was wandering abroad, when overtaken by the maniacal impulse. That conspired with his religious instincts to precipitate him unceremoniously into the synagogue. Consciousness was manifestly impaired at this moment; so that he failed to realise his position, and assailed Jesus as a destroyer. But this blind fury, this eclipse of consciousness, this appearance of deliberation, are integral parts of the malady from which this demoniac suffered; being essentially reflex, automatic, mechanical.

Madmen of this sort are extremely prone to crimes of horror and bloodshed. Probably this man was known already in Capernaum as a dangerous character; and his presence in the synagogue would therefore be the signal for a panic. His noisy demonstrations must have produced great consternation. Saved from a grave impending disaster, the former enthusiasm of the congregation returns, reinforced by a gratitude proportioned to the magnitude of the peril from which they had escaped. Hence the volley of interjections. What is this? A new doctrine! Fully authorised! He rebukes even foul spirits! And they obey him!

THE GERASENE DEMONIAC

When he was come to the other side into the country of the Gadarenes, there met him two possessed with demons, coming forth out of the tombs, exceedingly fierce so that no man could pass by that way. And behold, they cried out, saying, What have we to do with thee, thou Son of God? Art thou come hither to torment us before the time? Now there was afar off from them a herd of many swine feeding. And the demons besought him saying, If thou cast us out, send us away into the herd of swine. And he said unto them, Go! And they came out and went into the swine: and behold, the whole herd rushed down the steep into the sea, and perished in the waters. And they that fed them fled, and went away into the city, and told everything, and what was befallen to them that were demonised. And behold, the whole city came out to meet Jesus: and when they saw him, they besought him that he would depart from their borders. Matt. viii. 28–34.

And they came to the other side of the sea, into the country of the Gerasenes. And when he was come out of the boat, straightway there met him out of the tombs a man in an unclean spirit, who had his dwelling in the tombs: and no man could any more bind him, no, not with a chain; because that he had often been bound with fetters and chains, and the chains had been rent asunder by him, and the fetters broken in pieces: and no man had strength to tame him. And always, night and day, in the tombs and in the mountains, he was crying, and cutting himself with stones. And when he saw Jesus from afar, he ran and worshipped him; and crying with a loud voice, he saith, What have I to do with thee, Jesus, thou Son of the Most High God? I adjure thee by God, torment me not! For he said unto him, Come forth, thou unclean spirit, out of the man. And he asked him, What is thy name? And he saith unto him, My name is Legion; for we are many. And he besought him much that he would not send them away out of the country. Now there was on the mountain side a great herd of swine feeding. And they besought him, saying, Send us into the swine that we may enter into them. And He gave them leave. And the unclean spirits came out and entered into the swine; and the herd rushed down the steep into the sea, in number about two thousand; and they were choked in the sea. And they that fed them fled, and told it in the city and in the country. And they came to see what it was that had happened. And they come to Jesus, and beheld him that was possessed with demons, sitting, clothed, and in his right mind, even him that had the legion: and they were afraid. And they that saw it declared unto them how it befell him that was possessed with demons, and concerning the swine. And they began to beseech him to depart from their borders. Mark v. 1-17.

And they arrived at the country of the Gerasenes, which is over against Galilee. And when he was come forth upon the land, there met him a certain man out of the city, who had demons; and for a long time he had worn no clothes, and abode not in any house, but in the tombs. And when he saw Jesus, he cried out, and fell down before him, and with a loud voice said, What have I to do with thee, Jesus, thou Son of the Most High God? I beseech thee, torment me not. For he commanded the unclean spirit to come out of the man. For often it had seized him: and he was kept under guard, and bound with chains and fetters; and breaking the bands asunder he was driven of the demon into the deserts. And Jesus asked him, What is thy name? And he said Legion; for many demons were entered into him. And they entreated him that he would not command them to depart into the abyss. Now there was there a herd of many swine feeding on the mountain; and they entreated him that he would give them leave to enter into them. And he gave them leave. And the demons came out of the man, and they entered into the swine; and the herd rushed down the steep into the lake, and were choked. And when they that fed them saw what had come to pass, they fled and told it in the city and in the country. And they went out to see what had come to pass: and they came to Jesus, and found the man, from whom the demons were gone out, sitting, clothed, and in his right mind, at the feet of Jesus: and they were afraid. And they that saw it told them how he that was possessed with demons was made whole. And all the people of the country of the Gerasenes round about asked him to depart from them: for they were holden with great fear; and he entered into a boat and returned. Luke viii. 26-37.

Matthew's account is meagre, and is chiefly remarkable for the mention of two demoniacs. This discrepancy receives further attention and does not affect any conclusion regarding the nature of the disorder present; for the first Evangelist knows of no difference in the condition of the two men whom he mentions. From the medical standpoint, if not also from the historical, the two are one. Mark's narrative again takes us back to the eye-witness, while Luke's account adds nothing to the previous details; except by way of inference. The three Evangelists represent a Triple Tradition; but supply data which lead to one congruous result regarding the derangement under consideration.

The order of events as set forth by Mark is significant. It shows that the company sailed for the eastern shore of the Lake about sunset. The Jews had two evenings; the first beginning about the middle of the afternoon, the second at sunset. A comparison of Mark i. 32 (Matt. viii. 16), with Mark iv. 35 (ὀψίας), shows that the second Evangelist fixed the time of departure at the close of the day. The destination was a point in the region of Gerasa to the south-east of the Lake. Hence they "sailed down" to the country of the Gerasenes (Luke viii. 26). Evidently there were tokens of a coming tempest; so that without loss of time, they took Jesus "even as he was." The distance was not great; but the strong head-wind baffled the skill and the strength of the voyagers, so that the landing on the other side could scarcely have occurred before the dawn of the following morning. Anyhow, there was sufficient light for the party to see the demoniac(s) emerging from the tombs (Matt. viii. 28); and for the latter to single out Jesus as the leader of the company (Mark v. 6; Luke viii. 28). The landing itself was effected without difficulty and may not have been seen by the possessed. Sound rather than sight seems to have first excited his attention. Certain things confirm this supposition. The man was apparently within the tombs at the moment of disembarkation. There was likewise "a great calm" at the time (Mark iv. 39). Presumably there was also an excessive sharpness of hearing on the part of the demoniac, as is common in such cases. Owing to the extraordinary irritability of his acute mania, he was painfully susceptible to the slightest disturbances. The outward conditions concurred with the inward; and the result was the diversion of the attention of the possessed to the new-comers. The absence of all self-control is pathognomic of acute mania; and this lunatic's ungovernable fury manifested itself in charging down upon the enemy. The encounter took place close to the point where the party landed; for the man "ran"; and so met them "immediately." This violent haste was not the fruit of an amiable curiosity; but the proof of malevolent intention. It was natural on the part of one who had long been the pest of the locality; "exceeding fierce," so that none passed that way (Matt. viii. 28). Dangerous homicidal propensities were strikingly manifested as he rushed upon the party with menacing demeanour and furious yells, crying out, What have I to do with thee, Jesus? Yet such wild maniacs, though fierce in form, are but weak in will and destitute of steady purpose. That peculiar instability finds illustration here, in the sudden change from the most defiant insolence to a crouching attitude. This madman, overawed by the dauntless bearing and the forceful words of Jesus, "fell down before him" (Luke viii. 28), and "worshipped him" (Mark v. 6).

This rapid change of thought, feeling, and activity is highly characteristic of acute mania. There is a supersensitiveness to impressions derived from the organs of sense, tending to the instant reproduction of these in speech and action. This tumultuous activity is inevitable where normal self-control is lacking, and the power of self-suppression so greatly in abeyance. Under such circumstances, the passing fancy and impulse demand instant embodiment; so that waywardness of speech and eccentricity of conduct are pronounced features in the morbid process. Of that condition there is a notable example in the alternating use of the words "I" and "we," which Mark with wonted care has put on record, and which Luke implies. This is commonly cited as clear proof of a double consciousness and of a double personality, human and demonic. It has therefore been relied on to prove in the most positive manner, the presence of a demon within the demonised. But the inference is far from conclusive; because this feature is not at all exceptional. It is best explained on ordinary pathological principles as an example of that acceleration of mental processes which is common in certain phases of acute mania; giving the semblance of a twofold consciousness, only because the colligating factors are hidden from our view. We have here apparently no more than a regular part of the current disorder.

The amazing strength and the paradoxical endurance of this man also claim attention. The popular opinion is that maniacs are unusually strong. Even Herbert Spencer gravely endorses this fallacy, and finds here "a fact having noteworthy implications."[1] But the truth is that these manifestations of extraordinary strength among the insane are somewhat rare; and, if present at all, are temporary phenomena, occurring mostly at the beginning of the disorder. The Evangelists are faithful to the facts of observation when they furnish data which prove that these exhibitions were occasional. There had been "many times," when this man's strength had been insufficient to save him from capture and durance vile. There were also those other periods marked by invincible wakefulness night and day, by ceaseless wanderings to and fro, by incessant roarings which made the hours of light and darkness equally hideous. Even in captivity his energies were not arrested. These were then concentrated on his fetters, which were probably non-metallic; so that they were soon "rubbed to pieces." When his lower limbs were

[1] *Sociology*, i. pp. 228, 233, 416.

thus free, the rending of his bonds may have been a simple matter. The result was another spell of wild freedom and privation. But these exertions were mechanical rather than deliberate; reflex rather than intentional. Their incentive is to be sought in the pathological diversion of his energies into one morbid channel; rather than in any concentration of his will-power. Ill-informed critics who have hitherto found in these descriptions only a concatenation of pictorial details, have yet to learn that these painful performances are the genuine parts of a severe case of acute mania, whose parallels are still unhappily common in our asylums.

We can now understand how this demoniac, in reply to Jesus, calls himself Legion. Previous to his illness, he was, no doubt, familiar with the Jewish extravaganza which supplied the individual with a whole legion of demons; prepared to assault him for a trifling misdemeanour. He must also have been familiar with the movements of Roman troops. Six legions were stationed in Syria. Detachments of these were to be found in adjacent parts; such as Megiddo, then called Ligyon (Legion), and the towns of Decapolis. Serious disorders of sensation were associated with the mental derangement, producing the hallucination of portentous strength. Thus, a variety of circumstances, external and internal, concurred in the formation of this man's delusion. Under the fancy that he embodied the power and organisation of some six thousand demons, he felt himself more than a match for all invaders upon those domains which his ferocity had turned into a madman's paradise.

Insane ideas are again in evidence when this man in his antipathy to human society fled from the habitations of his fellows and cast off all social restraint. His dismal surroundings were in keeping with his dismal state of mind; though there may have been no aggravation of his condition from this source.[1] The pastures of the swine and the tombs of the dead were sought out as furnishing a convenient lair; not on the ground of any sentimental associations. He was liable to be hunted down like a wild beast, and experience had taught him that in those ghastly tombs he might find a secure retreat. There he would not be pestered by the attentions of his neighbours; who, if Jews, would shun the haunts of the swine; and whether Jews or Gentiles, would be chary of the sepulchres of the dead. Deliberate choice is not here to be thought of. Instinct rather than intelligence guided this demoniac to his strange quarters, where his brutish instincts would have full scope.

The shocking nakedness of the possessed is also in

---

[1] Farrar, in his *Life of Christ*, here draws attention to Sir Walter Scott's description of effects alleged to have been produced on the minds of the Covenanters by their cavern retirements. Historically, Sir Walter is in error. But the point to be noted is that no comparison can be instituted between the demoniac who, under the stress of mental disease, sought the caves of the mountain, and the men who were driven by sore oppression to seek such shelter. The solitude and foulness were agreeable to the lunatic of Gerasa; but were odious to any in their right mind.

place as a characteristic element of his formidable malady. Among those afflicted with acute mania, this is no uncommon thing; traceable variously to uneasy cutaneous sensations or sheer destructiveness or unmitigated brutishness. This patient had been ill for "a long time"; perhaps with intervals of improvement. Yet the nakedness seems to have been constant, and to have lasted through more than one season. In any case, it must have exposed this lunatic to severe experiences; for in Palestine, the diurnal range of temperature is considerable at all seasons. It was therefore the lot of this man to endure the scorching heat by day and the chilly air by night, in his ceaseless peregrinations among the mountains and the tombs. Clothed only in sunlight or starlight, he had "for a long time" braved the elements; yet apparently with no great detriment or discomfort. His behaviour in this respect is quite in harmony with that of his class, who have sometimes preferred to disrobe themselves on a cold winter's night in our more rigorous climate, without visible uneasiness. That is however but a proof of a diminution of normal sensibility, which is so largely present in these cases.

The same condition finds additional expression in self-mutilation. He "cut himself with stones"; not as a solitary act; but "night and day," as a constant practice. This is no penance, as Olshausen thought; but a well-recognised symptom of acute mental derangement. Here it concurred with the great fury of his delusion, and seems to have been the source of pleasure to him. Such delight in the pain of mutilation has received in Germany the technical designation,—"freudenschmerz." A curious classical parallel to this is the case of the Spartan king, Cleomenes, the subject of acute mania. When under confinement, he got possession of a sword and began to cut off the flesh of his thighs, and otherwise mutilated himself, till he perished (Herodotus, vi. 75).[1]

The impairment of memory is another notable feature in this case. Insanity always involves a breach of greater or less extent in the continuity of the life of the patient. Memory suffers as severely as any other faculty. Sometimes its contents are sharply sundered; so that the individual has a normal memory in his normal state, and a morbid memory when in his morbid mood. The facts of the normal life may thus be clearly separated from those of the morbid condition. This demoniac's memory was a blank for the former, so that he had forgotten what ought to have been nearest to him,—his own name. Yet for the facts relating to his previous attacks of insanity, his morbid memory was rather acute. According to the rough-and-ready manner of the times, he had often been put under close confinement, in chains and fetters. These were sore torments to this lunatic, who could only regard his wardens as

---

[1] Certain opium-eaters in Bombay stimulate their deadened sensibilities by the sting of a scorpion; deriving therefrom a pleasant sensation.

his tormentors. His old morbid associations still dominate his mind when he cries out in mingled tones of defiance and dread, What have I to do with thee? Thou didst come to torment me before the time! And truly, the tormentor always comes "before the time." Labouring under this fancy, it was quite natural for this madman to "run" with homicidal fury upon the strangers; prepared to fight with the will, if not with the strength, of a "legion."

The diagnostic indications need not be further pursued, as the conclusion is eminently beyond dispute. The whole of the symptoms point to acute mania of a formidable, but not of an exceptional, type. In conventional language, this patient had been "driven by the demon into the wilderness," and his disorder had lasted "a long time." The case was one of great urgency; for the tremendous excitement, the prolonged insomnia, the incessant wanderings, the cruel mutilations; coupled with the lack of proper food, clothing, and shelter, must have placed this demoniac in a most critical condition. Clearly this was his last chance. Death from sheer exhaustion must otherwise have put a speedy termination to his wretched existence.

Finally, we have to note the absence of any convulsions at the ending of this case. Olshausen, Ewald, Lange, Trench, and others, have without warrant introduced them. The proceeding is not more arbitrary than unscientific. The demoniac of Capernaum suffers from epileptic insanity; the demoniac of Gerasa from acute mania. Convulsions are in place in the former derangement; but out of place in the latter. The Gospel narratives are thus completely in harmony with clinical observation. The two parties ought in no wise to be confounded.

THE EPILEPTIC IDIOT

When they were come to the multitude, there came to him a man kneeling to him and saying, Lord have mercy on my son; for he is epileptic, and suffers grievously; for oft-times he falleth into the fire, and ofttimes into the water. And I brought him to thy disciples, and they could not cure him. And Jesus answered and said, O faithless and perverse generation, how long shall I be with you? How long shall I bear with you? Bring him hither to me. And Jesus rebuked him; and the demon went out of him; and the boy was cured from that hour. Then came the disciples to Jesus apart, and said, Why could not we cast it out? And he saith unto them, Because of your little faith. Matt. xvii. 14–20.

When they came to the disciples, they saw a great multitude about them, and scribes questioning with them. And straightway, all the multitude, when they saw him, were greatly amazed, and running to him, saluted him. And he asked them, What question ye with them? And one of the multitude answered him, Master, I brought unto thee my son, who hath a dumb spirit; and whithersoever it taketh him, it dasheth him down; and he foameth and grindeth his teeth, and pineth away; and I spake to thy disciples that they should cast it out; and they were not able. And he answereth them and saith, O faithless generation, how long shall I be with you? How long shall I bear with you? Bring him unto me. And they brought him unto him; and when he saw him, straightway the spirit tare him grievously; and he fell on the ground and wallowed foaming. And he asked his father, How long time is it since this hath come to him? And he said, From a child. And oft-times it hath cast him both into the fire and into the waters to destroy him: but if thou canst do anything, have compassion on us, and help us. And Jesus said unto him, If thou canst! All things are possible to him that believeth. Straightway, the father of the child cried out, and said, I believe; help thou mine unbelief. And when Jesus saw that a multitude came running together, he rebuked the unclean spirit, saying unto him, Thou dumb and deaf spirit, I command thee, come out of him, and enter no more into him. And having cried out, and torn him much, he came out: and the child became as one dead; insomuch that the more part said, He is dead. But Jesus took him by the hand, and raised him up; and he arose. And when he was come into the house, his disciples asked him privately, saying, We could not cast it out? And he said unto them, This kind can come out by nothing, save by prayer. Mark ix. 14-29.

When they were come down from the mountain, a great multitude met him. And behold, a man from the multitude cried out, saying, Master, I beseech thee to look upon my son; for he is mine only child: and behold a spirit taketh him, and he suddenly crieth out; and it teareth him that he foameth, and it hardly departeth from him, bruising him sorely. And I besought thy disciples to cast it out; and they could not. And Jesus answered and said, O faithless and perverse generation, how long shall I be with you, and bear with you? Bring hither thy son. And as he was yet a coming, the demon dashed him down, and tare him grievously. But Jesus rebuked the unclean spirit, and healed the boy, and gave him back to his father. And they were all astonished at the majesty of God. Luke ix. 37-43.

This outstanding case of possession deservedly receives a prominent place in the Triple Tradition. The narrative of Mark is realistic. Its diagnostic value exceeds that of the other two Evangelists. The complaint of this boy might seem to need no definition; for "all have knowledge" of it, as a case of epilepsy. There is the cry preceded by the unconsciousness, the sudden fall, the convulsive seizure, the gnashing of the teeth, the foaming at the mouth, the rolling on the ground; then the utter exhaustion, so that, in the graphic words of the father, the boy "is shrivelled up" ($\xi\eta\rho\alpha\iota\nu\epsilon\tau\alpha\iota$, Mark ix. 18). The latter is also the description of the distinguished Roman physician, Celsus. The comatose condition ensuing on the rapid repetition of severe fits, shows itself in the remark of many who said, He is dead! These features belong to a severe type of epilepsy (*haut mal*), and complete the popular diagnosis.

They do not, however, complete the points on which Jesus laid stress, no more than they would satisfy the inquiries of a physician whose skill is above that of a charlatan. It is very instructive to observe Christ passing beyond the coarse and pronounced symptoms of epilepsy; penetrating beneath the surface with the question: How long ago is it since this befell him? "Since childhood," says the father. That piece of information is peculiar to Mark; although the technical value of it could not have been realised by him. To one's surprise, Luke has nothing to say of the matter; though he tells us, evidently on the authority of Matthew, that the patient was still in the age of boyhood. That note is important; because it is capable of reduction to a numerical estimate, and throws much light on the condition of the boy.

The illness dated "from childhood" (ἐκ παιδιόθεν, Mark ix. 21). Possibly it was congenital. At any rate the convulsions began early in life, and had been frequent. At this date, the fits were so numerous that in the language of the times, "the demon hardly departed from the boy, wearing him away." Boyhood here denotes an age of some twelve years.[1] Here then are convulsions, beginning early in life, severe, and of frequent occurrence. These three factors are clearly brought out, and claim attention. The significance of them lies in the fact that they are the sure precursors of imbecility or idiocy. If any confirmation of this conclusion were needed, we find it in Christ's recognition of the fact that the boy's dumbness and deafness were constituent parts of the mental disorder (Mark ix. 25). They were correlated by Him with the broad epileptic symptoms which were open to all observers. Both sets of symptoms are traced by Jesus to one common underlying condition. That is in full accordance with the observation that sense-defects are common among imbeciles and idiots. In these cases, the loss of any one of the special senses is not to be taken into account as a separate matter; for such a loss denotes an addition also to the other disabilities under which the patient labours,—an

[1] So in Luke ii. 42, 43. Cf. Wagner's *Manual of Pathology*.

aggravation of the whole condition. The dumbness and the deafness here are great calamities *per se*; but they further signify increased mental defect or degeneration. Yet the mere physical health of those subjects may remain surprisingly vigorous, and the bodily strength may be well maintained. That seems to have been the case here; apart, of course, from the temporary exhaustion following the fits. It is clear that the boy did not remain indoors; otherwise he could not have fallen "often into the fire and often into the water." These words are explicit evidence that the lad was prone to wander abroad, apparently baffling the care of his guardians. Like other epileptic idiots, he was restless in his habits. Indications of wild impulses, unruly passions, destructive propensities, and suicidal intent, are furnished by the assertion that the "spirit often dashed him into fire and into waters, that it might destroy him." As in kindred cases, these outbreaks were likely to be mostly unprovoked and not easily circumvented. The dumbness and deafness, the multiplicity and severity of the convulsions, are proofs of serious organic disease or degeneration of the brain; issuing in this deplorable imbecility or idiocy, with its attendant perils. The case of this boy is almost desperate, even among epileptic idiots.[1]

---

[1] Jurists have drawn distinctions between imbecility and idiocy. Coke defined an idiot as one "who from his nativity by a perpetual infirmity is *non compos mentis.*" Alienists are content to assume the clinical standpoint and to regard both imbecility and idiocy as but degrees of weakmindedness.

SIGNIFICANCE OF THE DEMONIAC STATE

These then are the three "typical cases" of possession. From them we derive the meaning to be attached to the demoniac state as described in the New Testament. On the physical side, these are concrete instances of epileptic insanity, acute mania, and epileptic idiocy. In other words, they all belonged to the general category of "Lunacy and Idiocy." That, therefore, is the real significance of the demoniac state; and this definite conception is to be carried forward for the consideration of the more obscure cases.

THE SYRO-PHŒNICIAN GIRL

Jesus went out thence and withdrew into the parts of Tyre and Sidon. And behold, a Canaanitish woman came out from those borders and cried, saying, Have mercy on me, O Lord, thou son of David; my daughter is grievously vexed with a demon. Jesus answered and said unto her, O woman, great is thy faith, be it unto thee, even as thou wilt. And her daughter was healed from that hour. Matt. xv. 21, 22, 28.

From thence he arose, and went into the borders of Tyre and Sidon. Straightway, a woman whose little daughter had an unclean spirit, having heard of him, came and fell down at his feet. Now the woman was a Greek, a Syro-Phœnician by race. And she besought him that he would cast forth the demon out of her daughter. And he said unto her, For this saying, go thy way; the demon is gone out of thy daughter. And she went away to her house, and found the child laid upon the bed, and the demon gone forth." Mark vii. 24-26, 29, 30.

In point of time, this case precedes that of the idiot boy; but the previous study of the latter greatly facilitates the consideration of the present instance. The two have several notable points of contact with each other, which are specially noted by Mark. These common features are the sure guide to the proper diagnosis.

1. The ages of both patients are nearly the same. Mark applies to each of them the designation, "child" ($\pi\alpha\iota\delta\iota\rho\nu$, vii. 30, ix. 24). But the age of the boy was shown to be about twelve years. That also appears to be the age of the "young daughter" of the Syro-Phœnician mother.

2. The symptoms of their derangements are closely akin. The boy "suffers badly" (Matt. xvii. 15); the girl is "badly demonised" (Matt. xv. 22). The infesting spirit in each case is "filthy" (Mark vii. 25, ix. 25). In both there is the suggestion of wild roving habits. There is a note of surprise in the mother returning to find her daughter "laid upon the bed." The absence of deafness and dumbness in the case of the girl only proves that her illness has not yet reached its worst phases.

3. The termination of the two cases is in convulsions. The Authorised and Revised Versions, with admirable equivocation say that the girl was found "laid upon the bed." The common but false variant reading—$\beta\epsilon\beta\lambda\eta\mu\acute{\epsilon}\nu\eta\nu\ \acute{\epsilon}\pi\grave{\iota}\ \tau\hat{\eta}\varsigma\ \kappa\lambda\acute{\iota}\nu\eta\varsigma$—would denote "resting upon the bed."[1] But the correct reading here signifies that the "child" was *hurled upon the bed* ($\beta\epsilon\beta\lambda\eta\mu\acute{\epsilon}\nu o\nu\ \acute{\epsilon}\pi\grave{\iota}\ \tau\grave{\eta}\nu\ \kappa\lambda\acute{\iota}\nu\eta\nu$, Mark vii. 30). The second Evangelist

---

[1] Cf. Matt. ix. 2.

rightly draws attention to the fact that a convulsive seizure was the antecedent common to the healing of those two.

This brief comparison of their symptoms proves that the ailments were essentially alike. The diagnosis here is thus epileptic idiocy. But while the boy was brought to Jesus for cure, the girl was healed at a distance. There is then a difference in the sequel to those two cases. The lad was returned to his father in the full enjoyment of both mental and physical health; the girl was *hurled upon the bed*; freed from her mental derangement, but with her physical energies not as yet recruited. In the former cases, the commanding word and the invigorating touch of Jesus issued in complete restoration; in the latter the word was effective, but the touch was lacking. The lad had undergone a double miracle; not so the girl. The complete convalescence of the daughter of Jairus was left to rest and diet (Mark v. 43); and a similar course is indicated in the case of the daughter of this Syro-Phœnician mother.

THE DUMB DEMONIAC

And as they went forth, behold, there was brought to him a dumb man (κωφός), possessed with a demon. And when the demon was cast out, the dumb man spake. And the multitudes marvelled, saying, It was never so seen in Israel. But the Pharisees said, By the prince of demons, casteth he out demons. Matt. ix. 32–34; cf. Luke xi. 14, 15.

This brief and almost casual description of this demoniac's condition is very unpromising. Mental derangement is assumed on the grounds already stated. The dumbness with which it is associated puts us on the track for the discovery of its specific form. Dumbness may arise from many causes. It is often the sequel of deafness; for the normal antecedent of speech is hearing. Deafness, therefore, complete or nearly complete, if congenital or acquired early in life, through defect or disease or injury to the parts connected with the organs of hearing, is almost a certain precursor of dumbness. This close relation between deafness and dumbness is reflected in the Greek term κωφός, as in the Hebrew חרש, which alike denote deaf, or dumb, or deaf-and-dumb. But by far the commonest cause of true dumbness is that associated with mental disorder arising from cerebral defect or disease. The mental derangement implied in the demoniac state here coexists with dumbness which involves deafness. This triple conjunction of mental disease, dumbness, and deafness, leads straightway to the diagnosis of idiocy or imbecility.

THE BLIND AND DUMB DEMONIAC

Then was brought unto him one possessed of a demon, blind and dumb: and he healed him, insomuch that the dumb man spake and saw. And all the multitudes were amazed and said, Is this the son of David? But when the Pharisees heard it, they said, This man doth not cast out demons, but by Beelzebul as prince of demons. Matt. xii. 22-24; cf. Luke xi. 14, 15.

This case is not at all to be identified with the preceding, as if it were a duplicate of the same.[1] But, like the former, it is a case of idiocy or imbecility; with the additional feature of blindness. That is a new element of serious import here. Blindness may arise from congenital defects in the organs of vision, or it may be the outcome of local disease or injury. In like manner, it may be the result of disease or defect in those parts of the brain which are connected with the organs of vision. It may then coexist with intellectual incapacities. There is every reason to believe that the dumbness, deafness, and blindness, here present, are in organic union with the mental disorder, and therefore constituent parts of one underlying condition, namely, grave cerebral defect or disease. The idiocy or imbecility is thus of an aggravated type. Though life might not be immediately endangered, there was here a fourfold disaster which must have reduced the patient to a condition of most abject misery and helplessness.

MARY MAGDALENE

With him were certain women who had been healed of evil spirits and infirmities,—Mary that was called the Magdalene, from whom seven demons had gone forth. Luke viii. 2 (cf. Mark xvi. 9).

[1] See Appendix C, The dumb demoniac *versus* the blind and dumb demoniac.

This is the only demoniac who bears a name; and she is the unhappy possessor of seven demons. Talmudists have much slandered her; but in this matter they are hardly worse than those who confound her with the woman who washed the feet of Jesus with her tears (Luke vii. 37, 38); or have made her the patroness of unfortunates. John Lightfoot understood by the term "Magdalene," "a hair-curler," which metaphorically bears a suspicious significance. In this unfortunate conjecture, he has been followed by Lagarde and others. But the obvious interpretation is that which associates Mary with the town of Magdala, then largely engaged in dyeing and woollen manufactures. She was probably a widow in affluent circumstances, like Lydia of Thyatira (Acts xvi. 14). Her appearance in the company of the wife of Herod's steward, and her ministrations to Jesus in life and in death, confirm our conjecture as to her good social position. The interest of the situation lies in its indication of the existence of mental disease among the upper classes of the Jews at this date.

Celsus (not the Roman physician of that name, but the friend of Lucian) calls Mary a "half-frantic woman" ($\gamma \upsilon \nu \grave{\eta}\ \pi \acute{a} \rho o \iota \sigma \tau \rho o s$).[1] While insanity was doubtless present, it is not quite easy to assign a precise meaning to the "seven demons." To connect these with her "many sins" is a gratuitous assumption. Or to discover here, seven attacks of illness and

[1] Origen, *Contra Celsum*, ii. 55.

seven recoveries, is inconsistent with the fact that Jesus turned out the "seven" at a single operation. Renan associates the derangement of Mary with the Persian Asmodæus, "the cause of all the hysterical afflictions of women." But the ailment here is not hysteria. Nor is her case parallel with that where the single demon goes forth to consort with "other seven," more wicked than himself; for the demons of Mary are seven, not eight. The best explanation is that which leads us to recognise here the operation of Babylonian influences. In the "Magical Texts" of Babylonia, the "seven spirits" are of frequent occurrence. Possession by them was of the gravest significance; necessitating an appeal to Ea, Lord of spirits. The appointed remedy was the smoke of the cedar tree, on whose core was written the name of Ea, ascending to the roof of the chamber, coupled with the spell supreme, the spell of Eridu and of purity.[1] The mention of the "seven" thus attests the severity of Mary's disorder; proving that it surpassed the skill of ordinary practitioners. Evidently she too was brought to Jesus in a state of utmost distress. Her ailment is acute mania.

THE INFIRM WOMAN

And he was teaching in one of the synagogues on the Sabbath day. And behold a woman who had a spirit of infirmity eighteen years; and she was bowed together, and could in no wise lift herself up. And

---

[1] Sayce, *Hibbert Lectures*, pp. 459, 470, 471.

when Jesus saw her, he called her and said to her, Woman, thou art loosed from thine infirmity. And he laid his hands upon her. And immediately she was made straight, and glorified God. (Jesus said), Ought not this woman, being a daughter of Abraham, whom Satan hath bound, lo, these eighteen years, to have been loosed from this bond on the Sabbath day? Luke xiii. 10-13, 16.

Consideration of this case has been deferred, because it is not clearly a case of possession. The woman is said to have been bound by Satan, and to have had "a spirit of infirmity." Meyer puts her in the class of the demoniacs. For him, "the spirit of infirmity" is a demon who has "paralysed her muscular powers." "As a daughter of Abraham, she belongs to the special people of God, and must hence be wrested from the devil; since he, by means of one of his servants,—a demon, has taken away her liberty."[1] The proof of this statement must rest upon the report of the symptoms and the express testimony of our Lord.

1. *The report of the case.*—The symptoms enumerated are such as refer to the inability of the woman to assume an erect carriage. The points noted are—

(*a*) A constant and pronounced stoop.

(*b*) A marked loss of muscular power.

(*c*) A rigidity of certain structures.

(*d*) A disorder not psychical but surgical.

In the first instance, the case is described as one of "infirmity." In the second, as "spirit of infirmity." But the two terms are coextensive. The latter

[1] Meyer, *in loco.*

cannot contain any more than the former. Then mention is made of a "bond"; but its significance is demonstrably pathological. To its existence, the woman owed her inability to "look up at all." It has been variously interpreted as "gouty contraction," "muscular contraction," and "paralytic crippling." Another suggestion is "rheumatism." But until popular expositors condescend to enlighten us on the group of muscles thus affected, their conjectures are not worth a moment's consideration. The woman "was bowed together," and had been in that state for "eighteen years." The stoop was not more severe than prolonged. We regard this therefore as an exteme instance of spinal disease, in the form of "Pott's curvature." The passage is rich in medical terms, all pointing to the same conclusion. Hippocrates, speaking of curvature of the spine, uses the term λύειν, for its removal. Galen employs ἀνακύπτειν, for the straightening of the vertebal column. The ancient surgeons use ἀπολύειν, for the relaxation of tendons, membranes, and other structures; also ἀνορθοῦν, for replacing parts in their normal position. Luke employs the current terminology in these connections.[1] The crowning corroboration of this view is found in the term "bond." In disease of this sort, there is at the conclusion of the morbid process the formation of a "bond," by the fusion and cementing together of the disorganised tissues; entailing an "infirmity," through the atrophy of the dorsal muscles.

[1] Hobart, *Medical Language of St. Luke*, p. 21.

There is no evidence whatever for the belief that this spinal complaint concurred with mental derangement. The woman is a quiet member of the synagogue, approaching Jesus without confession or adjuration. In this respect, she is on a level with the sanest of her neighbours.

2. *The testimony of Jesus.* — This includes His acts as well as His words. In all other cases, the demoniacs are healed "by a word." Here, however, there is no exorcism, but imposition of hands. The latter is indeed expressly reserved for non-demonic cases; such as leprosy (Matt. viii. 3), fever (Mark i. 31), blindness (Matt. ix. 29), and common ailments (Mark vi. 5; Luke iv. 40). That further forbids the inclusion of this case among the demonised. The phrase "spirit of infirmity," which is Luke's, does not militate against this assertion; for both Hellenistic and Rabbinic custom permitted its use as an abstract form in place of the concrete term "infirmity," here employed by our Lord. What then are we to make of the description, " —whom Satan has bound"? Trench discovers in this comment "a deeper spiritual root" to the woman's calamity. "Her sickness, having its first seat in her spirit, had brought her into a moody, melancholy state," of which her outward condition "was but the sign and the consequence."[1] It will readily be granted that the kingdom of Satan has its physical as well as its ethical side. But the latter is not here in evidence. This woman is a devout

[1] Trench, *Notes on the Miracles.*

worshipper, "a daughter of Abraham," and therefore still an heir of the promises. She is no "profane person," no abandoned wretch, no God-forsaken Judas, into whom Satan has entered. The "binding" then has no reference to any ethical operation; but simply to the physical condition. Neither the symptoms of this case, nor the testimony of Christ, can be construed into proof of demonic possession.

THE PHILIPPIAN PYTHONESS

And it came to pass that as we were going to the place of prayer, a certain maid, having a spirit, a Python, met us, who brought her masters much gain by soothsaying. The same following after Paul and us, cried out saying, These men are servants of the Most High God who proclaim to you a way of salvation. And this she did for many days. But Paul being sore troubled, turned and said to the spirit, I charge thee in the Name of Jesus Christ to come out of her. And it came out that very hour." Acts xvi. 16–18.

The special features of this case suggest two theories,—fraud or insanity. The discovery of the truth here is not a simple matter. We start from the fact that somehow there was a decided change in the condition of this maid, which rendered her incapable of pursuing her former vocation. She was cured of something,—either fraud or insanity.

1. Was this a case of fraud and wilful imposition? The prophetic art, such as it was among the nations at this time, laboured under severe suspicion, though the age was notorious for its credulity. It is wrong, how-

ever, to suppose that the ancient oracles were mere manufactories of lies. Sometimes we find them advocating patriotic schemes, such as naval defence and foreign colonisation. Statecraft was here supplemented by priestcraft; but collusion need not be supposed. Even the delivery of ambiguous oracles cannot always be traced to intentional equivocation. The whole profession was a vast pseudo-science, whose agents, by the very rules of their art, had often to halt betwixt two opinions. That is the best that can be said for the oracles of old. The element of crookedness tended to enter into their transactions. Modes of tampering with seals were quite well known.[1] If, in the higher ranks of this calling, fraud was frequent, the same was much more common among the venal and rapacious soothsayers of the streets. Was this maid then a mere impostor? The foregoing considerations would point in that direction. But there are others which are quite decisive against the theory of wilful imposition. The august counterpart of this woman was the Pythoness of Delphi. Both were supposed to be inspired by Apollo. Both belonged to a religious system keenly antagonistic to that proclaimed by Paul. No mere trickster would have ventured to advertise this rival company as "servants of the Most High God who announce a way of salvation." But that was the very thing this soothsayer did, "for many days"; to the vast loss of the syndicate who owned her, and to the great grief of Paul. A shrewd

[1] Lucian, *Pseudomantis*.

adventuress would not have created those troubles for herself and her employers. If the Apostle had suspected her of mere deceit, her discomfiture would not have lingered so long. Before his "glittering eye," Elymas, the well-seasoned sorcerer, had already recoiled in terror. A sagacious fortune-teller would have instinctively avoided such company. So the theory of fraud entirely fails to substantiate itself.

2. Was this a case of insanity? There are abnormal symptoms of that sort; such as want of self-control, along with noisy demonstrations. Clearly, the woman was incapable of taking in the situation; whether it affected her masters, whose sordid selfishness she did not understand, or Paul, who was vexed with her monotonous wail. Her insanity was of a mild chronic type, quite harmless to the lieges. She had wit enough to distinguish Paul and his company day after day, and memory sufficient to pick up a few phrases among those strangers; such as "servants of the Most High God," and "way," and "salvation." The very mildness of her derangement was one of her best qualifications for discharging the functions of a Pythoness. Euripides remarks that "madness has a good deal of the prophetic art; for whenever the god largely enters the body, he makes the madmen foretell the future."[1] Plato similarly says that "the greatest blessings we possess, spring from madness, when granted by the bounty of heaven. For the prophetesses at Delphi and the priestesses at Dodona, when mad, have

[1] *Bacchæ*, 241.

done many and noble services to Greece, but in their sober senses, little or nothing."[1] How easily a lunatic might pass for a heaven-sent messenger, is seen from the words of Plato, as quoted by Clement of Alexandria, attributing "a certain dialect to the gods; concluding this specially from dreams and oracles, as well as from demoniacs, who do not speak their own language, but that of the indwelling demons." In the case before us, this maid had "a spirit, a Python": otherwise a soothsaying demon (δαιμόνιον μαντικόν).[2] "The inspired idiot" is a well-known phrase, recalling the preceding opinions. It remains a conviction with some who regard themselves as illuminated, but whose affinities in this respect are decidedly with the races of the lower culture.

THE EPHESIAN DEMONIAC

And God wrought special miracles by the hand of Paul; insomuch that unto the sick were carried from his body handkerchiefs or aprons, and the diseases departed from them, and the evil spirits went forth. But certain also of the strolling Jews, exorcists, took upon them to name over them that had evil spirits, the name of the Lord Jesus, saying, I adjure you by Jesus whom Paul preacheth! And there were seven sons of one Sceva, a Jew, a chief priest, who did this. And the evil spirit answered and said unto them, Jesus I acknowledge and Paul I am acquainted with; but who are ye? And the man in whom the evil spirit was, leaped on them, and mastered both of them, and prevailed against

---

[1] *Phædrus*, 47.
[2] Meyer, *in loco*; cf. *Æneid*, vi. 77-80.

them, so that they fled out of that house, naked and wounded. Acts xix. 11–16.[1]

There is a change here in the character of the cases of possession compared with those previously considered. The superstitions of the Ephesian Christians are thrust into unhappy prominence, as well as their magical practices. Paul had long laboured in Ephesus; the result being that "all those who dwelt in Asia heard the word of the Lord, both Jews and Greeks." His reputation as a worker of miracles was also firmly established; so that "from his person were brought to the sick, handkerchiefs and aprons," when demons and diseases alike departed. The Apostle had thus, in popular esteem, become a store of healing virtue, which required only a material vehicle to render it effective to the afflicted at a distance. At an earlier period, we find Peter in Jerusalem, the object of a similar veneration. People resorted to him for therapeutic purposes, trusting not in "handkerchiefs and aprons"; but in his "shadow" (Acts v. 15). There is no evidence whatever to prove that either Peter or Paul encouraged those practices, which savoured strongly of superstition. The grace of God is not of necessity bound to the correctness of a theory. Jesus responded to a genuine, though superstitious, faith in the case of the sick woman (Matt. ix. 22).

The cure of the possessed at Ephesus would have been reduced to its simplest ethnic terms, had clothes

[1] Appendix D, Fact-basis of the Ephesian narrative.

"touched to the body" of Paul been used alone. It is evident, however, that the Name of Jesus was the potent instrument in the cure of the demoniacs by the Christians. The strolling Jews were prompt to notice the point; and the sons of Sceva forthwith resolved to add the Name to their repertory of incantations. Their first attempt to operate with the new talisman was not more dangerous than ludicrous. A genuine experiment was aimed at by those exorcists. The demoniac was no selected impostor. He was apparently a sufferer from epileptic insanity, now enjoying a temporary intermission of his troubles. There are indications of a certain degree of mental vigour, and traces of religious monomania. The course of events becomes quite intelligible.

The initial state of this man betokened no immediate danger. He was in a house, when sought out by this enterprising couple. But his condition was one of excessive irritability; predisposing him to violent reaction on the application of even a trifling stimulus. The routine Jewish practice, as attested by Josephus and Justin Martyr, comprised adjurations and fumigations. The method was undoubtedly most provocative to a person "possessed." What more certain than that the alarming adjuration combined with the acrid smoke would produce an instant outburst of maniacal fury? The lunatic, now roused to the highest pitch of excitement by those sons of Sceva, summed up all his grievances in a comprehensive "assault and battery" on his tormentors. They had gone, no doubt, to that house in the brave attire of the magician;[1] but after being "jumped upon" and "mastered" (Acts xix. 16), they fled from the scene of their operations, bare and bleeding! That spectacle was highly edifying to those who had hitherto reconciled their profession of Christianity with the practice of "curious arts." Burning their books, they thenceforth purged themselves from this leaven of paganism.

[1] See Lucian's *Philopseudes*, *Necyomantis*, and *Pseudomantis*.

CHAPTER IV

MEDICAL ASPECTS OF DEMONIC POSSESSION—*continued*

NUMBERS OF THE POSSESSED IN THE TIME OF OUR LORD

AN approximation only is possible; but even that leads far afield. When, however, the indications available are carefully considered, a fair appreciation of the numbers of the possessed at this date is attainable.

A. *The regions whence the possessed were brought*

These were Judæa, Galilee, Peræa; also Decapolis, Tyre, and Sidon.[1] The three former districts comprised the great divisions of Jewish territory proper. The other three were outlandish, and inhabited by mixed populations. The cities of Decapolis are not uniformly defined by the ancient geographers. The number may have varied, as the towns composing this confederacy were loosely combined for mutual purposes of commerce and defence. Pliny mentions Scythopolis, Hippos, Gadara, Pella, Philadelphia,

[1] Matt. iv. 25; Mark iii. 7, 8; Luke vi. 17.

Gerasa, Dion, Canatha, Damascus, and Raphana. Ptolemy gives eighteen cities; but the numerical difference is immaterial. The point to be noted is that Damascus is common to both lists. That disposes of the attempt of Keim to remove it from the catalogue of "The Ten Cities." It also points to the reason for Christ's choice of Capernaum as a centre for effective work. *Capernaum was the focal point of the Eastern and Western Dispersions, because of its situation on the great commercial highway between the East and the West.* It dominated the following regions:—

1. The Euphrates Valley.
2. Decapolis and the towns of Galilee.
3. Tyre, Sidon, and other Mediterranean ports.
4. Jerusalem and its southern dependencies.

At this date the Jewish merchants of Babylonia and Alexandria almost monopolised the Indian and Eastern Trade of the Roman Empire. The former were interested in the sea-borne commerce which passed up the Persian Gulf, by the Euphrates Valley, through Palmyra, Damascus, and Capernaum; thence to such ports as Tyre and Sidon; and so to the cities of the West generally. Any event of uncommon importance occurring in Capernaum would within a few days be reported in the Eastern and Western Dispersions. The news sped along the great trade-routes radiating from Capernaum. After the stirring events associated with the beginning of the Healing Ministry of Jesus in that city, we can at once understand how multitudes should flock from all parts of the land of Israel; also from Decapolis, Tyre, and Sidon. The Jews of the Diaspora might have availed themselves of the gracious activity of our Lord in the healing of the afflicted.

B. *The population of Palestine*

The census returns of Augustus have vanished long ago; and we must rely on indirect evidence. The enumeration of Joab covered an area closely corresponding to "Judæa, Galilee, Peræa; Decapolis, Tyre, and Sidon." It indicates a population of not less than 4,000,000. Another account gives even a larger reckoning.[1] The figures may seem high for a land mainly engaged in agriculture; but the period was a prosperous one. That census may fairly represent the case also in the time of our Lord.

When Sennacherib captured "forty-six of the strong cities of Hezekiah, with innumerable fortresses and small towns," he "counted as a spoil 200,150 persons, great and small, male and female." This loss does not seem to have been much felt in the little Southern Kingdom, whose population could scarcely be less than 1,000,000. Comparing the area concerned with that traversed by Joab, we are prepared to accept 4,000,000 as the population under David and under the early rule of the Romans.

Josephus asserts that in his day, Galilee contained

[1] 2 Sam. xxiv. 5-9; cf. 1 Chron. xxi. 5, 6.

"240 cities and villages";[1] each containing "more than 15,000 people."[2] That gives a population of more than 4,000,000. But these figures are fabulous. They give a density of population of more than 3000 per square mile; whereas Lancashire, the most populous county of England, after Middlesex, has less than 2000 on the same unit of surface. Again, the exports of Galilee were enormous, and found an outlet in the markets of the world. But if the population of this district were 4,000,000, then the home consumption must have been very vast; not permitting exports of the magnitude indicated. We shall not greatly err, if we reduce the estimate of this historian by half, and take the population of the whole country at 4,000,000, as found within "Judæa, Galilee, Peræa; Decapolis, Tyre, and Sidon," in the time of our Lord.[3]

C. *The mental temperament of the people*

The history of the Hebrews is open to us for many generations. Abraham represents the Arabic strain in this race; Jacob, the Aramaic. The temperament of this nation was highly emotional, greatly impulsive, and prone to melancholy in critical situations. These pathological elements are not at variance with the

---

[1] *Vita*, 45. [2] *B. J.* III. iii. 2.
[3] The number of the passover pilgrims was some 3,000,000 (*B. J.* VI. ix. 3). Another account suggests 6,000,000; the kidneys of the paschal lambs being 600,000 (Pes. 64b). Many of these pilgrims were from the Diaspora; so that there is here no clue to the population of

possession of great excellences otherwise. The liability to excessive emotion reminds us of the weeping warriors of Homer. Thus, after a temporary reverse, Joshua and the elders of Israel fell to the earth, upon their faces, before the ark, till eventide; rending their clothes and casting dust upon their heads (Josh. vii. 6). A similar picture is given when the tribes were defeated by Benjamin; for they wept and fasted (Judg. xx. 26). In like fashion, David and his mighty men cried over their losses, till they had no more power to cry (1 Sam. xxx. 4). The ambassadors of Hezekiah similarly shed bitter tears over their ill success with Sennacherib (Isa. xxxiii. 7). Jeremiah describes the daughters of Zion, as sitting in silence on the earth, casting dust upon their heads, and girding themselves with sackcloth (Lam. ii. 10). Ezra gave way to temporary religious melancholy when he tore his mantle, plucked out the hair of his head and beard, and sat down dumb with astonishment (Ezra ix. 3). These instances of a strong neurotic element in the temperament of the people readily became conventional or theatrical, on the one hand; or easily developed into mental disease under adverse circumstances, on the other.

The records of suicide are not of much consequence in this connection; because the significance of the act is not always discernible. Abimelech was really a suicide (Judg. ix. 54). Saul and his armour-bearer, also Ahithophel, figure thus in the Old Testament, and Judas in the New. But Josephus and other writers attest an unhappy frequency of such rash acts at a later date.[1]

D. *The mental health of the people*

Here the concrete instances of mental derangement recorded in the Old Testament fall for description. To these are to be added certain general indications of the existence of such ailments, derivable from the same source—

1. *David's feigned dementia.*[2]—The easy and successful imitation of this condition by David argues its frequency at this date; in this locality at least. It would otherwise have been impossible to impose so completely on the court. David " changed his conduct "; scrabbling on the doors, and slavering on his beard. So aptly did he play his part, that the king curtly dismissed him with the remark: Lo, the man is mad!

2. *Saul's persecution mania.*[3]—The history of this case is most striking. From the first, Saul evinced a supersensitive disposition. When called to be king, he hid himself. His speedy assumption of the prophetic rôle was natural to him; though surprising to the spectators. Not long afterwards, he betrayed decided symptoms of mental disorder, for which his courtiers advised the services of a cunning musician. Saul's first outbreak of jealousy against

---

[1] Jos. *B. J.* III. viii. 5, 6, 7, VII. viii. 6, 7 ; Gittin 57b ; Chullin 94a.
[2] 1 Sam. xxi. 13, 14.   [3] 1 Sam. xvi. xviii.-xxi.

David occurs in connection with the ode of triumph—

Saul has slain his thousands,
And David his ten thousands.

From that day onward, he eyed David. The period of the insane interpretation of the conduct of others has now begun; also a deeply rooted aversion to David as the cause of all his troubles. Probably, the king suffered, like others of this class, from hallucinations; such as imaginary voices, urging him on to acts of violence. Preceding these outbreaks, there is a phase of mental exaltation, with much incoherent talk. He prophesied (raved R.V.) in the midst of the house. The sequel was a deliberate attempt on the life of David. Failing in this, he adopts a more politic course by giving David a commission against the Philistines. Again disappointed, he incites others to secret assassination; but in accordance with the usual course of this ailment, he shows himself, for a little, amenable to reason, upon the intercession of Jonathan. His derangement again suddenly asserts itself; and, yielding thereafter to his homicidal impulses, the king renews his attempts on the life of David. Being thwarted once more, he sends forth emissaries to kill him at dawn. His morbid suspicion is now fully organised; and in the pursuit of David, he passes again into the ecstatic state; stripping himself of his clothing; lying down unclad, all that day and all that night. After David's escape. Jonathan falls under suspicion as the accomplice of the absentee; and becomes in turn the object of homicidal passion. This third outbreak of maniacal fury is the antecedent to the characteristic complaint against the army as partisans of the son of Jesse. The outcome of this is the ferocious onslaught on the priests. Then follow two prolonged pursuits of David, which mark the progress of his malady.[1] It is not at all surprising to find again that Saul on each of these occasions, should again prove for a season amenable to reason. His mental vigour as yet does not seem to be impaired in other directions. His suicide saved him from the dementia in which such cases usually end. The whole case is a notable illustration of "persecution mania." Its affinities are wholly remote from the fine poetic creation of Robert Browning, entitled "Saul."[2]

3. *Nebuchadnezzar's lycanthropy.*[3] — The historical difficulties of the narrative are not under consideration; but the enumeration of a set of symptoms indicating the presence of that peculiar form of mental

---

[1] The two narratives are from different sources, and some regard them as duplicates (1 S. m. xxiv. 1–22, xxvi. 1–25). From the psychological standpoint, two separate pursuits are extremely probable.

[2] Josephus misunderstands the disorder of Saul. He speaks of "dreadful and demoniacal disorders," involving "suffocations" and "strangulations"; "an evil spirit and demon assailing him" (ἐγκαθιζομένων). He evidently relies on the Septuagint, which asserts that "an evil spirit from the Lord choked him" (ἔπνιγεν), rather than on the Hebrew, which declares that "an evil spirit from the Lord troubled him." Josephus thinks, no doubt, of epileptic seizures; and ascribes these to demonic agency. He is at the ethnic standpoint; not so, the first Evangelist.

[3] Dan. iv. 22.

disorder, in which the person imagines that he is changed into a beast, and attempts to act in character. This disease was much commoner in ancient times than now; judging from the numerous forms of the myth of the were-wolf. Here the king flees the habitations of men; eating grass like an ox; his body being wet with the dews of heaven, till his hairs were grown like eagle's feathers, and his nails like bird's claws. It is interesting to recall, in this connection, the story of the hero, Eabani, of Chaldaean legend. He was apparently the victim of lycanthropy also.[1]

In addition to these specific cases of mental disease, which were familiar to the Jews, there are other indications of the existence of a large amount of mental disorder. There is madness from drunkenness (Jer. xxv. 16, li. 7); from misfortune (Deut. xxviii. 34); from religious excitement (Hos. ix. 7; Jer. l. 38): from prophetic afflatus (2 Kings ix. 11; Jer. xxix. 26). In the progression of events, circumstances emerged unfavourable to the vigorous mental health of the nation. Their whole environment in the land of their captivity among Babylonians and Persians tended to aggravate latent elements of mental disease. "The Preacher" testifies to an extensive prevalence of insanity in his times. He professes to have made a special study of it (Eccles. i. 17); referring to the same in a series of passages.[2] This writer brings us near to

[1] See Maspero, *Dawn of Civilisation*, p. 576 ff.
[2] Eccles. ii. 2, 12, vii. 7, 25, ix. 3, x. 13.

the year 200 B.C. Renan suggests the year 125 B.C. These dates both introduce us to troublous periods in the history of the Jews. In the former case, they were distressed under the Seleucidæ; in the latter, they bore the hardships of the War of Independence. Any existing mental infirmity among the people would now tend to a disastrous issue. But the crowning aggravation of previous adverse conditions was the weary struggle against the might of Rome, with its tyrannies, its fanaticisms, and its copious bloodshed. These things prepare us for the discovery of a large amount of psychical disease among the Jews in the time of Christ.

E. *The representations of the Gospels*

1. Capernaum is the first scene of Christ's activity in this department; but not the first scene of His miraculous powers. In addition to the healing of the demoniac in the synagogue, we find a large concourse—

When the even was come, they brought unto him many that were demonised and he cast out the spirits with a word, and all that were ill he healed. Matt. viii. 16. Cf. Mark i. 32, 34. Luke iv. 40, 41.

2. The scene of a wider ministry is now Galilee, of which we have little more than summary notices—

Jesus was going about in the whole of Galilee, teaching in their synagogues and preaching the good news of the kingdom, and healing every disease, and every infirmity among the people. Matt. iv. 23. Preaching and casting out demons. Mark i. 39. Cf. Luke iv. 44.

3. The climax of this work appears in the great multitudes who were drawn from all parts of the country and from regions beyond—

The report of him went into the whole of Syria, and they brought unto him all that were sick, holden of divers diseases and torments, specially also¹ the demonised and the epileptic and the palsied; and he healed them. And there followed him great multitudes from Galilee, and Decapolis, and Jerusalem, and Judæa, and from beyond Jordan. Matt. iv. 24, 25. Cf. Mark iii. 7, 8, 10, 11. Luke iv. 14, 15.

4. This vast movement proved that the harvest was great and the labourers few, so that the choosing of the Twelve is in close relation to it—

He called unto him his twelve disciples, and gave them authority over unclean spirits, to cast them out, and to heal every disease and every infirmity. Jesus commanded them, saying, Heal the sick, cleanse the lepers, raise the dead, cast out demons. Matt. x. 1, 5, 8. Cf. Mark vi. 7. Luke ix. 1.

5. At a later date, the healing of the possessed is still proceeding apace—

Master, we saw one casting out demons in thy name and we forbade him. Mark ix. 38. Cf. Luke ix. 49.
Go ye and tell that fox, Behold I cast out demons to-day and to-morrow. Luke xiii. 32.

6. The mission of the Seventy is important in attempting to estimate the number of the demonised; both on account of the numbers employed and the success attained. The arguments of Strauss, De Wette, Gfrörer, Baur, and others, lack cogency to pro-

cure its rejection. A full examination of the subject leaves no doubt upon a candid mind regarding the reality of the Mission.[1] The record of it is brief and somewhat paradoxical—

Heal the sick and say to them, The kingdom of God is come nigh unto you. The Seventy returned with joy, saying, Lord even the demons are subject to us, in thy name. Luke x. 9, 17.

7. There may have been other occasions when the demoniacs were healed, though unmentioned; as when Jesus went forth and "saw a great multitude, and was moved with compassion towards them, and healed their sick" (Matt. xiv. 14); or as when they brought to Him the afflicted "out of the cities and villages and country" of Gennesaret (Mark vi. 55, 56). It is a mistake, however, to suppose that the demonised were always in evidence when the healing of disease was going forward. The testimony of Christ is explicit on the point. To the deputation from the Baptist, He said, Go and tell John the things which ye do hear and see. The blind receive their sight and the lame walk, the lepers are cleansed and the deaf hear, the dead are raised up and the poor are evangelised (Matt. xi. 4, 5).[2]

[1] Appendix E, The Mission of the Seventy.
[2] Luke repeats the words of Matthew with a notable addition as preface: "In that same hour, he cured many of their diseases and plagues and evil spirits, and unto many that were blind, he granted sight" Luke vii. 21. The mention of "evil spirits" is an independent touch.

F. *Comparison of the Jews with the Greeks and the Romans*

It has been shown that the hereditary factor was pronounced in the case of the Jews, and was much aggravated in later times. The narratives of the Synoptists prove the existence of a large amount of lunacy and idiocy among this people in the time of our Lord. Were they, then, any worse off than their neighbours in this respect?

1. *The Greeks.*—Latent elements of mental disorder are here also clearly perceptible. Lycanthropy was rather common in Arcadia. The daughters of Proetus were thus afflicted, and the contagion spread to the women of Argos. Bellerophon was insane, "shunning the trodden path of men." Sophocles, in his noble *Ajax*, skilfully describes a case of acute mania. Similarly, Euripides, in his thrilling *Hercules Furens*, depicts artistically a case of epileptic insanity. Herodotus records at some length the madness and self-mutilation of Cleomenes. Plato, in his *Republic*, provides for the adequate care of lunatics. Aristotle repeatedly refers to such ailments. Plutarch, in his *Superstitions*, gives an excellent description of religious melancholy. In his work on "The Failure of the Oracles," he relates the case of the Pythoness at Delphi, who became insane in the discharge of her office; being seized with "a speechless and evil spirit," and dying shortly afterwards.[1] In

[1] The Pythoness inhaled the vapours emanating from the oracular

accordance with these indications, we find insanity and allied diseases receiving scientific attention in the Greek schools of medicine, from the time of Hippocrates onwards. These meagre hints go far to show that in the matter of mental temperament and health, the Greeks were not superior to the Jews.

2. *The Romans.*—Hereditary factors are here also strong. That popular play-wright, Plautus, used to spice his comedies with the lighter phases of insanity, as in his Amphitruo, Aulularia, Captivi, Menæchmus, and Pœnulus. Horace gives an amusing instance of delusional insanity in the gentleman of Argos, who listened with rapt pleasure to imaginary actors in the empty theatre. He denounced his meddlesome friends for curing him of a most delightful delusion. In one of his satires (II. iii.), this poet gives a *locus classicus* on the subject; describing the simple mania of one who treasures up trash; the acute mania of him who pelts his neighbours with stones; the delusional insanity of him who takes a lambkin for his daughter; the dementia of the grey-beard whose joy is baby-games; the active melancholy of the slave who rushes through the streets, bawling out for immortality. Then we have also the valuable treatise of Celsus on mental diseases, and the appalling array of quack remedies preserved (*passim*) by the elder Pliny in his

---

cave. When under their influence, her movements and utterances were interpreted by the presiding priest. These mephitic fumes may have precipitated her insanity.

Natural History. The Emperor Caligula (37–41 A.D.) was full of the wildest ideas; being a sufferer from epileptic insanity. These fragmentary indications demonstrate that in regard to mental temperament and health, the Romans were not superior to the Jews.[1]

G. *Comparison of the Jews with the peoples of the British Isles*

Many other standards of comparison are available; this being merely a matter of convenience. An attempt is here made to reach the practical bearing of the preceding facts, namely, the discovery of the probable number of the possessed in the time of our Lord. The general similarity of the conditions prevalent among those different nations is much more striking than appears at first sight. A comparison is feasible, provided that two things are constantly kept in view.

1. *The factors of causation of mental diseases in general.*—These cannot be enumerated in detail; but with a wide outlook on all the elements of a perplexing problem, it may be asserted that the two cases are fairly on a par. In favour of the Jews was their greater temperance; to their disadvantage was their adverse environment at this date. The excessive use

---

[1] Suicide among the Romans throws little or no light upon the present subject; having practically become a philosophic adieu to life. The act is, however, always inconsistent with a healthy, self-sufficient temperament.

of stimulants in these Islands is confessedly responsible for more than twelve per cent. of the existing cases of mental disease. But the trying surroundings of the Jews, social and political, could scarcely be less baneful, in this regard. The "occurring" cases must therefore be regarded as nearly equal.

2. *The treatment of the possessed.*—The Jewish methods were magical and irrational; productive of much harm on the whole. That is part of the information conveyed in the parable of the demon returning reinforced by other seven, worse than himself (Matt. xii. 43–45). But the ill effects of the ancient methods acted in two directions. The rude empiricism of an ignorant age multiplied the numbers of the possessed. Injudicious treatment or neglect killed them off. The one factor balanced the other. Similarly, the beneficial effects of modern medicine act curiously in two directions. The scientific methods of to-day tend to the restoration of mental health and to a diminution in the numbers of the insane and idiots. But rational treatment and careful nursing prolong lives formerly sacrificed by the lack of these advantages. The total, therefore, of "existing" cases stands somewhere about the old level.

Where the factors of causation are so nearly identical, and where countervailing elements in treatment produce almost similar results, the proportion of "existing" cases of mental diseases in those two communities is practically the same. If so, then the following results accrue:—

Census returns for the British Isles (1891)—

| Total Population | . | . | . | 37,888,153 |
| Insane and Idiots | . | . | . | 115,641 |

Estimated returns for Palestine (*circa* 30 A.D.)—

| Total Population | . | . | . | 4,000,000 |
| Insane and Idiots | . | . | . | 12,000 |

That seems to be the nearest possible approximation to the numbers of the possessed in the time of our Lord. The application of the proper technical formulæ would readily disclose the average number cured within any given period. But such an attempt would be useless; because the healing of the possessed neither proceeded at a uniform rate, nor was it completed. Christ had at one time the assistance of the Twelve; and at another, the aid of the Seventy. Help was thus placed within the reach of all. Yet large numbers at a later date resorted to the Apostles in Jerusalem for the cure of such ailments (Acts v. 16). That fact, coupled with the representations of the Gospels, seems to corroborate the foregoing estimate of the numbers of the demonised in Palestine in the time of our Lord.[1]

---

[1] The Jews of Mesopotamia, Syria, and Egypt alone were reckoned at many millions. Being in very close touch with their brethren in the home-land, they were doubtless aware that "a great prophet" had arisen in Galilee. But their contribution to the number of the demoniacs cured by Christ must have been small, if any. The difficulties in the way of bringing such patients so far were enormous. Perhaps

NATURALNESS OF THE ETHNIC THEORY OF POSSESSION

The physical basis of the "demoniac state" has been shown to be "lunacy or idiocy." We have now to consider how natural the ancient theory of possession was. The demonstration need not proceed beyond the three typical cases.

1. *Epileptic insanity.* — During his convulsive seizures, the person seems to be throttled by an unseen foe, as he writhes and foams on the ground. During the fury of his maniacal excitement, conduct and character seem to have wholly changed. There is also an air of purpose and method in those outbursts of fury and destructiveness, which bespeaks a guiding agency. At the end of this abnormal state, the patient may have no remembrance of what has transpired, or he may give an erroneous account of himself. What simpler explanation of the matter, then, than that of the untutored mind? A demon has entered into the person, overpowering his soul, and compelling the members of the possessed to do its wicked will.

2. *Acute mania.*—The personality is here also changed; the thoughts, affections, and activities being

---

the heathen contributed more than those Jews to the multitudes of the demonised. There is the case of the Syro-Phœnician girl; possibly also that of the Gerasene. At least, Josephus calls the adjacent Gadara "a Hellenistic city." The natives of Decapolis, who in characteristic phrase, "glorified the God of Israel," may have witnessed the cure of the possessed in their midst; among the "many others" (Matt. xv. 30) disordered. Memory is dislocated. The person is out of harmony with his surroundings. He becomes indifferent to social customs and established usages: sometimes so violently hostile to them that he prefers wild solitude. He seems to have entered the society of invisible beings; holding ghostly conference with them; seeing what no other sees; hearing what no other hears; now crouching in dread before his spectral foes; now shouting out defiance; now relentlessly mutilating himself. What other interpretation can the unscientific mind put on these proceedings than demonic possession?

3. *Epileptic idiocy.* — The epileptic seizures are evidently the work of a wicked spirit. If the condition has begun early in life and is constantly progressing, then it is plain that the demon has been gaining the upper hand and usurping the body of its victim. If the attacks are severe and frequent, then it is evident that the "demon hardly departeth"; every fresh attack being a new onset of the foul demon; every cessation of the symptoms a departure of the assailant. Attempts at suicide are clearly the efforts of the malignant demon to destroy the life of the possessed. The simplest explanation is the primitive one. The person is demonised!

NATURALNESS OF THE TERMS "EVIL" AND "UNCLEAN"

Evil and unclean spirits are sometimes "spirits of

the tombs,"[1] "spirits of foul places," "spirits of unclean diseases," "souls of the wicked dead." But in connection with the demoniacs, this nomenclature has evidently a significance of its own. On ethnic principles, the conduct of the possessed was the clue to the character of the possessing demon. The use of the preceding descriptive terms arises naturally out of the circumstances; and remembering that the physical basis of the demoniac state is lunacy or idiocy, a further study of the subjects of those derangements at once discloses the rationale of the designations, "evil" and "unclean." Esquirol declared that moral alienation is the proper characteristic of mental derangement; adding that though "there are madmen in whom it is difficult to find any traces of hallucinations, there are none in whom the passions and the moral affections are not perverted or destroyed." These propositions may not command unlimited assent; but they represent the facts of a very wide experience, and help us now. A consideration of the three typical cases explains and justifies the use of the terms under consideration.

1. *The demoniac of Capernaum.*—His outburst of epileptic insanity was preceded by a certain amount of mental deterioration, shown in his aimless wanderings which implied inability to discharge the duties of his position, and loss of interest in his occupation. In cases of this sort, memory becomes defective; the temper is liable to exacerbations of violence or homi-

cidal fury. The finer sensibilities are impaired; low tastes or nasty habits are contracted. Religious monomania may coexist with erotomania. As the case advances to its worst, brutish instincts tend to predominate, and the very physiognomy may assume a brutal aspect. With such crass comminglings of religion and repulsiveness, the terms "evil" and "unclean" are sadly significant.

2. *The demoniac of Gerasa.*—This man, prior to his being healed, was in a most deplorable state. His normal memory was gone; his sense of propriety had vanished. He was quite unfit for the society of his fellows, and sought a congenial abode in the place of uncleanness. But things still worse were present. There was his delight in odious nudity, and his horrid self-mutilations. In him, as in others of his class, the moral sense is largely suppressed; the result being that brutish impulses become regnant. Through all these phenomena of degradation, physical, mental, and moral, there appears to have run, as so often under such circumstances, a strain of religious fervour. The terms "evil" and "unclean" are therefore most unfortunately in place.

3. *The idiot boy.*—The welfare of maturer years presupposes the acquisition of correct habits in childhood. The early onset of the boy's illness may have prevented him from surmounting the normal infirmities of infancy. To these initial defects, others would be added in the course of years. Where the primary instincts are distorted or depraved or sup-

pressed, the rudiments of a sound morality are wanting. Under those conditions, the impulses of youth are likely to defy the decencies of life. The instability of temper and the tendency to violence, common to epileptic idiots, are not to be lost sight of. What piteous emphasis is thrown into the appeal of the despairing father: If thou canst do anything, pity us and help us! In the lurid background are the spectres, "evil" and "unclean."

RESPONSIBILITY OF THE POSSESSED

Having discussed the *raison d'être* of the preceding terms, their natural sequel now claims attention, namely, the responsibility of the demonised. On ethnic principles, these unfortunates were supposed, through some fault or other, to have given occasion and opportunity to the demons to enter them. They were therefore answerable for their incipient condition as well as for its continuance. But the demoniacs were either lunatics or idiots, whose mental defects, according to the teaching of modern science, were a bar to their being held responsible for their doings. *Insanity or idiocy is always a devolution.* The higher centres of the brain are enfeebled, while the lower are more or less unchecked in their operation. Lunatics and idiots, being mentally below par, cannot be held responsible for their behaviour.

Was that also the opinion of Christ? Some have attributed to Him another view. No one emphasised moral responsibility more than He. With a keen outlook upon men and the facts of disease, He asserted at times a connection between the sufferer and his sins, in a tone which could not be misunderstood. To the man sick of the palsy He said, Courage, child, thy sins be forgiven thee (Matt. ix. 2). To the man at the pool of Bethesda He said, See, thou art now well! Sin no more, lest a worse thing happen unto thee (John v. 14)! The hideous physical and moral disabilities of the possessed could not be hidden from Christ; yet He never once hinted that they were monsters of iniquity, who were receiving the due reward of their deeds. He healed them of His own accord; dismissing them without reproach or rebuke. He regarded them evidently as beyond the common rule; and in this respect, His attitude towards those demoniacs was in perfect accord with the highest requirements of science and humanity.[1]

THE TREATMENT OF THE POSSESSED

This subject is really encyclopædic; and a meagre sketch of the same must suffice. Only a few typical methods can be adverted to, which were used either singly or in combination.

---

[1] It is hardly possible to take Olshausen, Trench, and others, patiently, when they affirm that Christ required even from the possessed a declaration of their faith in Himself. *It was not a fact;*

A. *Jewish methods of treatment*

1. *Coaxing demons.*—This method implies a timorous attitude towards the demons, rather inconsistent with the grandiose claims of the exorcists. It was however not uncommon. In the case of Saul, it took the form of music. Justin Martyr notes it in connection with adjuration. "Now assuredly, your exorcists make use of art when they exorcise, even as the heathen do; employing fumigations of incense and incantations." [1]

2. *Disgusting demons.*—The case of Sarah, the daughter of Raguel, is of great interest, whether regarded as a case of obsession or possession; the treatment being the same. Raphael, the angelic comrade of Tobias, has a fine conception of the malodorous. He advises that the heart and liver of the magic fish be laid upon the embers of ashes. The fumes from the putrid remains of the fish must have been outrageously irritating (sulphuretted hydrogen, acrolein, etc.),—"fiend-smiting" and "most healing"; amply sufficient to drive Asmodæus "post to Egypt," [2] or anywhere else. In Tanchuma 70, fumigations are also mentioned.

3. *Terrorising demons.*—Josephus affirms that he was witness of the performance of Eleazar, before the Emperor Vespasian and his army; when the exorcist put a ring that had a root of one of the sorts mentioned by Solomon to the nostrils of the demonised

---

[1] *Dial. with Trypho*, lxxxv.   [2] Tob. viii. 2.

(δαιμονιζομένου); after which he drew out the demon through the nostrils. When the man fell down instantly, he adjured the demon to return into him no more; still mentioning the name of Solomon, and reciting the incantations he composed. The root referred to is, no doubt, that which our author elsewhere calls "baaras," whose colour was like that of a flame; emitting towards evening a ray like lightning. The root could only be got by magical means, one of which involved the death of the dog yoked to it. The sole value of the plant depended on its anti-demonic properties.[1] It is really the mandrake (*Mandragora vernalis*). A little imagination with a little manipulation soon discovers in the root the semblance of a man; so that Semitic and Aryan races have deemed it the home of a spirit and possessed of supernatural qualities. Pliny gives the Latin rite for gathering the plant (*H. N.* xxv. 94). He knew that it possessed certain soporific and anæsthetic powers. The practice and the outfit of Eleazar are of great interest; because they clearly show the relation of Jewish demonology and exorcism to ethnic principles and customs.

---

[1] *Ant.* VIII. ii. 5. Cf. *B. J.* VII. vi. 3. The name "baaras" may have two references—

1. Burning,—בערה: in reference to its red and white flowers.
2. Stupid,—בער: in reference to its anæsthetic and soporific properties. The folk-lore of Shakespeare included the mandrake—

    The insane root that takes the reason prisoner. *Macbeth.*
    Give me to drink mandragora. *Antony and Cleopatra.*
    Not poppy nor mandragora. *Othello.*

(*a*) *The ring.*—This plays the part of the magic pentacle in the extraction of demons. Lucian, in his *Philopseudes*, mentions an iron ring, obtained from a gibbet, as used for a similar purpose. Among Egyptians, Babylonians, Persians, and others, spirits were supposed to enter the interior by the mouth or nostrils. The ear-ring was originally the nose-ring, designed to guard these portals. The former remains as an ornament; the latter has disappeared in the West, owing to adverse climatic influences. Eleazar, in imitation of Solomon, had his ring probably engraven with the Ineffable Name; so rendering it super-potent against all demons.

(*b*) *The root.*—This really included the whole plant (*B. J.* VII. vi. 3). Pliny, in the passage already cited, says that the odour of the mandrake was so potent that it sometimes struck persons dumb. It was inherent mainly in the root and the fruit. The application of the plant to the nostrils brought its powerful odour into operation; and at the same time utilised the bright colour of its flowers.

(*c*) *The incantation.*—Eleazar was not content with an appeal to the senses of smell and sight. He appealed also to the sense of hearing; making use of the rubric ascribed to Solomon. This reference to a "Past-Master" of the black art and the use of his incantations reminded the possessing spirit of the triumphs of the king over "the prince of male demons." The success of these menaces is as little to be doubted as their alleged authorship.

B. *Ethnic parallels to Jewish methods*

The demonology of the Greeks,[1] and their scientific system of medicine,[2] claim a place of their own. The treatment of the insane among this people is surprising for its excellence and its effectiveness. *The sufferer was a patient, labouring under mental disease, whose relief was to be accomplished by rational therapeutics. But among other peoples, the sufferer was the hold of an unclean spirit, which had to be dislodged by magical processes.* In the West, the foundations of scientific medicine were already laid in observation and experiment. In the East generally, professional lore was but superstition systematised. In these matters, the Jews were simply at the ethnic standpoint; only more humane. The following parallels are proof.

1. *Coaxing demons.*—Evil spirits are still soothed by the burning of incense in India and China. Music is also a recognised mode of effecting the same end. The offering of savoury foods for the pleasuring of demons has still its advocates. Tylor cites an excellent instance of the same, in the case of a Bengalee cook, who was seized with an apoplectic fit. His wife, among other things, laid out little heaps of rice, saying, Oh, ride him not! Ah, let him go! Grip him not so hard! Thou shalt have rice! Ah, how good it tastes! Among certain savage races, evil spirits are to

---
[1] Appendix F, Greek Demonology.
[2] Appendix G, Greek Medicine.

be extracted by stroking, sucking, licking, or caressing the person of the possessed.

2. *Disgusting demons.*—This implies an appeal to the senses of smell and taste. On the theory that a demon has been inhaled or swallowed, this method is obvious, and of easy application. Apuleius mentions the use of "artemisia," an aromatic plant, extolling also "aristolochia" for fumigations. Serenus Samonicus notes that "villainous odours often cure the insane." The concoction of "hell-broths" requires but little more ingenuity. The Babylonians had reduced the preparation of these to a fine art. Brecher mentions mixtures of wood, snake, mead, and raw flesh; tree root and dog's tongue; sheep's heart, skin, herbs, and reed. The Romans, according to Pliny (*H. N. passim*), were not less ingenious in the making of things loathsome to smell and taste. Not one whit behind the chief of exorcists are the witches of *Macbeth*—

> Fillet of a fenny snake,
> In the caldron boil and bake:
> Eye of newt, and toe of frog,
> Wool of bat, and tongue of dog,
> Adder's fork, and blindworm's sting,
> Lizard's leg, and owlet's wing,
> . . . . . .

These substances, powerfully odorous or fearfully nauseous, by their very loathsomeness to the senses of smell and taste, must often have produced violent emetic or drastic effects. The result would be an occasional success, in cases of epilepsy and hysteria;

sometimes even of insanity. Thus, the art of the exorcist would perpetuate itself, and plunge still more deeply into the vile and the loathsome, for the ejection of demons.

3. *Terrorising demons.*—This was virtually an appeal to the further senses of the demonised,—to hearing, sight, and touch. These had their respective functions to fulfil.

3a. *Terrorising by menacing words.*—The adjuration is the simplest of all methods; but as the fancy or the need of the exorcist directed, the appeal was made to various parties.

A. *The gods might be directly invoked.*—The ancient Egyptians applied to Thot, the Master of the Magic Formula, skilled in the fears, the infirmities, and the ritual, which dominated all superhuman beings. The magician being partner in this lore, was the equal of Thot; and from the utmost bounds of space could summon the mightiest of the mighty, against mischievous spirits. In like manner the Babylonians appealed to the gods of heaven, specially to Merodach, Gibil, and Ea. Of this trinity, Ea was the most powerful; being lord of spirits. Justin Martyr says to Trypho, Though you Jews exorcise any demon in the name of those who were among you—either kings, or righteous men, or prophets, or patriarchs—it will not be subject to you. But if any of you exorcise it in the name of the God of Abraham and the God of Isaac, it will perhaps be subject to you (*Dialogue*, c. 85). To the same effect is the testimony of Origen, who says that "many of those who give themselves to the practice of conjuring demons, employ in their spells the expression, 'God of Abraham'; though they do not know who Abraham is. And the same remark applies to Isaac and Jacob and Israel; which names, though confessedly Hebrew, are often introduced by those Egyptians who profess to produce some wonderful results by their incantations" (*Contra Celsum*, i. 22).

B. *The superior demons might be directly invoked.*—After Ea had been confounded with Mul-lil, lord of spirits and ruler of the under-world, appeals to this "prince of demons" for the ejection of lesser demons, became current. At the present day in China, the same idea holds sway. Where the native doctor fails to cast out a demon, spiritualists are called in. A charm is written out and then burnt, that it may reach any spirit hovering about. Incense is also burnt. If no name is written on the paper, the nearest demon accepts the invitation to eject his feebler congener. The first comer may offer "a robustious and rough oncoming"; so that another charm is prepared, and inscribed to Lu-tou, a more facile demon. These are instructive illustrations of one satan casting out another. This pagan rite was Christianised, when the angels were invoked instead of the superior powers of evil (*Clem. Homil.* v. 5).

C. *The infesting spirit might be directly menaced.*—The Jewish adjuration addressed to the demon of epilepsy is a fine sample of "a railing accusation": O thou demon that art hidden, thou son of foulness, thou son of abomination, thou son of uncleanness, be thou cursed, crushed, anathematised, as Schmagas, Marigas, Istemaa (Shab. Bab. 67a). Words were often used, devoid of any significance, save perhaps to the demons thus menaced. Plutarch relates that the magi advised the demonised to read and repeat the "Ephesian Letters" when alone (*Sympos.* vii. 5). These words were said to have been uttered with great effect by Crœsus on the funeral pyre; and were also said to have been used by an Ephesian wrestler, whom his Milesian antagonist could not overcome, till these "Letters" were removed from his ankle, when the Ephesian was overthrown thirty times in succession.[1] The "Letters," often referred to, but never quoted, are cited by Clement of Alexandria and by Hesychius:—askion (darkness), kataskion (light), aix or lix (earth), tetrax (year), dammameneus (sun), aision (true). The Milesians had a similar set of words for the plague-demon:— bedu, zaps, chthon, plectron, sphinx, knaxbi, chthyptis, phlegmon, drops. Lucian testifies also to the use of occult Hebrew and Phœnician names in his *Pseudomantis*. On a grade little inferior to the foregoing are the noisy demonstrations of the Indian "medicine-man," aided by drum and rattle, who barks the demon out of his patient.

3b. Terrorising by startling sights.—Here the appeal was to the sense of sight. Fire was commonly used in this connection; and the rite became Christianised at an early date, when it was thought sufficient to

[1] Eustathius. Homer, *Od.* 24.

warn the demons of the fire of hell in store for them. Exorcists have always sought to enhance their dignity by grotesque exhibitions and fantastic dress. The following quaint tale illustrates a regal method of imposing upon a stubborn demon. When Rameses XII. was suzerain over Mesopotamia, he met and married one of the daughters of a subject chief. At a later date, came a request to Egypt for a physician to cure the sister of the queen, who had become possessed of an evil spirit. A physician was sent; but his best efforts were futile. Eleven years later, came another request; this time not for a physician, but for a god, to heal the patient. Accordingly, the god Khonsu of Thebes was sent in his ark, taking some eighteen months on the journey. Confronted by the god, the demon cried out, Great god, that chaseth demons, I am thy slave, I will go to my place whence I came! They sacrificed therefore to the spirit, and it went in peace. But the father-in-law of Rameses coveted this mighty god, and resolved to cheat the Pharaoh out of his property. This knavish design was frustrated by a dream, in which the chief saw Khonsu flying off to his own country in the form of a golden sparrow-hawk; while the would-be thief was suddenly seized by illness. Thus admonished again of the power of the demon-compelling deity, the latter was returned, after an absence of some seven years from his Theban home.[1]

[1] Lenormant, *Ancient History*, i. p. 270 f. Mahaffy, *Prolegomena to Ancient History*, p. 300.

3c. Terrorising by painful sensations. — Here the appeal is to cutaneous sensibilities. This method is heroic, and has been unhappily popular in all ages. Cyprian put the matter in its true ethnic form when he asserted that Christians were able to compel evil spirits, to overcome them, and to force them to confess what they were, by threats and rebukes; and by harsh stripes, press them to depart; to augment their punishment more and more, till they were forced to struggle, to lament, and to groan; to beat them with stripes and to burn them with fire. These things were done upon the theory that they operated invisibly on the demons, and were manifestly a punishment to the possessing spirits.[1] Among savage races, beating, squeezing, and kneading of the possessed are still common methods for expelling those baleful foes. Torture by fire is frequent. The Sumatrans enclose the possessed in a hut, which is then set on fire: leaving the occupant to escape as best he can, — *minus* his demon. In China, the thumbs of the demonised are tied together; also the great toes. A pill is then placed at the root of the finger-nails, and another at the root of the toe-nails. These are kindled and kept in place till the flesh is deeply burned. During the process the demon cries out: I am going! I am going at once! I'll never dare to return! Oh, have mercy on me this once! I'll never dare to return! In that country also, needles are not infrequently plunged into the tips of the fingers, likewise into the

---

[1] *Epistle to Donatus.*

nose and the neck of the possessed, for the removal of the demon.

COMPARATIVE RESULTS

It has been shown that between the Jewish and the ethnic doctrine of demons there is substantial agreement. Both bespeak a hoary antiquity. But the treatment of the possessed is only the practical application of current theories to individual cases. Harmony in regard to underlying principles, carries with it harmony in concrete methods. The preceding parallels are the demonstration of that essential agreement in therapeutic practices. The belief of the exorcist was that the demon was to be reached through the avenues of sense. By these channels, influence might be brought to bear upon the possessing spirit in the way of coaxing, or disgusting, or terrorising it; the result being the dislodgement of the enemy and the restoration of the possessed. But it is to be very distinctly noted that the success of all these methods depended on the comparative soundness of the organs of sense.[1] Given a fairly healthy organism, the possessing demon was open to assault through the medium of the senses, either singly or in combination.

1. *Through the sense of smell, by fumigations, pleasant or odious.*

---

[1] Where the sensory organs were but little affected, the illness was slight and likely to proceed to spontaneous cure. That result would be claimed by the exorcist as his; hence the perpetuation of superstitions

2. *Through the sense of taste, by "hell-broths," or vile mixtures.*

3. *Through the sense of hearing, by violent threats or withering abuse.*

4. *Through the sense of sight, by fantastic or terrific exhibitions.*

5. *Through the sense of touch, by the infliction of manifold tortures.*

These circumstances are of special importance in clearing up the cases of the dumb demoniac, the blind and dumb demoniac, and the idiot boy. To the two former, is attached the charge of Christ conspiring with the prince of demons. In the light of the preceding, their former obscurity vanishes.

CHRIST AND CURRENT METHODS OF TREATMENT

The Gospels show that Christ's method was neither magical nor medical. The cures of Christ were effected quite apart from the popular superstitions of the East or the scientific methods of the West.[1] He cured "by a word" (Matt. viii. 16), and "instantly" (Luke xiii. 13). If so, then the treatment of the possessed by Jesus was transcendental in character and attainment. But that is the very conclusion which a negative criticism has always deprecated. It has its philosophic inventory of things in heaven and earth, and aught beyond that is inconceivable. Its mood has changed for the moment. Where an older scepticism once denied the miraculous with offensive assurance, a more recent rationalism gives effusively with one hand what it artfully removes with the other. A striking feature of the present situation is the concurrence of an ostentatious acknowledgment of the miraculous with a real negation of it. The *psychological explanation* is the grand instrument of the modern Naturalistic School. The views of its principal representatives demand consideration.

1. Strauss attempts to explain the cure of the possessed by two remarkable canons.

(*a*) The more strictly the malady was confined to mental derangement on which the word of Jesus might have an immediate moral influence, or to a comparatively slight disturbance of the nervous system, on which He would be able to act powerfully through the medium of the mind, the more possible was it for Jesus, "by a word" or "instantly," to put an end to such states. On the other hand, the more the malady had confirmed itself as a bodily disease, the more difficult is it to believe that Jesus was able to relieve it in a purely spiritual[1] fashion and at the first moment.

(*b*) To any extensive spiritual[1] influence on the part of Jesus, the full recognition of His dignity as a prophet was requisite; whence it follows that in districts where He had long had that reputation, He could effect more in this way than where He had it not.

[1] Psychological.

Strauss here contemplates three degrees or forms of the malady: (1) affecting the mind; (2) affecting the nervous system; (3) confirming itself as a bodily disease. Yet he regards possession as "a species of madness." But mental disease is not an entity, separable from the nervous system, or from the body. The brain is the organ of mind; and mental disease has always a physical basis, the pathological traces of which are to be sought in the brain. To throw the prophetic character of Christ into the scale is most misleading; for that, as will be shown, was not at all apparent to the possessed. Apart from the heated imagination of its author, this pathology of Strauss is purely "mythical."

2. Renan holds that the disorders which were explained by possession were often very trifling. "In our times, in Syria, they regard as mad or possessed by a demon (these two ideas were expressed by the same word—*medynoun*), people who are only somewhat eccentric. A gentle word in such cases often suffices to drive away the demon. Such were, doubtless, the means employed by Jesus. Who knows if his celebrity as an exorcist was almost spread without his knowledge? Persons who reside in the East are constantly surprised to find themselves possessed of a great reputation as doctors, sorcerers, or discoverers of hidden treasures, without being able to account to themselves for the facts which have given rise to these strange fancies."

Here again is a total lack of appreciation of the

gravity of the disorders, manifested in the three typical cases of possession. Renan's explanations are even less satisfactory than the pseudo-scientific canons of Strauss. Slight eccentricity may sometimes pass for possession in the East; but to present such cases as genuine parallels to the three foregoing instances, described in detail by the Evangelists, is to ignore the facts of observation. To call persons suffering from grave forms of epileptic insanity, acute mania, and epileptic idiocy, "only somewhat eccentric," is an abuse of language. To suggest that such would be cured by "a gentle word," betrays the profoundest ignorance of the ailments under consideration.

3. Keim holds that it was the superstition itself, the superstitious idea of possession, and not any actual phenomenon, which formed the generative cause of the disease. In the cure of demoniacs, therefore, Jesus did not put foreign guests to flight; but only freed an enslaved self-consciousness from the morbid dispositions and the melancholy with which the superstition of the sufferers themselves, and of others, were wont to trammel men. If incantations, magic formulæ, fumigations, anointings, and ablutions were conceivably beneficial to the insane, restoring them to health for a longer or shorter time; then must we attribute much greater success to the impressions and influences produced and exercised by the person of Jesus, by His holy calm, His imposing confidence, and His authoritative word of command; even without semi-magical formulæ. The influence of Jesus was

brought to bear with triple energy upon the possessed, through His name in the mouths of the people, His look, and His authoritative utterance. Keim adds that modern science is unanimous in accepting this view of Christ's influence; Paulus, Schleiermacher, Hase, Neander, De Wette, Bleek, Winer, Strauss, Schenkel, Holtzmann, Weizsäcker, and others, being cited in this regard.

Medical experts have still to learn that these authorities are representatives of "modern science"; whatever their worth otherwise. It is natural that one who finds the cause of possession in the mere superstitious conception, should laud psychical and moral agencies for the cure of such troubles. Yet even hallucinations and delusions have an organic basis; and the correction of the psychical processes attends the adjustment of the physical functions. The demoniacs of Keim are certainly not those of the Gospels; but figments of his own imagination. His pseudo-scientific therapeutics are on a level with his imaginary patients.

4. Matthew Arnold asserts that "medical science has never gauged—never perhaps set itself to gauge —the intimate connection between moral fault and disease. To what extent, or in how many cases, what is called *illness* is due to moral springs having been used amiss, whether by being over-used or not being used sufficiently, we hardly know, and we too little inquire. Certainly it is due to this much more than we commonly think; and the more it is due to this,

the more do moral therapeutics rise in possibility and importance. The bringer of light and happiness, the calmer and pacifier, or invigorator and stimulator, is one of the chiefest of doctors. Such a doctor was Jesus; such an operator, by an efficacious and real, though little observed and little employed agency, upon what we, in the language of popular superstition, call the *unclean spirits*, but which are to be designated more literally and more correctly as the *uncleared, unpurified* spirits, which came raging and madding before him."

The littérateur, doubtless, finds more " sweetness " in the term " uncleared "; but the scientist more " light " in its alternative—" unclean." Psychological medicine takes account of " moral causes " in the production of mental disorders; but holds aloof from " moral springs," and allows to the former only a limited field of operation. In like manner, it takes cognisance of moral treatment, in the prosaic form of rational discipline; but has not yet generally, if at all, risen to the moral glorious term " moral therapeutics." These, however, are points of minor consequence. What we have to notice is the assertion of Matthew Arnold that " by an efficacious and real agency," " upon unpurified spirits," Jesus proved Himself in such cases " the bringer of light and happiness, the calmer and pacifier, or invigorator and stimulator." In a word, He acted as " one of the chiefest of doctors." But that is essentially an under-statement. Take again the three typical cases of possession, which on their physical side are instances of epileptic insanity, acute mania, and epileptic idiocy. If Jesus here operated "by an efficacious and real agency," then He cured those patients. Hence it follows, that He did what no other has ever been able to accomplish; for we freely challenge the records of medicine to produce three similar cases of epileptic insanity, acute mania, and epileptic idiocy, where the cure was effected "by a word" and "instantly." He Who confessedly attained to such results is not merely "one of the chiefest of doctors,"—HE IS INDEFEASIBLY THE CHIEFEST! In a sense wholly unique, He proved for those patients "the bringer of light and happiness, the calmer and pacifier, or invigorator and stimulator." It will be time enough to discuss the *modus operandi* of our Lord, when the followers of Arnold furnish us with a scientific definition of "moral springs,"[1] and a complete system of "moral therapeutics." Till then, the student of science must regard these elegant disquisitions as superfluous verbiage.

It is needless to go beyond these representatives of the Naturalistic School. Their fundamental mistake is an inability to discover, or a refusal to recognise, the fact that mental diseases of a most formidable type can never be equated with simple eccentricity

[1] What had the idiot boy, whose illness dated "from childhood," to do with the excessive use or the disuse of "moral springs"? Had the Gerasenes some fore-glimmerings of the value of "moral therapeutics," when they tried to "tame" their demoniac (Mark v. 4)? In Jerusalem the method was unknown or lightly esteemed, judging by the remark: He has a demon and is mad! *Why hear ye him*

or common hysteria. The pathological factors can neither be minimised nor dismissed. It remains, therefore, for the negative critics, either to acknowledge outright the supernatural success of Jesus or to renew their Sisyphean labours.[1]

PROOFS OF THE EXPULSIONS OF DEMONS

Josephus relates that when Eleazar wished to demonstrate to the Emperor Vespasian and his army the ejection of a demon from his demoniac, he placed a cup or foot-bath, filled with water, a little in front of the spectators. The demon was charged to upset the vessel on his exit; to furnish ocular demonstration of his departure. The evil spirit, from fear or courtesy, complied with the injunction, to the satisfaction of all. Philostratus, in his *Life of Apollonius*, tells how the sage discovered a demon in a young man, who laughed and cried, without apparent reason. The evil spirit, when disclosed, broke out into all the foul language used by people on the rack, and swore to depart for good. Apollonius rebuked the demon as a master does a saucy, cunning slave; bidding him depart. At once the spirit cried out and promised to go; the proof of departure being the overturning of a certain statue. That was done accordingly, amid great uproar. The young man then woke up, as out of sleep, and thereafter amended his ways according to the precepts of Apollonius. A modern instance of a similar sort is that recorded by Nevius, in his *Demon Possession*. It occurred in the house of one Chang, a Chinaman, in 1883. Different women of the family were demonised. Worship was demanded for the demons in their name; but refused by Chang. Thereupon, food, clothing, and valuables were stolen in the most mysterious way. Furniture and dishes shook and rattled without perceptible cause; fires also broke out without apparent reason and destroyed several buildings. On one occasion, two women were possessed. One of them set herself to the drinking of wine; tossing her arms about, using strange language, and giving way to tears. A religious service was held by some Christians, at the conclusion of which the woman was lying unconscious or asleep.[1] After a time she woke up, and sought out her visitors who were still in the house. She said she had had a long sleep and was her old self again; having had no idea of what had happened during her abnormal state. "About this time, just before dark," there was a great commotion among the fowls and swine of the house, which continued for some time, and was believed to be due to the entrance of the demons into them. We need not tarry over the credibility of these events; but note that ethnic custom required tangible proof of the departure of possessing demons. The onlookers had to be convinced of the reality of success by spectacular results. How different the practice of our Lord! He offered no ocular demon-

[1] Tipsy!

stration of the ejection of spirits. The stampede of the swine is no exception to that rule. *Such a sign would have been useless to the man under any circumstances.* If really cured, he had the witness in himself in the sense of restoration. If still uncured, no hecatombs of swine would have convinced him that he was sane. The old hallucinations and delusions would have remained. In these cases, Jew and Greek and Chinaman trust to lying vanities; but Christ is wholly superior to such devices. He effected the cure and left it to bear its own testimony.

CHAPTER V

THE EXISTENCE OF GENUINE DEMONIC POSSESSION

BY placing the symptoms of the possessed alongside of their modern parallels, it has been shown that all cases designated "demoniac" belong to the category of "LUNACY OR IDIOCY." But was there aught in these cases which went beyond the mere pathological phenomena? Were there forms of possession with which real demons were directly concerned? Two simple rules must guide this inquiry.

(*a*) Whatever is explicable on the principles of modern science is to be regarded as natural.

(*b*) Whatever is inexplicable on the principles of modern science is to be regarded as supernatural.

Corresponding to those axioms, two classes of the possessed emerge potentially.

(*a*) Cases simply natural and not genuinely demonic.

(*b*) Cases truly supernatural and genuinely demonic.

The latter appear as a residual phenomenon; transcending the former. As the issue may seem to turn here upon a single point, the real strength of the position is to be recognised. That introduces a new element.

THE HISTORICITY OF THE GOSPEL NARRATIVES

There is no need to travel far afield, as the facts to hand have a cogency of their own. The narratives of the three typical cases are varied; but at the same time, congruous and complementary. They afford clear testimony to the veracity of the different authors.

1. *The Capernaum demoniac.*—Keim says, "This incident did not happen." That dictum only proves that he has no eye for the luminous background which is patent to the expert alienist. The significance of the symptoms here described was not open to the spectators and reporters of this miracle. They merely narrated what they saw and heard; interweaving the same with collateral events in the synagogue. But the product is the correct representation of a set of complex morbid phenomena with a complex local environment. Invention is entirely out of the question; because it is so manifestly beyond the capacities of the writers or their informants. They are saved from inevitable blunders, only by faithful delineation of an actual case of epileptic insanity.

2. *The Gerasene demoniac.*—This example is equally instructive and reveals the same fidelity to fact. Here the symptoms are manifold and the details of time and place plentiful. The stampede of the swine is an integral part of the narrative which greatly complicates the whole situation. Yet it is in a precise

and natural relationship to the cure of the possessed. The occurrence gave rise to a theory of the occurrence; but the objective phenomena are thoroughly in harmony with each other. That result is accomplished only by unswerving adhesion to the concrete facts, in a manner which is wholly beyond the power of any literary artist who lacks either the training or the guidance of an expert in mental diseases.

3. *The idiot boy.*—His condition is set forth with large enumeration of features whose meaning was quite beyond the comprehension of the spectators; such as the query about the onset of the illness, and the remark about the lad being cast "both into the fire and into the waters." The command of Jesus and the subsequent convulsions are essential parts also of one great whole, which is fitted together, not by art, but by precise attention to the solid facts. The close and necessary inter-connection of the diverse parts of this spectacle is not within the ken of the observers. Yet the Gospels furnish a consistent succession of events which could only be derived from an actual example of this ailment.

The correlation of so many diverse elements in those three cases, in a manner which satisfies the highest scientific requirements, spontaneously produces the impression that we are here on the impregnable rock of solid fact. This is one of the most delicate tests of historicity which can be applied to the records under consideration. There are other arguments of a technical sort, whose nature, force, and relevancy

THE SIGNIFICANCE OF THIS CONFESSION OF JESUS

This phenomenon is without parallel anywhere. It therefore demands the most careful scrutiny. Attempts to explain it have usually ended in explaining it away. The following hypotheses really cover the whole ground :—

1. *Accident.*—This theory recognises that in the case of the insane, the unexpected is that which happens. Their mental instability renders them extremely sensitive to external influences; so that the issue is beyond prediction. Their freedom from conventionality of speech and imagination, and their tendency to refer their novel sensations and experiences to the mysterious but plastic element of religion, predisposes them to all manner of erratic things. But the confession of Jesus as the Messiah is not an accident. This striking feature is manifested under the most diverse circumstances, by different persons who suffer from different types of mental disease. This strange constancy among a class notorious for caprice and inconsequence is the condemnation of any theory of accident.

2. *Clairvoyance.*—This we may call the theory of Lange; who does not define his terms. He declares that the nervous and insane subjects of our time, as well as the demoniacs of the Gospels, are capable of divining the disposition and intention of persons around them, by an intensified power of foreboding. They are in a morbid state of psychical agitation and

in closer affinity to the psychical movements of bystanders than healthy persons; having specially an extraordinary sensitiveness to states of mind which are in contrast to their own. And as *clairvoyantes* can be disturbed by the nearness of impure persons, so demoniacs and lunatics often become excited by the approach of saintly persons. They feel the operation of a power which even at a distance comes into collision with their own, and presses punitively on the secret consciousness of psychical terror with which commonly their state of bondage is connected. That the demoniacs were the first to proclaim Jesus as Messiah, may be accounted for, by the activity and perceptive vigour of their intensified power of foreboding, which brought them into a peculiar relation with the consciousness of Christ and with the secret thought of their own time. Such is Lange's theory. The truth or falsehood of clairvoyance is immaterial to the issue on hand. What is "intensified power of foreboding"? Whatever else it may stand for, in this sample of obscurantism, it clearly implies a concentration of attention. But that is the very point wherein the insane are specially defective. It is not at all too much to say that even believers in modern spiritualism would have found the intense mental disturbances of the demoniacs of Capernaum and Gerasa, an insuperable obstacle to the conditions supposed to be necessary for clairvoyance. Reactions produced on lunatics by the mere presence of saintly persons are the wildest fancies. This theory of clairvoyance is ineffably impossible as an explanation of the recognition of the Messianic dignity of Jesus by the demonised.

3. *Verbal information.*—The question before us touches the possible sources of information. Jesus Himself could not have been the informant; because He uniformly and vehemently repelled the testimony proffered by the demoniacs. His attitude determined that of the Apostles in this matter; whatever their private hopes or convictions might have been thus far. These did not receive formal expression till late in the ministry of our Lord, at Cæsarea-Philippi (Matt. xvi. 13–20). On that occasion also the strictest silence was enjoined upon the disciples. Nor could the information have been derived from persons outside of the circle of Jesus, because, up to the moment of Peter's confession, public opinion had not ventured beyond the timid conjecture that Jesus might be John the Baptist risen from the dead, or Elias, or Jeremias, or one of the prophets (cf. Matt. xvi. 14). Any authoritative declaration from any external source was not available for the information of the possessed. Yet their confessions of Jesus as Messiah are coincident with the beginning of the ministry of Christ, and are made without reserve or hesitation. Truly, flesh and blood had not revealed this secret unto them.

4. *Genuine discrimination.*—This theory has found considerable favour where the recognition of Jesus is regarded as the resultant of the Messianic hope and the impression produced by the august personality of

Christ. "The Messianic hope was immanent in the hearts of the Jewish people, ever ready to break forth into expression, and it was quite to be expected that, when the Messiah came, among the first to recognise Him should be those diseased in their minds, especially those whose thoughts moved within the religious sphere. Insanity is much nearer the kingdom of God than worldly-mindedness. There was, doubtless, something in the whole aspect and manner of Jesus which was fitted to produce almost instantaneously a deep spiritual impression to which children, simple, ingenuous souls like the Galilean fishermen, sinful yet honest-hearted men like those who met at Matthew's feast, readily surrendered themselves. Men with shattered reason also felt the spell, while the wise and strong-minded too often used their intellect, under the bias of passion or prejudice, to resist the force of truth. In this way we may account for the prompt recognition of Jesus by the Gadarene demoniac. All that is necessary to explain it is the Messianic hope prevalent in Gadara as elsewhere, and the sight of Jesus acting on an impressionable spirit. The view of the Blessed One acting on the remnant of reason drew the poor sufferer to His presence in instinctive trust and expectation of benefit. The same view acting on the dark element produced repulsion and fear. Hence the self-contradictory attitude, as of one saying, It is the Christ; He is come to save me; He is come to destroy me."[1]

[1] Bruce, *Miraculous Element*, p. 187.

Certain things here are really preposterous;[1] certain others are to be freely admitted; such as the impressiveness of the person of Jesus, and the wide prevalence of the Messianic hope. The latter may even have crossed the seas to an alien race.[2] But the bearing of these things on the sane is one thing, and on the insane (demonised) is quite another.

The Messianic hope was both variant in form and complex in character. Jewish literature, canonical and extra-canonical, reveals different types of it. But that hope, wherever found, was in essence a mental image of "The Coming One," projected into the near future, as the object of the national desire. The image, however, was not innate. It was the product of education. Its initial development in the case of those whose early years were severely marred by mental disease was an impossibility.

Supposing even that the image of the Messiah had been duly fixed in the mind, there was always the risk that through the accident of mental disease, it might be obscured, or distorted, or blotted out. It is notorious that such an event affects the mental landmarks; denuding some, destroying others, and more or less confounding the whole. The demoniacs of Capernaum and Gerasa may have at one time shared the hope of the nation. If so, that hope was not at all operative on their encounter with Jesus. The

[1] Appendix I, Fallacies.
[2] See Suetonius, *Vesp.* 4. Tacitus, *Hist.* v. 13. Cf. Josephus, *B. J.*

suspension of memory, judgment, and susceptibility, so prominent on these occasions, was wholly inconsistent with the recognition of Jesus as Messiah, in the manner suggested. The vast incoherences, contradictions, and confusions of their mental life, thoroughly disqualified the possessed for such discrimination.

5. *Demonic Inspiration.*—The preceding theories cover the whole field of what can be called the human and the natural. Their rejection logically carries us into the sphere of the superhuman and the supernatural. The agency behind these ostentatious confessions of the Messianic dignity of Jesus, was evidently hostile. That is implied in their vehement rejection on the part of Christ. Such disclosures were really dangerous to the person of the King and the establishment of His kingdom. They were an incitement to the populace to precipitate a crisis with the Roman authorities. Any day there might arise an attempt to make Jesus a king; creating thereby an intolerable situation. These proclamations from the unseen world were also misleading. Moral progress must proceed according to moral principles. Confessions of Jesus as Messiah which failed to do justice to His ethical claims upon humanity might create excitement, but not faith. Such testimonies were not more embarassing than mischievous. Their intent was malicious; their source was tainted. There is no escape from the simple statement of the Evangelist, that " the demons knew that Jesus was the Christ" (Luke iv. 41). Once we find our Lord refer-

ring to David as speaking "in the Holy Spirit" (Mark xii. 36); *i.e.* "inspired by the Holy Spirit." The same Evangelist notes that the demoniacs of Capernaum and Gerasa were "in an unclean spirit" (Mark i. 23, v. 2). By parity of reasoning, therefore, we conclude that the confessions emanating from the mouths of the possessed were due to demonic inspiration.

CLASSIFICATION OF THE POSSESSED

The preceding investigation has brought into clear light two distinctive characteristics of genuine demonic possession.
1. Insanity or idiocy of some sort, forming the natural element.
2. The confession of Jesus as Messiah, forming the supernatural element.

The former is established on scientific grounds and cannot be shaken; the latter on exegetical, and equally invincible. This confession is a residual phenomenon which is not reducible by any means to the purely natural. Where this classical criterion is found, there we postulate without hesitation, the activity of an evil spirit. To this category belong the cases of the demoniacs of Capernaum and Gerasa: with the general cases similarly attested. But there remain other cases labelled "demoniac," where this criterion is not mentioned. At this stage, then, we recognise two classes of the possessed in a tentative manner.

1. Those manifesting the natural features of mental disease, coupled with the supernatural feature of the confession of Jesus as Messiah.
2. Those manifesting the natural features of mental disease, without report of the supernatural feature of the confession of Jesus as Messiah.

Does the absence of the report of the confession denote the non-existence of that confession? Presumably that is the case. No one has ever suggested that the writers of the New Testament aimed at belittling the power of Christ. The opposite is often asserted. But this confession of Jesus was a feature surprisingly novel, and absolutely unique. It could not fail to be profoundly impressive to memory and imagination. Is it conceivable that such a striking phenomenon should have been overloooked or suppressed? We may hold, then, that the absence of the record of confession denotes the real absence of the same. But we are not left to mere presumption or conjecture. Several instances corroborate this view of the matter.

(*a*) *The idiot boy.*—The illness of this lad antedated the ministry of Christ. The father described a series of symptoms which had persisted with painful regularity from childhood onwards. These, neither more nor less, according to the narrative, were witnessed by Jesus when the patient was brought for cure. The symptoms thus enumerated or witnessed are such as are purely natural; being readily matched by others in the present day. They present nothing inexplicable on the principles of scientific pathology. There is nothing corresponding to the criterion of genuine demonic possession.

Further, as the lad was dumb, it is not possible to see how a demon could utilise him for perverting the minds of the spectators. What testimony could be borne to Jesus otherwise than by articulate speech? The sudden scream, the violent fall, the writhing limb, the ghastly aspect of one as dead, could have no theological significance whatever. Distinct utterance was the only weapon wherewith a demon might adversely disclose the Messianic dignity of Jesus. Other movements could not be thus construed. So the lad was useless for the end in view. We therefore conclude that the absence of any report of the confession of Jesus as the Christ, points to the exclusion of this case from the category of genuine demonic possession. A confirmation of this view may be sought in the peculiar remark of Jesus, This kind (of thing) goeth forth by nothing than by prayer (Mark ix. 29).[1]

(*b*) *The Philippian Pythoness.*—Was there anything more than insanity here? She followed Paul and his company, crying out, These men are servants of the Most High God who announce to you a way of salvation! Is this the equivalent of the confession of the demoniacs of Capernaum and Gerasa? At first

---

[1] See International Critical Commentary, *in loco*.
[2] Appendix J, The use of popular language by Jesus.

sight, that is credible; but closer inspection of the narrative does not confirm that view. Her declaration contains elements that are of a neutral character, such as "Most High," and "salvation." The former term is really international, and applies to such deities as Jupiter and Baal. It appears even in the "Pœnulus" of Plautus as an imported phrase—"Alonim valoniuth," "gods and godesses most high."[1] The term "salvation" has also a non-sectarian significance; belonging to poetry, philosophy, politics, commerce, and common life. These words, if used by Paul, would be easily taken up by this woman; and appear to be a blurred remembrance of words uttered by him. The recognition of Paul as a servant of the Most High God was not immediate. That is to be expected of one who was weak of intellect; not from one truly possessed of an evil spirit. The mental capacities of this person did not unfit her for picking up a few catchwords, such as "way," "salvation," and "announce." These were fused together in an incoherent manner, so that the combination was not distinctively Pauline; though its parts might be such. In this proclamation, there does not seem to be anything inexplicable on natural principles, nor anything at all approaching the immediate and unhesitating confession of Jesus as Messiah, which is the criterion of genuine demonic possession.

Further, this woman belonged to the order of the Puthones ($\pi\acute{v}\theta\omega\nu\varepsilon\varsigma$). Plutarch relates that they were formerly called Eurukleis (Εὐρυκλεῖς), after Eurukles, mentioned by Aristophanes. He was a famous ventriloquist, who was supposed to deliver true oracles. Galen notes that the ventriloquists (ἐγγαστριμύθοι) were so called, because they spoke with their mouths shut, so as to seem to speak out of their belly. In any case, it is not feasible to rate this woman higher than a common ventriloquist or fortune-teller; in whose case no genuine demonic activity is discoverable. Was Paul then mistaken when he charged the spirit to go forth? It is possible that at this stage he was not fully emancipated from the traditions of the fathers; but even that cannot be proved. Rabbinic custom permitted a certain amount of personification in the nomenclature of disease. Paul may have used an ethnic formula without endorsing ethnic doctrine.[1] It is remarkable that in none of his Epistles does he refer to the ejection of evil spirits as one of the "gifts" (χαρίσματα) of the Church; while the *charisma* of healing is repeatedly mentioned (1 Cor. xii. 9, 28, 30). Whatever view of the matter be now taken, we note that the woman was miraculously healed and the Name of Christ magnified.

(*c*) *The Ephesian demoniac.* — The extraordinary strength alleged to belong to this man is quoted as proof of demonic agency. But while he put to flight his would-be saviours with sovereign rage and contempt, supernatural strength is not demonstrable.

[1] Appendix K, The demonising of the heathen gods.

When operating in the presence of what was believed to be a dangerous demon, Jewish exorcists were in a state of high nervous tension, ready to flee at the first approach of peril. Here we recall the tale of the Rabbi saved by the friendly cedar and similar stories. The dangers inherent in the treatment of the demonised were real, and here emerged with explosive violence. The hearty onslaught of this demoniac on those parties is no proof of superhuman vigour; but an exhibition of portentous cowardice on the part of those miserable vagabonds.

The mention of the names of Jesus and Paul is no indication of a supernatural knowledge. To begin with, the demoniac was in a quiescent state. He was not under bonds, but free to go abroad and shift for himself in some sort. That argues a capacity for receiving and retaining impressions of current events. Now the preaching of Jesus by the Apostle was the great topic of conversation in the city. Wherever this man might go, he was sure to hear of Jesus and of Paul. But even if he had no previous knowledge of this kind, these two names were put into his mouth by those exorcists: We adjure you by Jesus whom Paul preacheth! The reply of the demoniac is an echo of that formula: Jesus I know, and Paul I am acquainted with; but who are ye? There is nothing here, then, corresponding to the confession of Jesus as Messiah by the demoniacs of Capernaum and Gerasa.

The cases of the Syro-Phœnician girl, the dumb demoniac, the blind and dumb demoniac, and Mary

Magdalene, need not be discussed. Presumably, if not certainly, they belong to the same order as the foregoing. By the application of the criterion of genuine possession, a twofold classification of the possessed has become possible—

1. Cases self-attested and clearly supernatural.
2. Cases not self-attested and simply natural.

These two classes must have been very conspicuous to the contemporaries of Jesus. The first was absolutely novel and unique. The second class was commonplace. The "sons of the Pharisees"[1] dealt with the latter: attaining a show of success. It is not necessary, with Pressensé, Steinmeyer, and others, to deny this. Their remedies were perhaps heroic upon occasion, and no doubt beneficial at intervals, because of their pungent, drastic, or emetic effects, in cases of hysteria, epilepsy, and mild insanity. Jesus acknowledged so much, and in doing so confirms the preceding classification.

RESULTS OF THIS CLASSIFICATION

1. In the cases "not self-attested," there seems to be an unwarrantable reduction of the miraculous. But that is not so; for even where there is no more than the removal of physical disease, there is no disparagement of the power of Jesus to save unto the uttermost. He is adequate to every occasion.

Members of the order of the Pharisees: בני הפרישין ; like "members of the order of the Elohim": בני האלהים.

2. In the cases "not self-attested," there is a real enhancement of the authority and dominion of our Lord. There come into clear light two facts of immense importance, which have hitherto received no recognition—

    (*a*) *The remarkable paucity of the cases "self-attested."*
    (*b*) *The restriction of them to the earlier portion of Christ's ministry.*

Here then is proof that the demons did obey the injunction of Jesus that they should cease to "make Him manifest." They were already "muzzled." Here also is a demonstration that the "strong man" has been bound by the Stronger.

3. This enables us to understand why certain cures of the demonised are put on a level with the healing of non-demonic ailments—

In Thy Name have we not cast out demons, and in Thy Name done many mighty works? Matt. vii. 22.

Heal the sick, cleanse the lepers, raise the dead, cast out demons. Matt. x. 8. Cf. Mark vi. 7. Luke ix. 2.

In that hour He healed many of their diseases, and plagues, and evil spirits, and to many that were blind He granted sight. Luke vii. 21.

Certain women who had been healed of evil spirits and infirmities. Luke viii. 2.

Go ye and tell that fox: Behold, I cast out demons and I do cures to-day and to-morrow. Luke xiii. 32.

This classification of the demoniacs thus fully approves itself. The cases "self-attested" were clamorous and aggressive. The historical imagination can form but the feeblest conception of the powerful impression which demonic confessions were fitted to produce on the minds of the contemporaries of our Lord. *It was never so seen in Israel; no, nor anywhere else! That fact spontaneously determined a cleavage in the ranks of the possessed.*

THE ANTECEDENTS OF GENUINE DEMONIC POSSESSION

Moral depravity has been generally cited as the precursor to the demoniac state. Proof of the same has been sought in the Beelzebul controversy, where the ejection of spirits is coupled with the overthrow of the kingdom of Satan. But that passage is not decisive in favour of this view. The kingdom of Satan has its physical as well as its ethical aspects, corresponding to the cases "natural" and "supernatural." The remark of Christ on the return of the Missioners carries us no further. The language of Jesus is highly pictorial: I beheld Satan as lightning fall from heaven. It is to be remembered that Christ offered Himself to men as the Healer of disease and the Vanquisher of sin; so that the successful establishment of His kingdom involved the curtailment of the devil's power in both directions, though these processes do not advance *pari passu*. The ethnic theory always assumes fault of some sort on the part of the unfortunate sufferer. That idea appears in the early Church, and has maintained itself in some sort until the present day.

The author of the *Clementine Recognitions* describes

Simon Magus as one possessed and incurable; "because his sickness arises from his will and is become spontaneous," the demon not dwelling in him against his will (ii. 72). It is further asserted that a demon has no power against a person, unless one submit of his own accord to its desires (iv. 34). Likewise also, Origen declares that demons gain a lodgment in minds which have been already laid open to their entrance by intemperance (*C. C.* III. iii. 2). Jerome likewise, in his *Life of Hilarion*, tells us that a maid, who had been cured by the saint, had before her possession, induced the demon to take up his abode within her, by her unseemly conduct. These ancient authors are all on the plane of the old-world superstitions, and it is needless to multiply evidence from this source. It is remarkable that these old pagan theories should reassert themselves in modern times, and should receive specific formulation from eminent theologians. The following are sufficiently representative:—

John Lightfoot asserts that the demons were common in the time of Christ above all the times of the Old Testament, and beyond any instances in any other nation. Whether this were due to the fact that the spirit of prophecy had so long departed from them (cf. 1 Sam. xvi. 14); or that the Lord would in justice confute the cursed doctrine of the Sadducees (cf. Acts xxiii. 8) by this dreadful experience; or that He did evince His great displeasure against the sinfulness and falsehood of those times which was now grown intense, by the delivery of so many to the power of the father of sin and error; or that He would by this painful experience read all men a lesson as to what a misery it is to be in the power and subjection of Satan, and so make them more intent to hearken after Him that was to break the Serpent's head; or all these things together; it certainly did greatly redound to the honour of Christ and to the magnifying of His divine power, and did mightily prove that He had come to destroy the works of the devil, when, finding so many that lay so visibly under his power, He enlarged them all and brought them from under that power, and bound the strong man who could not resist Him.[1] In another passage, the same author holds that the cause of the trouble was that the "Jewish people, having arrived at the very summit of impiety, now also arrived at the climax of those curses which are recited in Lev. xxvi. and Deut. xxviii." Further, this "nation beyond measure addicted to magic arts, did even affect devils and invited them to dwell with them."[2]

Olshausen in his commentary on Matt. viii. 28–34, advocates a similar view. He says that the demoniac state presents psychical and physical features which always seem to presuppose some form of moral delinquency, "not so much as wickedness, properly speaking, but more as predominant sensuality (probably lasciviousness in particular), indulged in contrary to their better self." Hence a weakening of

[1] Lightfoot, *Horæ Hebraicæ*, i. 639 (1684).
[2] *Ibid*. ii. 175.

the bodily organisation, specially the nervous system, due to such sinful indulgence. This reacts on the inner life, which suffers derangement, apparently proportionate to the former acuteness of conscience. The latter testifies against the demoniac, as to his personal responsibility and his inability to save himself from the fetters of sin and the kingdom of darkness, to whose influence he has resigned himself. In such cases there is, however, a desire for deliverance, a spark of hope and faith which makes the subjects of it susceptible to the powers of a higher life. This hope is expressed by all the demoniacs, and faith is the necessary condition of their healing. The individual consciousness of the possessed is suppressed or absorbed in the influence of the power of darkness, but returns to the surface. The condition is not therefore to be conceived as if two or more persons were contained in them. The hostile power may be alternately in the ascendant or in retreat. Demoniacs are very miserable, but not the most wicked of mankind. Their state is distinguishable from that of those who are "decidedly wicked." In the former there is a contest against evil; whereas in the latter, the hostile force has been admitted undisturbed and unopposed into the recesses of the heart. The first class is salvable; the second is not.

Dieringer, a Roman Catholic theologian, puts the matter thus. Fallen man is in inward sympathy with fallen spirits, and this inward affinity exposes him to their seducing and tormenting influence. The extent to which this influence is exercised, depends on the moral self-assertion of the individual and the decree of God. The antecedents to possession proper are temptations, snares, besieging, blockade. These preliminaries are hostile influences to which all men are more or less exposed; and possession occurs when the self-assertion of the human over against the demonic personality, present in the blockading, ceases; so that the demonic force has appropriated the use of the bodily organs, and the soul appears to be in bondage. The latter is not destroyed but may reassert itself, when the possession reverts to obsession.[1]

Trench's views are practically those of Olshausen. He holds that the demoniac state presents a blending of the physical and the spiritual. Demoniacs are not merely great sufferers, but great sinners also; "greatly guilty, though not the guiltiest of all men." Lavish sin and specially indulgence in sinful lusts, superinducing a weakness of the nervous system, may have laid such sufferers open to the incursions of the powers of darkness. There is present in such cases a sense of misery, of the true life utterly shattered, of an alien power which has mastered them wholly and is ruling in the high places of their soul, having cast down the rightful lord. The demoniacs feel that by their own acts, they have given themselves over to the tyranny of the devil, so that his power is no longer outside of them as a power which they can successfully resist or from which they can save them-

[1] Delitzsch, *Biblical Psychology*, p. 351 f.

selves. The demoniacs do not, however, acquiesce in their misery but cry for redemption, when a glimpse of hope offers; and this yearning for deliverance makes them the objects and subjects of Christ's saving power. Otherwise, there would be nothing for the divine power to lay hold upon. Faith is the condition of their healing. While the individual consciousness may for a moment reassert itself, the foreign power forces itself upon the demoniac, taking possession of him so that he speaks and acts as its organ. Demoniacs are among the most miserable of men; but not of necessity, the most guilty. They are distinguishable from "surpassingly wicked men," who with heart and will and waking consciousness, do the devil's work. In the latter case, there is a unity with evil and no cry for pardon.[1]

Weiss regards sin as the precursor of possession. " The radical matter of fact was simply this, that the sinful condition had reached a height where the man no longer had the mastery of sin, but sin of him; and when sunk in his utter impotence, and possessing no will of his own, he yielded to the enslaving power of sin, this dominion is referred to a superhuman spiritual power which held sway over him and deprived him of all volition." "What was most striking about the appearance of these so-called demoniacs was the conjunction with this yielding to Satan and the power of sin, of a state of disease whether of a psychical or bodily character, which is regarded as the result of

[1] *Notes on the Miracles.*

their moral condition." "These sufferers retained a consciousness of their moral bondage by the powers of darkness, such as did not usually appear before the beginning of their moral deliverance."[1]

Further evidence to the same effect is superfluous. The relevancy of that already adduced is easily disposed of, without inquiring into the correctness of Lightfoot's conjectures, or the views of Olshausen and Weiss regarding the nature of demonic beings. The only antecedent to all "self-attested" cases of possession is mental disorder of some sort or other.

THE LIMITS OF GENUINE DEMONIC POSSESSION

To attempt the unattempted is somewhat audacious; but the enterprise here is not without promise of success. The phrase, "moral and intellectual damage," has passed into international politics. It comes to hand conveniently. We have again to recall the two factors pertaining to every case of possession which answers to the criterion already laid down—

1. The physical element or the presence of mental disease.
2. The super-physical element or the presence of demonic agency.

(a) *The moral damage.*—It has been shown that the terms "evil" and "unclean" have only a pathological significance in relation to the conduct of the possessed. Their aberrant behaviour is completely explained by the facts of psychlogoical medicine. The depravity present is but an integral part of the disease. Jesus did not therefore hold demoniacs responsible for their condition; nor did He at any time ascribe to possessing spirits moral influence over the possessed, so that the condition of the latter should be ascribed to the former. Following that ruling, no moral damage can be attributed to the possessing spirits.

(*b*) *The intellectual damage.*—The symptoms of the possessed have their parallels among the insane of to-day: the confession of Jesus as Messiah alone excepted. But the pathological features existed in the possessed prior to their confrontation by Jesus. There is not the slightest indication of any aggravation of the purely physical derangement when the demonised of Capernaum and Gerasa were brought face to face with Christ. Luke says expressly concerning the former that the demon went forth, "having done no harm." The new feature in these and kindred cases was "the confession"; but that was an intercurrent and momentary phenomenon, entailing no intensification of the mental disorder. No intellectual damage is therefore imputable to the possessing spirits.

(*c*) If "moral and intellectual damage" be thus excluded, then the range of the action of possessing spirits becomes rather limited. It can have reference only to the residual, the super-physical phenomenon, *i.e.* to the classical criterion of genuine demonic possession,—THE CONFESSION OF JESUS AS MESSIAH. While the morbid concomitants of the demoniac condition pre-existed in the cases under consideration, this confession was an instantaneous act, evoked in, with, and under, the *presence of Christ*.[1]

(*d*) Hypnotism is generally supposed to offer a true analogy to the action of a possessing spirit upon one possessed. That is a twofold error. Hypnotism is a physiological or pathological process always induced through the organs of sensation. But the operation of a spirit is not conceivable on this wise. It is further supposed that the hypnotic state is due to the imposition of the will of the hypnotiser on his subject. But the will has really nothing to do with it; for the operator may suggest one thing, and with all his power will another, without altering the result. Space forbids any theorising on the *modus agendi* here. The fact of experience is to be recognised,— the reality of psychical influences or interactions.

---

[1] In the cases "not self-attested" or "natural," the whole of the phenomena belong to psychological medicine. That is that the question of antecedents is simply to go back upon the causation of insanity and idiocy in general. Moral depravity may occur as one among many other causes of these disorders. It could have no place in regard to the idiot boy, whose illness dated "from childhood."

CHAPTER VI

The Beelzebul Controversy

THE OCCASION OF THE SAME

THERE are three cases of possession whose intrinsic relations, historical, medical, and theological, set them apart as a special group. These are—

1. The dumb demoniac.
2. The blind and dumb demoniac.
3. The epileptic idiot.

The healing of those three produced an astounding effect; being in each case as follows:—

1. They wondered, saying, It was never so seen in Israel. Matt. ix. 33.
2. They were amazed and said, Is not this the son of David? Matt. xii. 23.
3. They were all amazed at the majesty of God. Luke ix. 43.

Compare with this emotion, that aroused by the three raisings from the dead. In connection with the daughter of Jairus, the son of the widow of Nain, and Lazarus, we read respectively—

1. They were astonished with a great astonishment. Mark v. 42.

2. There came a fear on all, and they glorified God. Luke vii. 16.

3. Caiaphas said, It is expedient that one man die. John xi. 50.

The comparison is instructive; because it suggests that the people regarded the cure of those demoniacs as a task rivalling the raising of the dead. The sensation produced on those occasions is wholly unique. Instances of a similar feeling are to be found occasionally; but only as the product of cumulative causes. The healing of the paralytic is accompanied with the forgiveness of sins; and the cure of the Gerasene is connected with the destruction of the swine. So in other cases, where there is a great astonishment, the antecedent is not single but composite. The foregoing point is worthy of consideration.

That brings us back to the diagnosis of these three cases of possession—

1. Idiocy, with deafness and dumbness.
2. Idiocy, with deafness, dumbness, and blindness.
3. Idiocy, with deafness, dumbness, and epileptic seizures.

There is an undoubted increase in the severity of these cases, as in the admiration of the multitudes. There is likewise a change in the attitude of the enemies of Christ—

1. They said, He casteth out demons in the prince of demons. Matt. ix. 34.

2. They said, He has Beelzebul, and in the prince of demons casteth out demons. Mark iii. 22.

3. They (with the others) were all amazed at the majesty of God. Luke ix. 43.

Here then we have the beginning, the culmination, and the sequel of the Beelzebul controversy. We soon discover how this personage comes into view.

These three demoniacs suffered from idiocy, with deafness, dumbness, and other sensory defects. The exorcist, charged with his superstitious lore, has to study his cases for their appropriate treatment. The dumbness is immaterial to him; because, *per se*, it offers no bar to his operations. But the deafness shut one door of access to the demon. Adjurations were quite useless. The deafness had virtually rendered the demon curse-proof. But other avenues of approach remained for attacking the loathly tenant: provided that the other organs of sense were comparatively sound. But idiocy involves many and grave defects; in advanced cases such as these were. Was the sense of smell greatly impaired? Then the most cunning fumigations were naught. Was the sense of taste much disordered? Then the most odious concoctions were irrelevant. Was the sense of sight grievously defective? Then the most startling exhibitions were worthless. Was cutaneous sensation much below normal? Then the severest inflictions were out of place. The foul spirit was sheltered under the very sense-defects of the possessed. The exorcist was baffled at every turn. His resources were completely exhausted. *The case was hopelessly incurable! The hapless demoniac was abandoned to his malignant demon!*

That then was the condition of those three. They were wholly beyond professional aid. But in the last resort, they had been brought to Jesus. He succeeded with ease where all others had failed. The further surprise of the situation was that He used no fumigations nor other devices of the vulgar exorcist. Candid observers could not withhold their tribute of admiration. Prejudiced onlookers cast about them for an explanation which would be plausible with the multitude yet detrimental to Jesus. The ethnic doctrine of demons aptly met all the requirements. It fancied a world of demons or satans where the greater lorded it over the lesser. To an exorcist on a friendly footing with "The Prince," nothing was impossible in the way of expelling recalcitrant spirits. Hence on the cure of the dumb demoniac, the knowing Pharisees said, He casteth out demons in the prince of demons! "The Prince" was then a well-known personage; now he is little more than a great enigma.

WHO IS BEELZEBUL?

The theory of the Pharisees embodied current conceptions regarding the orders and functions of spiritual beings. These must therefore be kept steadfastly in view. Thus we learn first of all what Beelzebul was not.

1. He is not Ashmedai. To the latter, the title of

"Prince" is commonly applied. But his authority extended over "male demons" only. The other wing of the demonic host was controlled by Lilith, as queen of "female demons." These spirits are of the same order as Beelzebul; but his authority is superior to theirs. He is sovereign over all foul demons.

2. He is not Satan, the great devil. Beelzebul is a "foul spirit" (Mark iii. 30); and belongs therefore to the order of the Shedim, who are semi-sensuous beings. He is also a possessing spirit (Mark iii. 22); the result of his action being in part conceived as a driving of Jesus out of His senses (Mark iii. 22).[1] But these attributes are in sharp contrast with those of Satan. The latter, though "head of all the Mazziqin," is no "half-spirit," like the Shedim; but belongs to the order of purely spiritual beings. While demon-possession is common; Judas is the sole instance of Satan-possession; the result of the latter is not insanity; but moral and spiritual ruin. This "prince of demons" is clearly not to be identified with Satan.[2]

Had this "prince of demons" ever enjoyed the honours of divinity? There is a suggestion of that in the variant reading of the name — Beelzebub. The authority for it is certainly not the highest; but Jerome accepts it. As science can ignore no fact or

---

[1] Appendix L, Jesus out of His Senses?

[2] Beliar, Berial, Malkira, Mastemah, Mekembekus, Matanbukus, Mastiphat, Mansemat, Asbeel, Satanail, occur as names of Satan in extra-canonical writings; but not Beelzebul. That is distinct confirmation of the foregoing conclusion.

suggestion, however trifling in appearance, the hint must not be overlooked. It leads us therefore to consider the fly-gods of the ancients, in the hope that we may thus discover a clue to the antecedents of "The Prince"—

1. *The Egyptian fly-god.*—This was the venerable Scarab-Beetle. According to Maspéro, the scarab was "khopirru," and was confounded with Khopri—He that is—the sun of the morning. Khopri is thus represented as a disc enclosing a scarab, or as a man with a scarab for his headpiece.[1] The scarab was likewise adored as an emblem of Phthah, the Creator. In the following fragment, wrongly ascribed to Orpheus by Gregory of Nazianzen and Philostratus, this deity seems to be referred to—

Most glorious Zeus, greatest of gods, enwrapt in dung.
Ζεῦ κύδιστε, μέγιστε θεῶν, εἰλύμενε κόπρῳ.

But no connection is traceable between the scarab-god and the prince of demons. The function of the latter pertains to Thot among the divinities of Egypt.

2. *The Ekronite god.*—Strictly speaking, the name Baalzebub denotes "owner of flies." It is thus a title of office rather than a personal name. This deity was probably of Babylonian origin, and a relic of Babylonian supremacy in the West, like his neighbour Dagon. This Ekronite god had more than a local reputation as a giver of oracles; having been applied to by King Ahaziah (2 Kings i. 3). In

Babylonia, flies were believed to possess a competent knowledge of the future, and were consulted accordingly.[1] But the function of the ancient Baalzebub is quite remote from "the prince of demons," and cannot be in view here.

3. The classical divinities,—Zeus and Hercules. They bore distinctive titles in connection with this useful but humble function:—$μυί-αγρος$,—hunter of flies, and—$ἀπόμυιος$,—averter of flies. Hercules is said to have banished flies from Olympus by sacrificing to Zeus. Pliny relates that the Eleans acted similarly for the removal of flies which were bringing on a plague. Clement of Alexandria records that the Romans, in like manner, sacrificed to Hercules. The Jews also understood that the divine presence repelled flies. Two Rabbis were discussing how the Shunammite knew that Elisha was "a holy man of God." The reply was, She never saw a fly cross his table (Ber. 10*b*). Again it is written, In the place of sacrificing, no fly is seen (Pirqe Abh. v. 6, 7). But even so, there is here no clue to "the prince of demons."

It is necessary therefore to turn to the etymologies of the better reading—Beelzebul. Only two of these are of any consequence.[2]

---

[1] Lenormant, *La Divination*, p. 95.

[2] Beelzebul might be derived from Beelzebub in two ways. Baudissin suggested a change in the final letter, in the interests of euphony. Beelzebul might also be a pun on Beelzebub; the prophets even being fond of punning (cf. Micah i. 10 ff.). Both conjectures are unproven; though not without precedent. These suggestions are of no value, as at most they lead back to Beelzebub, which has been already discussed.

1. *Lord of dung.*—So the name is rendered by John Lightfoot, followed by Fritzsche, De Wette, Bleek, Gesenius, and others. The arguments of Lightfoot need not be reproduced. They are vastly unconvincing. The insuperable objection to this view is that the proper word for dung is not "zebul," but "zebel."

2. *Lord of the dwelling.*—That is the interpretation of Michaelis, Paulus, Jahn, Hitzig, Hilgenfeld, Volkmar, and others. This gives to the name its natural significance; and has also in its favour the analogous title of the Phœnician Saturn. There is perhaps not much in the discovery of Meyer that the Greek term for "the master of the house" is the exact equivalent of the Hebrew Beelzebul.[1]

The first interpretation is discredited on many grounds; but the second is plausible. If, however, we can proceed no further than mere etymologies, our knowledge is little increased. The meaning and source of this title are to be further inquired into.

WHO IS THIS "LORD OF THE DWELLING"?

When describing the case of Mary Magdalene, evidence was found of the prevalence of Babylonian influences. Among Jewish cultivators of occult arts, these influences were making themselves energetically felt. In this direction, then, we may seek an explanation of the name Beelzebul.

---

[1] Meyer, *in loc.*

Prominent in the Babylonian pantheon was the god Ea. He became also a Semitic Bel. Bel-Ea signifies exactly—"Lord of the dwelling." It is therefore the precise equivalent of the designation—Beelzebul. But we may go beyond this coincidence. The name of Ea has reference to the region over which he ruled. That was the home of man and animated things. His domain was the earth, the sea, the air. As spirit of the world and animating it, he possessed all knowledge. As the soul of the zone of the world of living things, he was the god who saw that all was in order; defending the frame of nature against the attacks of evil spirits. Having all knowledge, he knew all the tricks of demons and was able to baffle all their enterprises. He knew all the magic formulæ for subduing evil spirits, and was thus of exceptional helpfulness to the magician and the exorcist. His aid was sought where no rite or word or talisman of any other god or goddess availed to destroy the power of the demons.[1]

But the god Ea became identified with Mul-lil, "lord of the ghost-world," and "king of all the spirits of the earth," whose messengers were diseases, nightmares, and demons of the night." Like Ea, he too became a Semitic Bel. In the Magic Texts of Babylonia, he is invoked—[2]

O spirit of Mul-lil, king of the world conjure!

---

[1] Lenormant, *Babylonian Magic*, p. 158 ff.
[2] Sayce, *Hibbert Lectures*, pp. 140–147; p. 155 et seq.

Mul-lil had thus become an expeller of spirits as Ea had been; and when thus merged in the latter, his title and function are those of Beelzebul—

Bel-Ea	Lord of the dwelling.
Bel-Mul-lil	Lord of evil spirits.
Bel-Ea-Mul-lil	Lord of the dwelling and of evil spirits.

Here at last then we have found "the prince of demons," who is also "a foul spirit." The identification seems to be complete. We can easily understand how exorcists who practised upon refractory spirits, according to the Babylonian rubric, should have but one explanation of the phenomenal success of Jesus. That is reflected in the words of the Pharisees: He casteth out demons in the prince of demons.

This first accusation belongs to an early period in the ministry of Christ. It spread with amazing rapidity. When sending forth the Twelve, Jesus warned them, If they have cast up Beelzebul to the Master of the house, how much more to them of His household?[1] That charge had a twofold merit. It satisfied at once the claims of science falsely so called, and served to discredit Christ as an ally of the powers of darkness. It had, therefore, an ingenious and malignant vitality about it which ensured its repetition. As the enmity of the scribes and Pharisees gathers way, the names of "glutton and winebibber" come to be well fixed. The Synagogue Ministry is now over; and the house to house visitation of the Twelve also. The training of the Apostles now

[1] Appendix M, Was Jesus nicknamed Beelzebul

engages attention. "The Teaching on the Mount" is concluded. Jesus returns unexpectedly to Capernaum, and the word goes round, He is home (Mark iii. 19). These are the antecedents to the more embittered accusation which is connected with the healing of the blind and dumb demoniac. The whole *nuance* of the narrative presupposes the performance of this miracle in the neighbourhood of Capernaum.[1]

CHRIST POSSESSED OF BEELZEBUL

Such was the wretched counterblast of desperate men in their most desperate mood. The people had said, Is not this the son of David? Meyer notes this as the "question of imperfect but growing faith." But faith in Jesus was the very thing which these Pharisees deprecated, and for the prevention of which they had already sent forth their cunning accusation. The people had shown an ability to judge for themselves which was most ominous to the future supremacy of those lordly hypocrites who claimed to do the thinking for all. This prospective loss roused them to fury. Incipient independence must be crushed instantly and for ever. But, upon principle, Pharisaic godlessness proceeds in godly fashion. So those saintly villains said, He has Beelzebul, and in the prince of demons casteth he out demons.[2]

---

[1] Appendix N, Scene of the healing of the blind and dumb Demoniac.
[2] Appendix L, Jesus out of His Senses?

But with this passionate declaration there mingled a deep note of insincerity. It was reckoned not only possible to form compacts with demons, but even highly respectable to do so. Had not Solomon, in his halcyon days, summoned male and female demons to dance before him? Had he not also through those agents got possession of the worm Shamir, in the highest interests of religion? Had not this darling of the people likewise been the familiar of Ashmedai, the prince of demons? Could any man therefore forbid those excellent Pharisees to follow these royal precedents? A public avowal of those sentiments might not at this juncture enhance the reputation of those Pharisees; but none the less were they convinced that an alliance with Beelzebul meant —POWER! That surely was a consummation to be devoutly coveted? How fervently those deceivers wished to be potent as Jesus now!

CHRIST'S REFUTATION OF THE PHARISAIC THEORY

There was no question as to the reality of the cure of the blind and dumb demoniac. The only point at issue was, Whence hath this man this power? Is it devilish or divine? Jesus refutes His enemies calmly and magnificently, by simply pushing their theory to its furthest issues.

1. *The logical issue.*—The Pharisees believed in a kingdom of evil organised on the common ethnic model. It was a loose organisation, wherein the

satanic units possessed no real community of interest, sentiment, or activity. One member could therefore cast out another. The displacement was a mere question of caprice or strength. But Jesus showed the utter absurdity of such a conception. Under those conditions, the kingdom of Satan must have an end. But its continuance proves that it is a compact organism; wherein the several units are pervaded by an essential identity of interest, sentiment, and activity. There is one head of this kingdom and therefore one responsibility. In this sense, then, How can Satan cast out Satan? He is not divided against himself. The ethnic conception of the kingdom of evil is irrational; because it involves division and consequent instability. The Pharisaic theory is logically untenable.

2. *The social issue.*—This is an *argumentum ad hominem*. If the Pharisaic theory was correct, then it was also defamatory to the confrères of this party, who busied themselves with the ejection of demons. " Jesus reasons *ex concessis.*" He does not deny that the Pharisaic exorcists might sometimes attain a modicum of success. He is fully aware of the nature and limits of it. He argues that if the degree of His success is to be taken as the measure of His alliance with Beelzebul, then the same rule must apply to " the sons of the Pharisees." If a surpassing infamy attaches to Him because of His surpassing success, then highly respectable exorcists must bear a proportionate dishonour. The Pharisaic theory,

already shown to be crassly absurd, now becomes socially monstrous.

CHRIST'S PROPOSAL OF AN ALTERNATIVE

The healing of the blind and dumb demoniac remained as a supernatural fact. The achievement was either devilish or divine. There was no *tertium quid*. Jesus had shown that the former alternative was impossible. He had burst up the old theory from the bottom, and had covered its advocates with shame and confusion. But He never sought a cheap triumph even over His enemies. In a conciliatory manner, He makes a new suggestion. The success of the ordinary exorcist was at best, occasional, accidental, and mostly temporary; the result of spells and fumigations. But the success of Christ was uniform, immediate, and always permanent;[1] the result of "a word." Collusion with Beelzebul was an infamous absurdity. How could Jesus succeed otherwise than "in the Spirit of God"?[2] The only reasonable conclusion was that the power resident in Him was truly divine. Here emerges the moral argument. Miracles which curtail the dominion of Satan are proofs that a new era has dawned. There stands One already in their midst Whom they know not. The Messianic King achieves His saving purpose "in the Spirit," as "the Lord and Giver of life."

[1] Appendix H, Testimonies to the success of Jesus.
[2] Luke xi. 20, "With the finger of God."

Therefore the announcement is to all: The kingdom of God has come upon you (ἔφθασεν ἐφ' ὑμᾶς, Matt. xii. 28).

But the moral argument is capped by the prophetic. The victory obtained over Satan that day implied a prior one. The spoiler was already spoiled; the captor already captured. The strong man has been bound by the Stronger. Therein is the ancient oracle fulfilled: Shall the prey be taken from the mighty or the lawful captive delivered? But thus saith the Lord, Even the captives of the mighty shall be taken away, and the prey of the terrible shall be delivered; for I will contend with him that contendeth with thee, and I will save thy children (Isa. xlix. 24, 25). In the rescue of that blind and dumb demoniac, the Pharisees had presented before them the promise and the potency of the true Messiah. What was the event?

THE SIGN FROM HELL

Jesus had rectified the errors of His adversaries and had proposed the true alternative for their acceptance. But Pharisaic superstition and malignity were invincible. Christ endeavoured in vain to cure the one and abate the other. The only result was a demand for a sign from heaven. For these Pharisees, then, neither moral proof nor Messianic miracle possessed the slightest value. They had contemptuously brushed aside the most cogent evidence,

and had thus come indefinitely near to the sin that
hath no forgiveness. They refused to be enlightened,
and had now the poor satisfaction of learning that
they were "an evil and adulterous generation." No
other description was more appropriate. That age
had witnessed a real return to sorcery and mongrel
worship. Lilith, Ashmedai, and Beelzebul were conspicuous proofs of the same. The people which
united an illicit regard for those principalities and
powers with professed allegiance to Jehovah was
deservedly reprobated as an "evil and adulterous
generation." "Teacher, said they, we wish to see a
sign from heaven." The response was most disquiet-
ing. *The sign was from hell,—THE RETURN OF THE
DEMONS!*

THE PARABLE OF THE LAST STATE

It is quite necessary to remember that Jesus spoke
here "in parables" (Mark iii. 23). The parable is
essentially "an illustrating analogy." This one moves
in the region of popular conceptions.[1] Elements of
the ethnic doctrine of demons are numerous here;
such as the arbitrary going forth of the unclean
spirit; his roaming at large in the waterless desert;
his longing for a material organism wherein to rest;
his commandeering of seven others more malignant
than himself; the united invasion of the house that
was empty, swept, and garnished; the increased de-

[1] Appendix O. Did Jesus practise accommodation

structiveness of the more wicked fiends; so that the last end of the possessed is worse than the first. But glancing backwards at Christ's attitude towards popular superstitions, we find those points anticipated and refuted. At the very beginning of this discourse, Jesus showed His aversion to ethnic superstitions. At the end of it, He does not return to the same. He uses, as the basis of His argument, the language of His opponents; *and He had a right to do so.* These men refused to be divorced from their stubborn misconceptions. For them no illustration could possibly have been more clear and telling than this one. The aptness of it was its completest justification. Moreover, the parable was in process of fulfilment. In the eager study of occult lore and in the practice of the black art, the demons of the prime had returned, and had recovered for themselves a place in the imagination and the creed of the populace. Modern Judaism with its strange customs and doctrines offers the best commentary on the prediction of a latter state worse than the former.

THE SEQUEL TO THE BEELZEBUL CONTROVERSY

Instead of reaping the rewards of zealous piety, these scribes and Pharisees had the mortification of being exhibited as pagan theorists. Moreover, their pretty suggestion that Jesus was confederate with the prince of demons was now so deftly, yet withal so forcefully, knocked about, that they never had the courage to air it again. The reproach of possession reappears in Jerusalem; but not the old accusation.[1] *The very name of Beelzebul henceforth sinks into such disrepute that it vanishes from Jewish literature.*

Though worsted in argument, the wounded vanity of the scribes and Pharisees did not permit them to retire from the arena. The cure of the idiot boy at the Hill of Transfiguration is the true sequel to the Beelzebul controversy. In the narratives of Matthew and Mark that is the recognised order of events.[2] Though silenced in public, those malicious enemies continued to dog the footsteps of Jesus, even as far as the remote regions of Cæsarea-Philippi. Here in the absence of the Master, the idiot boy was brought for cure. At first sight, there is no reason manifest why the Apostles should not succeed. On their first Mission, they had not known of failure (Mark vi. 13). But somehow the Nine failed at this critical juncture. The scribes must have been rendered jubilant over their impotence; for the power which wrought in them was the self-same power as wrought in Jesus. The drying up of the stream implies the exhaustion

---

[1] John vii. 20; viii. 48, 52; x. 20.
[2] Luke has reversed the order; but without clear reason for it. "The Ebionitic tendency of the third Gospel," if any, does not clear up the matter. The charge of conspiring with Beelzebul has been shown to attach itself naturally to the healing of the dumb demoniac. Its repetition in a more aggressive form is equally natural in connection with the severer case of the blind and dumb demoniac. Its total absence in relation to the worst of these three cognate cases is wholly inexplicable, unless on the assumption that it has already been suppressed. Matthew and Mark have, doubtless, preserved the true chronological sequence.

of the fountain. Had the ceaseless vigilance of these men at last obtained its reward? Were their former charges now to be proved up to the hilt? So they seem to have thought. Hence their enthusiastic haste to examine the crestfallen disciples (Mark ix. 14). That precious opportunity, which they were so fervently embracing, was sadly marred by the return of Christ, Who cut short their inquisitorial proceedings. The malevolent intention of the scribes was at once unmasked; and they were asked to show cause for this magisterial action. After a leading question or two had been put to the father, the lad was healed. A sharp lesson was read to all concerned. He rebuked them, saying, O faithless and perverse generation, how long shall I be with you? How long shall I bear with you? The distribution of the blame has puzzled commentators; but the answer is now self-evident. The faithlessness is that of the Apostles in particular; the perversity, that of the scribes and their sympathisers in general. The disabling unbelief of the former was disappointing; the aggressive violence of the latter, intolerable. But in the end all discordant voices were hushed; even the scribes were overawed. "All were astonished at the majesty of God."

"WHY COULD NOT WE CAST IT OUT?"

This case was apparently of a novel character. Among demoniacs, it is the worst on record. Cases of this sort must have been rare in the land. The mortality, always high among such patients, must have been phenomenal in Palestine, owing to neglect or maltreatment. We are therefore entitled to believe that the Nine had never been confronted with a case of such extraordinary severity. But what was the special feature which must have impressed them as an invincible barrier to the healing of this lad? Clearly, the deafness! Whereas the ordinary exorcist supplemented his adjurations by a variety of methods, the Apostles had to rely on the Name alone. But how could the Name operate when the sense of hearing was defunct? That seemed fatal to success. According to current notions, the demon was thus entrenched in security behind the deafness. By such false ideas, the Nine were reduced to helplessness. The old leaven of superstition was their undoing. The power delegated to them was not to be exercised in any magical or mechanical fashion; but only on the basis of intelligent faith and earnest prayer, sustained by an inward harmony of thought, desire, and will, with Christ. Dark superstition is to rational belief as night to day; they are mutually exclusive. "This kind (of thing) can go forth by nothing but by prayer."[1] The later records of the New Testament prove that the lesson was laid to heart by the Apostles. There ended their enfeebling superstitions.[2]

[1] Appendix P, Ejection of demons by "fasting."
[2] Appendix Q, The popular treatment of epilepsy.

CHAPTER VII

The Difficulties of the Gerasene Affair

HUXLEY referred to this with unnecessary vehemence as "the Gadarene pig affair." In this connection, he remarks: "(Mr. Gladstone's) strategic sense justly leads him to see that the authority of the teachings of the synoptic Gospels, touching the nature of the spiritual world, turns upon the acceptance or the rejection, of the Gadarene and other like stories. As we accept, or repudiate, such histories as that of the possessed pigs, so shall we accept, or reject, the witness of the synoptics to such miraculous interventions." A critique of the potential fallacy underlying this statement is not called for at this stage. Truth rarely consorts with the purely controversial mood. If the difficulties of the narrative have been felt to be real, there remains the possibility of a restatement of the whole case, with the prospect of diminishing or removing most of them.

THE SCENE OF THE EVENT

The locality has been variously assigned to the Gadarenes, Gerasenes, and Gergesenes—

	MATT.	MARK.	LUKE.
Lachmann	Gerasenes	Gerasenes	Gerasenes.
Tregelles	Gadarenes	Gerasenes	Gerasenes.
Tischendorf	Gadarenes	Gerasenes	Gergesenes.
Westcott and Hort	Gadarenes	Gerasenes	Gerasenes.
Revised Version	Gadarenes	Gerasenes	Gerasenes.
Authorised Version	Gergesenes	Gadarenes	Gadarenes.

Origen clears up the matter; remarking that the precipitation of the swine is recorded to have taken place in the country of the Gerasenes. In a few manuscripts he found mention of the country of the Gadarenes. He objects to Gerasa, which was a city of Arabia (Gilead), having neither sea nor lake near it; also to Gadara, noted for its warm springs, but its lake or sea was not at all near to precipices. There remained Gergesa by the Lake of Tiberias, near which was a precipice adjacent to the Lake, from which it was pointed out that the swine were precipitated by the demons. Origen thus makes it clear that in his time, "Gerasenes" was the prevalent reading; "Gadarenes," that of a few manuscripts; "Gergesenes," being unattested.[1] The weight of textual authority thus favours the reading, "Gerasenes."

The indications of the site are sufficiently explicit—

1. A place over against Galilee.
2. A place with tombs adjacent to it.
3. A place sloping steeply towards the Lake.

[1] Keim calls Gergesa a mere guess of Origen; but Jerome affirmed the existence of a village of that name, "still shown above the mountain, close by the Lake of Tiberias."

The site of the ancient Kerza or Gersa, discovered by Thomson, answers all the requirements of the case. The ruins of the old town are described as but a few rods from the shore; but there is no bold overhanging cliff, or "jumping-off place." Sir C. W. Wilson notes that about a mile south of the town, the hills approach within forty feet of the water's edge; not terminating abruptly, but in a steep evenly slope. That spot would accord with a desire on the part of the demoniac(s) and the swineherds to avoid the town. Neither Gadara nor Gerasa affords the proper environment. The former on the Hieromax (Um-Keis on the Jermuk), some ten miles from the Lake, was the capital of a district which apparently included Kerza. The latter was east of the ancient Ramoth-Gilead; being some twenty miles from the Jordan, and some forty miles from the Sea of Galilee. It may be affirmed, on physiological grounds alone, that the swine were unequal to the physical task of galloping without rest from either of those towns to the Lake; even though ridden by a whole legion of demons. These considerations lead to the unhesitating acceptance of Kerza as the scene of this affair. That is also the verdict of numerous competent travellers.

The mention of the locality introduces us to the "Huxley-Gladstone controversy," which has already an antiquarian flavour.[1] It is immaterial, whether

[1] *Nineteenth Century*, "Agnosticism," Feb. 1889; "Keepers of the Herd of Swine," Dec. 1890; "Huxley and the Swine-Miracle," Feb. 1891. Cf. *Impregnable Rock of Holy Scripture*, p. 268 ff.

we hold with Huxley that "the legal provisions which alone had authority over an inhabitant of the country of the Gadarenes were the Gentile laws sanctioned by the Romans"; or believe with Gladstone that the Gadarenes were "Hebrews bound by the Mosaic law." The ownership of the swine is completely hidden from us, and the conclusions on either side are open to a twofold objection. The arguments really proceed,— *e silentio*. Moral issues cannot rest upon mere topographical considerations.

THE NUMBER OF THE DEMONIACS

That Matthew should have two demoniacs where the other Synoptists have but one, is a surprising but not a singular occurrence.[1] Attempts to make the diverse accounts agree with each other have met with small success, and the tendency is to get rid of one of the possessed. Thus Chrysostom, Augustine, and Calvin thought of the greater importance of one of the demoniacs compared with the other. Ammon's suggestion of a madman and his keeper is too ridiculous to deserve attention. The difficulty is hardly removed by the supposition of communicated insanity (*folie à deux*); for Matthew contemplates no difference either in the type or in the severity of the symptoms of the two possessed. We have thus to consider two men suffering from the most furious mania, both manifesting the same homicidal pro-

[1] Cf. Matt. xx. 30; Mark x. 46; Luke xviii. 35.

pensities, both harbouring the same delusions, both practising the same mutilations, and both uttering the same menaces. How two lunatics animated by such terrible passions, could dwell together in unity, "for a long time," surpasses comprehension. The theory of *folie à deux* is inadequate to the occasion, and the circumstances raise an inherent, if not an invincible, doubt as to the accuracy of this detail.

Various conjectures have been offered as to the source of this discrepancy. Matthew does not aim at a heightening of the miraculous here. The concentration of the demons in one subject comes much nearer to that. Nor does the first Evangelist introduce the two demoniacs here to make up for his omission of the possessed of Capernaum. Ebrard, Bleek, Holtzmann, and others, overlook the fact that Matthew is usually precise in distinguishing things that differ. He separates the epileptics from the demonised, and differentiates the dumb from the blind-and-dumb demoniac. Another explanation, usually associated with the name of Weiss, is that Matthew found the term "demons" in his original; and for the plurality of these postulated a plurality of demoniacs. Yet Jewish, not less than ethnic, doctrine contemplated the possibility of a single person becoming the hold of many unclean spirits. Matthew was therefore under no necessity of introducing two subjects of possession where one sufficed. The suggestion of Weiss thus becomes of none effect, and there is still left an unsolved antinomy.

THE ALLEGED TRANSMIGRATION OF THE DEMONS

The statements of the Synoptists are as follows:—

1. The demons, having gone out, departed into the swine; and behold, the whole herd rushed down the steep into the sea and died in the waters. Matt. viii. 32.
2. The filthy spirits, having gone forth, entered into the swine; and the herd rushed down the steep, some two thousand of them, and began to be choked in the sea. Mark v. 13.
3. The demons, having gone out of the man, entered into the swine; and the herd rushed down the steep into the lake and were choked. Luke viii. 33.

On the understanding that the transmigration of the swine is a fact, there have arisen questions of motive which must be considered.

A. Motives have been assigned to the demons—

1. Their desire was to prejudice the Gerasenes against Jesus, whose permission of the demons to enter the swine involved the pig-owners in loss. But those people raised no threat of legal action. They offered no violence to the party. They wished simply to get rid of Jesus quietly as an *uncanny* personage.

2. Their desire was to escape from the torments of hell; an organism, animal or human, being supposed to afford the requisite shelter. This poor apologetic elicited the cheap sneers of Strauss, Keim, and others, who pointed out how little the demons were to be congratulated on their foresight; the possession of the swine proving a short cut to the abyss. But these remarks are puerilities. If demons are spirits, then the ethical element must enter into

their "torments," and from these no physical environment can save them.

B. Motives have been assigned to Jesus—

1. The destruction of the swine was intended to alleviate the final paroxysm of the demonised, caused by the exit of the "legion." But this is a triple error. As a matter of fact there were no final paroxysms. Even had such existed, their alleviation by transference to an animal organism is a physiological impossibility. Finally, the death of the swine could afford to the demonised no demonstration of his cure.

2. The destruction of the swine was intended to test the Gerasenes as to whether they would prefer eternal life to the loss of their property. But they had no option in the matter. They were apprised of their loss after its occurrence. In any case, Jesus never attempted conversions by physical methods. He came not to judge but to save. The foregoing suggestion is an absurdity.

We need not proceed further with the enumeration of motives on either side. It is evident that no light comes from these sources, and it is therefore necessary to consider anew the fundamental facts.

DATA FOR A CONSTRUCTION

We recognise here a solid nucleus of fact, which remains after the application of the canons of historical criticism. That unassailable residuum comprises the cure of the demoniac and the precipitation of the swine.

We recognise here also a certain theory of this occurrence. The facts are separable from the theory, and furnish material for testing its validity. The facts remain unchallenged; the soundness of the theory is legitimate matter of inquiry. The record is as follows:—

The demons besought him, saying, If thou cast us out, send us away into the herd of swine. And he said unto them, Go! Matt. viii. 31, 32.

Jesus asked him, What is thy name? And he said unto him, My name is Legion; for we are many. And he besought him much that he would not send them away out of the country. And they besought him, saying, Send us into the swine, that we may enter into them. And he gave them leave. Mark v. 9, 10, 12, 13.

Jesus asked him, What is thy name? And he said, Legion; for many demons were entered into him. And they besought him that he would not order them off to hell.[1] They besought him that he would give them leave to enter into the swine. And he gave them leave. Luke viii. 30–32.

These remarkable differences of the Triple Tradition give us the theory emergent from the facts—

1. The prayer of the demoniac becomes the prayer of the demons themselves.
2. Leave to remain in the district becomes a request to escape the abyss.

---

[1] Luke regards the nether region of hell ἄβυσσος) as the proper home of the demons, not the country (χώρα) round the Lake. Cf. Luke viii. 31; Mark v. 10. *But the sea was a recognised route to hell.* The Jews knew of three gates to Gehenna—one in the wilderness (Num. xvi. 33); another in the sea (Jonah ii. 2); another in Jerusalem (Isa. xxxi. 9). See Erubin 19a.

3. The word, Go,—is interpreted as permission to enter into the swine.

It is to be noted that the possession of animals by demons is an ethnic idea, which found entrance into the early Church. Origen asserts that demons enter into birds, serpents, foxes, wolves, and weasels. Jerome relates the success of Saint Hilarion in casting a demon out of an unspeakable Bactrian camel. The transference of demons from human beings to objects, animate and inanimate, is likewise an ethnic conception.[1] Charles VI. of France, the Mad or the Beloved, was experimented on by a bold priest for the removal of his demon; twelve men being chained up for its reception. The Indian exorcist of Cumana, when called in for the treatment of one possessed, after much toil brings up a thick black phlegm, having in its centre a little hard black ball. The latter is carried into the field with the words: Go thy way, devil! Farrar asserts that the passage of unclean spirits from the demoniac to the swine was "a thoroughly Jewish belief." Edersheim takes exception to the statement. But the proof-passage of the former is no proof; and the denial of the latter is not an argument. The idea of such a transference could not have been quite foreign to the Jews. The point of paramount importance relates to the question, Did Christ sanction that belief by directing or permitting the demons to invade the swine?

1. The case seems to be regarded as one of

multiple or manifold possession. "Many demons were entered into him." But that was an opinion which Jesus did not hold. The evidence on the point is perfectly clear.

Mark has these oscillations—

The man is in an unclean spirit. v. 2.
He cried, What is there between me and thee? v. 7.
Jesus said, Come out of the man, unclean spirit. v. 8.
The man besought him not to send the demons away. v. 10.
The unclean spirit besought him, Send us into the swine. v. 12.
Jesus suffered them to enter the swine. v. 13.
The spirits, having come out, entered the swine. v. 13.

Jesus allows of only one demon throughout; Mark has one also in c. 2. The demoniac surmises a multitude; so does Mark in v. 12, 13.

Luke has these oscillations—

The man has demons. viii. 27.
He cried, What is there between me and thee? viii. 28.
Jesus commanded the unclean spirit to go forth. viii. 29.
The unclean spirit had seized him many times. viii. 29.
He was driven by the demon into the wilderness. viii. 29.
He said, Legion; for many demons had entered into him. viii. 30.
The demons besought him not to order them off to hell. viii. 31.
The demons besought permission to enter the swine. viii. 32.
The demons, having come out of the man, entered the swine. viii. 33.

Jesus allows of only one demon throughout; Luke has one also in viii. 29. The demoniac surmises a multitude; so does Luke in viii. 30, 31, 32, 33.

Entirely in harmony with this view of our Lord is the demonic confession—

What have I to do with Thee, Jesus, Son of God Most High? Mark v. 7.

What have I to do with Thee, Jesus, Son of God Most High? Luke viii. 28.

The textual variations have long been known; but no one has ventured to draw the proper inference. The statement of Jesus is precise and unfaltering. *He did not regard this as a case of manifold possession.*

2. What meaning then is to be attached to the words: Send US into the swine? They obviously imply a plurality of demons in the man; whereas Christ expressly recognised one only. Was this the prayer of "many demons"? Evidently not; for Jesus did not believe in the existence of such a host. Was this then the prayer of the single demon? Clearly not; for it belies itself in the contradiction of terms. The correct formula for the single possessing spirit would have been: Send ME into the swine! There is therefore no demonic request to invade the herd. The utterance is human, and proceeds naturally from a lunatic who harbours the delusion that he is possessed of a "legion." No real reply to this man's request was possible. Did Jesus then offer a pretended reply? Was this a case of accommodation? Within narrow limits, the practice is a legitimate one in the treatment of the insane. The danger is that recognised by Cælius Aurelianus of old, viz., the con-

firmation of the existing delusion. An instance taken almost at random illustrates the method. Thus, a person who believed that a snake was present in his internals was cured by a pretended operation. But he thereafter took up the notion that, while the serpent itself was removed, its ova were left behind, ready to be hatched into a new brood of vipers. He was relieved, however, by the dexterous reply that the snake was a male.[1] Accommodation is thus a form of condescension (συγκατάβασις). The insane person assumes the leading rôle; the physician, for the time being, abdicates his intelligence. But such procedure in no wise corresponds to the case under consideration. The demoniac is never regnant. From first to last, Jesus is supreme. The very conditions of accommodation are conspicuous by their absence. There could be no response, real or pretended, to the words of the possessed: Send US into the swine. That statement is wholly unrelated to anything that follows.

According to Matthew, Christ uttered one word: Go (ὑπάγετε)![2] The same term is implied, not expressed, in the narratives of Mark and Luke. A severe and enlightened criticism must find in it the nearest approximation to the *ipsissimum verbum* of our Lord on this occasion. It can have no reference, logical or practical, to the demoniac himself; but only to his possessing demon. The word—ὑπάγειν—occurs in the New Testament in two distinct senses—

[1] *Guy and Ferrier's Forensic Medicine*, "Mania."
[2] Plural for two demoniacs.

(*a*) As the symbol of an absolute command.

(*b*) As the vehicle of a simple permission.

The first Evangelist clearly favours the former interpretation; the second and third evidently contemplate the latter. If it be granted that a demonic request is contained in the words: Send US into the swine; then it must also be granted that the answer to that request is contained in the word, Go. But excellent reasons have been offered in proof of the conclusion that no demonic request for permission to invade the herd is to be found there. Petitions for leave to enter into the swine are but the vagaries of one who has lost his reason. *Where there was no genuine prayer by the possessing demon, there could be no genuine permission by the sovereign Christ.* The term, Go, must therefore bear the former interpretation in preference to the latter. It thus denotes an imperial injunction which shows that Jesus is in unbending opposition to the enemy. "Go," is but the repetition of the first behest: Get out of the man, thou filthy spirit! Neither direction to enter the swine, nor permission to do so, nor compensation for disturbance, can be thought of here. The first is an assumption. No command to this end is recorded in the Gospels. The naked mandate is: BEGONE! The second is an inference. No passage of the demon into the swine was visible. The former is a spirit. The third is an impossibility. Demonic confession was an offence to Christ. No mitigation of its evil desert is conceivable; least of all by hiding in the swine.

THE STAMPEDE OF THE HERD

As the panic among the swine seems no longer explicable by the action of a legion or a unit, the cause of this incident must be sought elsewhere. The conceited dogmatism of Krug, Schmidt, and Volkmar, lacks even the saving grace of "most ingenious and beautiful poesie." The more serious attempts to understand this event require brief consideration.

1. Paulus supposed that the demonised in the last paroxysm of their illness, rushed upon the herd with loud cries, hunting them over the cliffs, while the keepers fled. There was, however, no final paroxysm; and there is no trace of such a driving of the swine into the sea.

2. Lange, along with final paroxysms, fancies that the cries of the demonised rose to a most horrible shout—the thousand voices of the demons now being expelled. This acted like an electric shock, causing a panic among creatures "susceptible of dark sylvan terror"! But this author's imagination so occludes his practical understanding that the matter remains obscure as ever.

3. Farrar conceives that the shrieks and gesticulations of a powerful lunatic might strike the swine with uncontrollable terror; adding that the "spasm of deliverance was often attended with fearful convulsions, sometimes perhaps with an effusion of blood."[1]

---

[1] A curious integration — Shrieks (Bleek, Lange), gesticulations (Ewald), spasms (Paulus), etc.

The last is a notable addition, not attested in the records. It is really irrelevant to the issue. In swine, the senses of sight and smell are highly developed. Their being "far off" at the moment, might possibly be no bar to their seeing and scenting effused blood, if any. But while cattle and some other animals are sensitive to the sight and smell of blood, swine are psychically indifferent to the same, whether animal or human. No panic could therefore arise from this cause.

4. Rosenmüller suggests that hot weather might have something to do with the stampede of the herd; one perhaps being morbidly affected, and beginning to run about wildly, then followed by the whole flock.[1] If the first point be conceded, the rest might follow. But whatever the season of the year, the heights round Gerasa, on which the swine pastured, must have been cool at this particular hour. The strong wind of the previous evening had been sweeping these hills for hours. This suggestion cannot be accepted; and in any case it would leave the panic of the herd more mysterious than ever.

5. Lutteroth thinks of the incidence of giddiness upon the swine, permitted by Christ, Who thereby intended to give the demonised a sign of deliverance, and so remove his fixed idea.[1] But a fixed idea connotes physical disease as its substratum; and, as already noted, a sign for the confirmation of the man's sense of restoration was superfluous and absurd.

Further, the smiting of some two thousand swine with vertigo defeats the end of this suggestion. If the herd were smitten with giddiness, their plunging into the Lake, by a movement, direct and rapid, would have been impossible. The effect of severe vertigo is the suspension of all power of locomotion. This proffered solution is a multiplication of existing difficulties.

With the failure of these explanations, we are driven back upon the simple narrative. Clearly, Jesus issued no injunction, direct or indirect, for the destruction of the herd. It is equally certain that there is some connection between the healing of the demoniac and the rushing of the swine into the sea. The time and place must be carefully scrutinised once more as a clue to the solution of this difficulty. Specific notes are furnished by the three Evangelists—

1. All are agreed that the cure of the possessed coincided with the panic among the swine.
2. At this juncture, the demoniac and the herd were separated from each other by a considerable distance ($\mu\alpha\kappa\rho\acute{a}\nu$, Matt. viii. 30).

The term—$\mu\alpha\kappa\rho\acute{a}\nu$—is an elastic one. Meyer translates it in a relative sense; Weiss renders it— "afar off." The latter contradicts the Vulgate— "non longe." These sharp differences only prove that the ordinary philological methods are of little use in dealing with a colloquial term like this. The combination of the descriptions of Matthew and Mark happily furnishes a concrete basis for determining the *lineal value* of the word under consideration—

There was a good way off (μακράν) from them a herd of swine. Matt. viii. 30.
Having seen Jesus afar off (μακρόθεν), he ran and worshipped. Mark v. 6.

The two terms are equipollent and commensurate. The distance is reckoned from the point of landing. That was the centre of a circle; the demoniac being at the extremity of one radius, the herd at the extremity of another. These adjacent extremities were the *loci* from which the running in each case began. But it was shown that the demoniac, when within the tomb, became aware of the arrival of Jesus and His party through the sense of hearing. The interval between them was not great. They were within earshot of each other. When the demoniac "ran," he met them "instantly."

But the terms—μακράν and μακρόθεν—are often applied to distances within which distinct vision is possible—

Hagar watches Ishmael,—μακράν; as it were a bowshot off. Gen. xxi. 16.
The father recognises the ragged prodigal,—μακράν. Luke xv. 20.
Those at the cross are—μακρόθεν; but within earshot. Mark xv. 40; John xix. 26-27.

In these instances the distances do not exceed two or three hundred yards at most. This would amply suffice to harmonise all the philological and topographical data of the narrative here. It is a reasonable estimate, and brings us within sight of the solution of the problem, viz., the cause of the stampede of the swine.

The herd was some two or three hundred yards from the spot whereon the party of Jesus was gathered and whereon the demoniac was cured. Prior to these events, there may have been an initial restlessness among the herd. It is a striking fact in the natural history of these animals, that they are peculiarly sensitive to aerial disturbances in the open field. Like the horse, they are very liable to panic. During the preceding evening a strong gale had been blowing off shore. It may have engendered a state of excitement not allayed towards morning. But the point need not be pressed. There was more than enough in the following events to produce a stampede.

There were the fierce yells of the maniac as he rushed down the hill. Now the shrieks of a homicidal lunatic are particularly penetrating, even when he is under confinement; but if heard, when he is at large, they are unspeakably disconcerting. They can never be forgotten. But above those wild shouts of the demoniac rose the voice of Christ: Get out of the man, thou filthy spirit! The response was the fierce defiance, What have I to do with Thee, Jesus, Thou Son of God Most High? I adjure Thee by God that Thou torment me not! Then finally, the great commanding word of Christ, addressed to the demon: BEGONE!

The mad rush of the demoniac and these many loud voices were more than sufficient to arouse the most stolid creatures. Each interjectional episode was stormier than its predecessor, till the terror of the swine, passing beyond all control, projected them, down the steep declivity, over the narrow foreshore, almost in a solid mass, into the waters. The whole series of events was probably comprised within a few moments.

But let us return for an instant to the state of the demoniac. The departure of the demon does not follow upon the first word of Christ; the cure is not instantaneous. There is a brief period of physical reaction, during which strange thoughts flit through the mind of this man. His abnormal sensations had formerly produced the hallucination of gigantic strength, which took local form and colouring in the delusion that he was possessed of a "legion." Something similar is happening now. He is conscious of a change in his condition, and seeks an explanation of his novel sensations. His imagination couples the subsidence of his more acute symptoms with the increasing excitement among the swine. Hence the idea of a transference of his demons and his prayer for their welfare. Then, with one word of majesty, Christ completes the stage of convalescence, and the man sits "clothed and in his right mind, at the feet of Jesus."

THE LOSS OF THE SWINE-OWNERS

Travellers in the Orient may deem the destruction of the swine a welcome riddance. Probably it was so to some of the people of Gerasa; for those beasts did not add to the amenities of the place. Still the death of these creatures meant loss for the owners; the swine being in demand among the Gentiles for dietetic and sacrificial purposes. The damage has probably been overrated hitherto. At least there are certain countervailing factors—

1. The estimate of two thousand is approximate. It may be a little high; having been made under unfavourable circumstances. There is no suggestion that precise information was furnished on the point. The keepers fled, and the others "were afraid."

2. The loss may have been diminished by retrieving the carcases and utilising them afterwards. The removal of the dead hogs from the Lake was a necessity for "the long-shore folk," both on hygienic and ceremonial grounds. Witness the results of the sea-fight of Tarichæa, as related by Josephus.[1] There is perhaps something in the serio-comic suggestion of Wetstein that the flesh of these drowned animals may have been pickled or made into smoked hams! If so, some of the Gerasenes or their neighbours may not have been worse than certain degraded classes in India and China, whose long living on the margin of existence has created a penchant even for carrion.

[1] *B. J.* III. x. 9.

3. The plunging of the herd of swine into the waters may have been less fatal than is commonly supposed. These animals are excellent swimmers. No higher authority for this statement can be found than Heilprin. When discussing the migration of animals, he says: The domestic pig, even at a very young age, has been known to swim five or six miles; and it is not exactly impossible that the wild hog, in cases of absolute necessity, might successfully attempt a passage of three or four times this distance.[1] Huxley betrays no inkling of this fact, which is rather damaging to his advocacy of the imaginary claims of the "Gadarene Swinefolk."

THE WORTH OF SOME CRITICISMS

In connection with this miracle, Christ has been repeatedly accused of being a law-breaker and an injurious person. Woolston asserted that no jury would have acquitted one arraigned and accused in such case; coarsely adding that our laws and judges of the last age would have made such a culprit "swing for it."[2] Strauss lauded the greater justice of Pythagoras, who is said to have compensated some fishermen for his alleged liberation of fish from their nets. Huxley has given us this flourish of trumpets: "Everything that I know of law and justice convinces me that the wanton destruction of other

---

[1] *Distribution of Animals*, p. 42.
[2] *Miracles*, pp. 35-39 (1727-1729).

people's property is a misdemeanour of evil example."[1] But as neither command nor permission from Jesus is discoverable in this regard, these ponderous accusations must take their place among exploded fallacies.

[1] "Keepers of the Herd of Swine," *Nineteenth Century*, Dec. 1890.

CHAPTER VIII

Alleged Continuance of Genuine Demonic Possession

POSSESSION IN SUB-APOSTOLIC TIMES

IT has been shown that apart from the earlier portion of the ministry of our Lord, cases of genuine demonic possession, as attested by the criterion of the Gospels, are not discoverable. No case of this sort is reported by the Apostolic Fathers who shared the illumination of the Apostles. As a whole, their writings fall well within the first half of the second century; while the regions represented by them include Egypt, Italy, and Asia Minor. They possess very varied degrees of culture; but are at one in their freedom from the superstitions of possession and exorcism, so prominent in later ages. The sequel proves that they had abundant opportunity for the expression of such views, had they entertained them.

1. The Didache or Teaching of the Twelve Apostles, was written, apparently in Egypt, about 100 A.D. It forbids one to become "an omen-watcher or enchanter or astrologer or purifier," or "to

be willing to look" on the same (iii.). The way of death includes magic arts and sorceries (v.); and earnest counsel is given against things offered to idols: "for it is a worship of dead gods" (vi.). Possession is not mentioned.

2. The Epistle of Clement of Rome, to the Corinthians,[1] written about 92–101 A.D., shows a knowledge of Apocryphal literature in its quotation from the Book of Judith (lv.), whence we may presume a knowledge of the extra-canonical books. But the writer makes no mention of demons; and knows of no such powers disturbing the harmony of the universe (xx.). Their oppression of the human race is not contemplated by him.

3. The Shepherd of Hermas, written by a contemporary of Clement, in Italy, is a crude kaleidoscopic affair, a very primitive *Pilgrim's Progress*. Spirits and angels, good and evil, are much in evidence. In the building of the Tower (Church), twelve holy spirits appear as virgins—Faith, Continence, Power, Patience, Simplicity, Innocence, Purity, Cheerfulness, Truth, Understanding, Harmony, and Love (*Sim.* ix. 13, 15). There are also twelve evil spirits, appearing as women in sable robes and dishevelled hair—Unbelief, Incontinence, Disobedience, Deceit, Sorrow, Wickedness, Wantonness, Anger, Falsehood, Folly, Backbiting, and Hatred (*Sim.* ix. 15, 18). Doubt is an earthly spirit, daughter of the devil (*Mand.* ix.); Lust is another (*Mand.* xii. 2).

Slander is a restless demon (*Mand.* ii.); Passion, an unclean spirit which straitens and strangles the Holy Spirit, Who then departs. From folly is begotten bitterness; and from bitterness, anger; and from anger, frenzy. When all these evils dwell in one vessel (the heart), in which the Holy Spirit also dwells, the vessel overflows. The tender Spirit, not being accustomed to dwell with the evil spirit, withdraws; and the man is henceforth filled with evil spirits (*Mand.* v. 1, 2). Grief is said to be "more wicked than all the spirits," and crushes out the Holy Spirit (*Mand.* x. 1). Self-will with empty self-confidence, is likewise a "great demon" (*Sim.* ix. 22). The spirit of the false prophet is empty, powerless, foolish, and devilish; fleeing from the assembly of the righteous, who are possessed of a spirit of divinity (*Mand.* ix.). There are also two classes of angels; indeed every man has two such attendants. When the angel of righteousness ascends into the heart, then he talks of righteousness, purity, chastity, contentment, and of every righteous deed and glorious virtue. When the angel of evil enters, then ensue anger, harshness, and a whole train of other vices (*Mand.* vi. 2). The enumeration of the works of the evil angels include sins already called demons. It is therefore evident that the language of Hermas is greatly pictorial. There is no reference to possession or exorcism. No suggestion of that sort can lie in the statement that one is saved in the Name of the Lord (*Vis.* iv. 2), nor in the declaration that one cannot enter the kingdom of heaven except in the Name of the Beloved Son (*Sim.* ix. 12). Conybeare's inference is untenable: the clear Scriptural significance of these phrases being otherwise.[1] The magical element is absent from this Epistle, and the ethical is exalted in quaint, rustic fashion.

4. The Epistle of Barnabas was written about the beginning of the second century; possibly by a Gentile, judging from the statement that before conversion the heart was "full of idolatry and an house of demons" (xvi.). It hails apparently from Alexandria, and is severely anti-Judaistic. It savours of the jungle in its references to the hare, the hyena, and the cloven foot (x.); and might be expected to reflect vulgar superstitions. Satan is said to possess the power of the world (ii.); and men are warned to hate the works of iniquity, lest "the black one" (ὁ μέλας) should enter into them (iv.). Over the way of light are the light-bringing angels of God; over the way of darkness are the angels of Satan (xviii.). In the way of darkness are such soul-destroying things as magic (xx.). Yet there is no reference to possession or ejection of demons.

5. The genuine Epistles of Ignatius are the preface to his martyrdom (110–118 A.D.).[2] These

---

[1] See *Jewish Quarterly Review*, July 1896, p. 596.

[2] To the Ephesians, Magnesians, Trallians, Romans, Philadelphians, Smyrnaeans, and Polycarp. The spurious Epistle to the Antiochians contains the following passage:—"I salute the holy presbytery. I salute the sacred deacons, and that person dear to me (Hero, the deacon). Him may I through the Holy Spirit, behold, occupying

writings refer to the gradation of angels (*Tral.* v.), and to "things in heaven and earth" (*Eph.* xiii.). Satan obtains frequent mention as the wicked one, the seducing spirit, and the author of all evil. After the resurrection, Jesus is said to have addressed the disciples: Lay hold, handle me, and see that I am not a bodiless (ἀσώματον) demon (*Smyr.* iii.).[1] In the account of the martyrdom, there are several references to demons, of a popular sort; but these are not citable as evidence, because this narrative contains elements that are confessedly unhistorical. Possession and exorcism are conspicuously absent from the genuine Epistles.

6. The Epistle of Polycarp, written to the Philippians shortly after the martyrdom of Ignatius (xiii.), enjoins prayer and fasting: but only as aids to the religious life (vii.). There is a quotation from the Book of Tobit: Alms delivers from death (x.); but the writer evinces no taste whatever for the superstitions of that book or for kindred absurdities.

7. The unknown author of the Epistle to Diognetus writes "not before Trajan, and not much later." He has a vigorous polemic against idols; but says nothing which would imply their animation

by demons. Far less does he think of the latter as infesting man. The Fragments of Papias—"a hearer of the Apostle John," and "a companion of Polycarp"—are of a similar tenor.

POSSESSION IN ANTE-NICENE AND POST-NICENE TIMES

From the large mass of material available, only a few testimonies of leading writers can be cited. It is convenient to consider these under two categories—

A. *The general doctrine of demons*

Justin Martyr (105–167 A.D.) represents Samaria and Ephesus. He was deeply versed in Hellenic lore; having studied the Stoic, Peripatetic, Pythagorean, and Platonic systems of philosophy. He despised the Epicurean. The general date of his writings is approximately 150 A.D. He is largely responsible for the invasion of the Church by ethnic demonology. According to Justin, demons are the children of the fallen angels (*Ap.* ii. 5); striving to enslave men by dreams or magic; corrupting women and boys by apparitions; and terrifying them by fearful sights into the belief that they are gods (*Ap.* i. 14. 5). They endeavour to seduce men from God and Christ: producing their counterfeits of Christ and Christian ordinances (*Ap.* i. 58. 54. 62. 66). They subdue men variously by magic writings, fear, and punishment; or by teaching them to offer sacrifices, incense, and libations. They sow murder, war, adultery, intemperate deeds, and all wickedness (*Ap.* ii. 5). These things are ascribed to the gods; but they are the work of demons, who likewise invent the foul tales told of the former (*Ap.* i. 21. 25, ii. 5). They inspire magicians like Simon Magus and Menander, and raise up heretics like Marcion (*Ap.* i. 26. 56. 58).[1] They persecute the wicked, demanding sacrifices and services (*Ap.* i. 12). They everywhere persecute the righteous; having put Heraclitus, Musonius, and Socrates to death (*Ap.* ii. 8. 1, 5, ii. 7). They decree death against those who read the books of Hystaspes or the Sibyl or the prophets; their object being to prevent the knowledge of good and retain men in slavery (*Ap.* i. 44). Demons instigated the Jews to persecute Christ (*Ap.* i. 63), and now incite the persecution of Christians (*Ap.* i. 57). They are overthrown by the Name of Christ (*Ap.* ii. 8), and will finally be shut up in hell (*Ap.* ii. 8). Possession is also ascribed to the souls of the dead (*Ap.* i. 18).

Minucius Felix flourished about 150 A.D. He was a Roman advocate and wrote his *Octavius* about this date. He argues that as the magi, the philosophers, and Plato, have shown, the demons as impure spirits lurk under statues and images and by their afflatus attain the authority of a present deity; while they are breathed into prophets, dwell in shrines, animate the fibres of the entrails, control the flight of birds, direct the lots, and work miracles. They are

---

[1] Cf. 1 Tim. iv. 1, "Seducing spirits and doctrines of demons."

both deceived and deceivers, because ignorant of the simple truth; and for their own ruin confess not what they know. They thus bend down from heaven and call men away from the true God to material things. They disturb life, render all men unquiet, creep secretly into human bodies, as being subtile spirits. They feign diseases, alarm the mind, and distort the limbs, that they may constrain men to worship them; so that being gorged with the fumes of altars or the sacrifices of cattle, they may seem to cure what they had bound, by remitting the same. These raging maniacs who are seen rushing about, are also themselves prophets without a temple. In them also is a like instigation of the demons, but an unlike occasion of their madness. A great many people know all these things. Saturn himself, and Serapis, and Jupiter, and whatever demons are worshipped, confess before Christians, who they are. When adjured by the only true God, these wretched beings unwillingly shudder[1] in the bodies (of the possessed), and either spring forth at once or vanish by degrees, as the faith of the sufferer assists, or the grace of the healer inspires. They thus fly from Christians when near at hand; though they harassed them at a distance in their assemblies. They take possession of minds and obstruct hearts, that men may begin to hate Christians before they know them; lest if they knew them, they should either imitate them, or not be able to condemn them (*Oct.* xxvii.).

[1] Cf. Jas. ii. 19, "The demons believe and shudder."

Tertullian (150–230 A.D.) has an elaborate doctrine of demons, worthy of North Africa. He starts with the axiom that there are demons, since Socrates himself waited on the will of one. This evil spirit attached itself to him, even from childhood; and doubtless turned his mind from good. The poets also acknowledge demons; even the untutored populace use them for cursing. Indeed, they call on Satan, the arch-demon, in their execrations as if prompted by some instinctive knowledge of him. Plato also believed in angels, and the magi witness to the existence of both angels and demons. The Scriptures further teach how there sprang from the fallen angels a more wicked demon-brood; condemned of God, with the authors of their race and the demon-chief. The great business of these demons is the ruin of mankind. Hence they inflict on the body, illness and physical calamities; and on the soul, sudden and excessive fits of madness. Their marvellous subtility and tenuity gives them access to both parts of our nature. These demons, being invisible and impalpable, can inflict much harm on men who are not conscious of their action, save by their effects. Just as when some secret blight in the air affects fruit and grain in the flower, killing them in the bud or blighting them in their maturity; or as when in some occult manner, the tainted atmosphere spreads abroad its pestilential exhalations; so by a contagion equally obscure, the breathing of angels and demons corrupts the mind and goads it into madness or cruel lusts, with various delusions. The most prevalent of these deceits is that by which the demons enthral and delude men to believe in the gods, that thus they may obtain the sustenance appropriate to them,—the savour of the flesh and blood of the sacrifices offered to their images and images: as well as the turning of the minds of men from the true God by the deceits of false divination; that being to them a more pleasant repast. These deceits are effected by the demons being winged like the angels, so that they are everywhere in a moment. The whole world is as one place to them. Hence with equal ease, they know and report all that is done over the whole earth. Men do not know what their real nature is and take their swiftness for a mark of divinity. Often they foretell evils, and wish to be thought the authors of the same. They often have ill news to announce, but never good. From the lips of the prophets of old, the demons stole the counsels of God, and the same course is followed by them when they overhear them in the churches. Thus acquiring some knowledge of the future, they set up as rivals to the true God, while they steal His oracles (*Apol.* xxii.). By the help of angels and demons, the magi put dreams into the minds of men, and by the latter powers, goats and tables are made to divine. In proof of the assertion that the gods of the heathen are demons, Tertullian charges the pagans to bring before their tribunals one who is though elsewhere he has declared himself a god. Similarly, let one supposed to be god-possessed be taken, one of those who by inhaling the fumes of the altar has conceived divinity, and who is bent double in belching forth his prophecies; let the virgin Cœlestis, the promiser of rain, or Æsculapius, the inventor of medicine, be taken; if these do not at once confess to being demons (for they dare not lie to a Christian), then slay upon the spot that most impudent Christian (*Apol.* xxiii.).

Origen (186–253 A.D.) represents the culture of Alexandria. His demonology is practically that of the Neo-Platonists. He placed himself under Ammonius Saccas, the founder of the School,— an apostate Christian. The doctrine of Origen is mostly contained in his work *Contra Celsum* (*C. C.*). He applies the term "demon" to wicked powers freed from the encumbrance of a grosser body (*C. C.* v. 5); the body being naturally fine and thin, as if formed of air, and by many considered incorporeal (*Princip.* Proleg. 8). The earth-spirits are intent on frankincense, blood, fumes of sacrifices, and sweet sounds (*C. C.* iv. 32, vii. 35, viii. 61). They haunt the images of the gods (*C. C.* viii. 43); feeding on blood and fumes and odours of victims (*C. C.* vii. 35, 64). They enter certain animals, as weasels, birds, serpents, foxes, and wolves (*C. C.* iv. 92, 93). Evil spirits may take complete possession of the mind; allowing their victims, neither the power of understanding nor of feeling. This constitutes possession or insanity, as in the

Gospels (*Princip.* III. iii. 4). Wicked spirits cause sterility, plagues, tempests, and other calamities, also famine, blight of fruit trees, and pestilences among men and beasts (*C. C.* i. 31, viii. 31). This is done by them as executors of divine judgment or agents of divine chastisement. These evil powers lead men astray, fill them with distractions, and drag them down from God and super-celestial things to those below (*C. C.* v. 5). The demons that haunt unclean places and the denser parts of bodies, possess oracular power: hence their choice of the bodies of animals. The spread of Christianity destroys the worship of idols, and thus cuts them off from their former supplies. In this way, some starving demon incited Celsus to vilify the Christians (*C. C.* vii. 56). It is their interest to arrest the Gospel and to cause persecutions (*C. C.* iii. 29, viii. 43, iv. 32). Yet the demons have no real power over Christians (*C. C.* viii. 34, 36). Experience has taught them that they are defeated by the martyrs, whose confessions are tortures to them (*C. C.* viii. 44). Origen holds that magic is a consistent system, having words known to a few. These, when pronounced with the appropriate modulations, are of great power; but useless when translated: for the local demons have local names and must be cited accordingly (*C. C.* i. 24, 25). The Name of Jesus has expelled myriads of demons from the bodies and souls of men. It is still effective for the removal of mental distractions and diseases (*C. C.* i. 25, 67). Unclean spirits fear the Name of Jesus as that of a superior being, or reverently accept Him as their lawful Ruler (C. C. II. 36).

The testimonies of Athenagoras, Irenaeus, Cyprian, Lactentius, and many others make no substantial addition to the teachings already adduced. The superstitions which invaded the Church, in the writings of Justin Martyr and others, are in most striking contrast to the pinion of the older Fathers.

fled from the touch of … … … ions upon them; being overwhelmed by … … plation and representation of the fire in store for … (*Apol.* xxiii.).[1] Cyprian alleges that demons … … … the bodies of … possessed, by … … … Christians; being … … by spiritual stripes, … crying and groaning at the voice … … and … … of God, fleeing … strip… … blows (*Ep… ad Demetr.*). Origen knew of a variety of methods for curing the demonised, such we the imposition of hands (*Hom. xlv.*); the invocation of the God of all things and of Jesus, with the … of the history of the latter (*C. C.* iii. 4); also prayer and simple adjurations, without magic or incantations (*C. C.* vi. 4); likewise, prayers and other means which might be learned from the Scriptures (*C. C.* vii. 67). This last method sufficed for the ejection of demons from the souls of men or from places where they had established themselves, or from the bodies of animals which were often injured by them. It was natural for Origen to complain of the scientific medicine of his day, which discovered mental disorder where he found demonic agency.[2] Lactantius believed in "the sign of the passion," coupled with the Name of the Master, for the ejection of evil spirits (*Inst.* iv. 27). The Arabic Canons of Hippolytus prescribed adjurations, with the sign of the cross upon the breast, the brow,

---

[1] Cf. Cyril … … … : The impious … … … … … … … … it becomes a fire to the unseen foe.

[2] See comment on Matt. xvii. 15.

the ears, and the mouth (Can. xix., xxix.). Jerome tells how the demonised resorted to the tombs of Elisha, Obadiah, and John the Baptist, at Samaria. His description makes it evident that most of the sufferers were lycanthropes (*Epist.* 108). Chrysostom reports the case of Stagirius, whose health had broken down under the strain of monastic life. He had recourse to the saints and the tombs of the martyrs; but his peregrinations were vain (*De Provid.*). He suffered from suicidal melancholy. Martin of Tours (319–400 A.D.) is credited with an unsavoury triumph over a demon. His biographer, Sulpitius Severus, relates how one day, on going into a house, the saint paused on the threshold, saying, I see a horrible demon in the porch of the house. The good bishop ordered the demon off; but thereupon it seized the cook (?) who still lingered inside. This wretched man then began to gnash with his teeth and to tear all that he met. The house was in an uproar; the people fled. Martin presented himself to the madman and bade him stand. But when he gnashed with his teeth and threatened with open mouth to devour, Martin thrust his fingers into the man's mouth, saying, If you have any power, eat these! Then the possessed, as if he had taken a piece of red-hot iron into his jaws, retracting his teeth, would not touch the fingers of the saint. The demon, when compelled by punishments and tortures to depart, not being allowed to escape by the mouth, passed out "*fluxu ventris*"; leaving sad and foul traces behind it

(*Vita*, xvii.). But dismissing the embellishments of this tale, there is here an undoubted case of insanity, induced by superstitious horror, and cured (!) by " punishments and tortures."

The treatment of the possessed[1] generally tended to pass from superstition to barbarity. But there was another side to it. From the Canons of the Council of Carthage, we learn that, in certain places at least, the care of the demonised had become systematic, if not rational. They had their abode in the church. The official exorcist laid his hands on them each day. They had to sweep the floors of the church, and received their meat in due season (Can. iv. 90, 91, 92). Chrysostom also notes that they had a place in the prayers of the Church. The beautiful "Bidding Prayer" of the *Apostolic Constitutions* is still extant (viii. 6, 7)—

(After the dismissal of the catechumens), let the deacon say: Ye energumens afflicted with unclean spirits, pray. And let us all earnestly pray for them, that God, the Lover of mankind, will by Christ rebuke the unclean and wicked spirits, and deliver His supplicants from the dominion of the adversary. May He that rebuked the legion of demons, and the devil, the prince of darkness, even now rebuke those apostates from piety, and deliver His own workmanship from his power, and cleanse those creatures which He has made with great wisdom. Let us still earnestly pray

---

[1] Δαιμονιζόμενοι, κατεχόμενοι, ἐνεργούμενοι, χειμαζόμενοι, κλυδωνι-

for them. Save them, O God, and raise them up by Thy power. Bow down your heads, ye energumens, and receive the blessing.

And let the bishop add this prayer and say: Thou Who hast bound the strong man and spoiled all that was in his house, Who hast given us power over serpents and scorpions to tread upon them and upon all the power of the enemy, Who hast delivered to us the serpent, that murderer of men, bound as a sparrow to children, Whom all things dread, and before the presence of Whose power all things tremble, Who hast cast him down as lightning from heaven to earth, not with a fall from a place but from honour to dishonour, on account of his wilful disposition to evil, Whose look dries the abyss and Whose threatening melts the mountains, and Whose truth endureth for ever, Whom infants praise and sucklings bless, Whom the angels hymn and adore, Who lookest upon the earth and makest it tremble, Who touchest the mountains and they smoke, Who threatenest the sea and driest it up, Who makest all the rivers as a desert, and the clouds as the dust of Thy feet, Who walkest upon the sea as upon solid land, Thou only-begotten God, Thou Son of the great Father, rebuke those wicked spirits, and deliver the work of Thy hands from the power of the hostile spirit; for to Thee is due, glory and honour and worship, and by Thee to Thy Father, in the Holy Spirit, for ever. Amen.

At first, the ejection of demons was not a specialty among Christians. It belonged to all. Origen says thus made evident the grace of God and the despicable weakness of the demons (*C. C.* vii. 4). In the *Apostolic Canons*, it is still an exercise of voluntary goodness (viii. 26). With increasing complexity in the functions discharged by the Church, the order of exorcists arose. The office was a subaltern one: the exorcist not being ordained unless required for the office of bishop, priest, or deacon (Apost. Can. viii. 26). On appointment, the person received a book of formulae, containing prayers and adjurations (Con. Carth. iv. 7). About the middle of the third century, Cornelius of Rome had fifty-two exorcists, readers, and doorkeepers (Euseb. *Hist. Eccles.* vi. 43). In this century also, baptism came to be surreptitiously connected with exorcism. But candidates for baptism were not on the same plane with the energumens. The latter were only eligible for that rite upon recovery or *in extremis*. The anointing of catechumens with "exorcised oil," preparatory to baptism, as practised under Cyril of Jerusalem, does not bear transcription.

POSSESSION IN MEDIÆVAL AND MODERN TIMES

During the Middle Ages, the old demonism continued to flourish; but was partly overlaid by a novel diabolism. Gregory the Great (542–604 A.D.) reflects the standpoint of his times when he relates how a nun, in godless haste, proceeded to eat without first making the sign of the cross; the consequence being that she swallowed a devil in her lettuce (*Dialog.* i. 4). This pope, in sending forth his missionaries to the barbarians, did not aim at the extirpation of pagan rites. His policy was rather to Christianise them. His laxity or liberality opened wide the door for the introduction of heathen superstitions. A quasi-Christian mythology arose, in which fairies and goblins freely mingled with angels and demons. Under a sanction, sometimes traditional, sometimes ecclesiastical, the old pagan ceremonies contrived to maintain themselves and to acquire a new importance. Satan played the part of dupe or clown, appearing now as a beast or a black man; again as an angel or a fair woman. Yet with all his versatility, he was only a poor stupid, who might be confounded or put to flight, with ridiculous ease. Relics, rosaries, proven amulets, holy water, the sign of the cross, and canonical adjurations, reduced him to a state of impotence; wherein he was fain to vent his displeasure by sulphureous fumes as he fled. From the tenth century, he began to be taken more seriously: and witchcraft, as a hybrid between paganism and Christianity, came into prominence.[1] That is, however, a side-issue, and attention is to be directed to a few of the alleged instances of possession in mediæval and modern times—

The demonomania of South-Eastern Europe.—This appeared in the eighth century, and spread through

[1] Appendix K, Witchcraft.

Calabria to Greece, Constantinople, and the Egean Islands. Phantoms were said to have come near and conversed with the subjects of this disorder. On its physical side, it was a contagious insanity, wherein the hallucinations of the afflicted reproduced themselves in others.

The dancing manias of the Middle Ages.—The first appeared at Erfurt in the thirteenth century, but was of moderate dimensions. In 1374, the most notable outbreak of this sort occurred. The lunatics danced hand in hand, in pairs or circles; on the streets, in private houses, even in the churches; without rest and without shame. They were insensible to ordinary sights and sounds or other impressions. They professed to have visions of spirits whom they could name. The wild screams of the dancers were regarded as the invocations of demons. When this fierce delirium had produced exhaustion, convulsions and severe pains set in. The condition was ascribed to possession, and solemn exorcisms were performed. After a time the disorder ceased; but burst forth again in 1418. The dancers raved and pranced as before; also fasting for prolonged periods. This time the possessed were put under supervision and taken to the chapel at Rotestein. Masses were said for them, and they were led in procession round the altar, for the ejection of their demons. On the physical side, these dancing manias are recognisable as ancient insanities which have become recrudescent and contagious. Their parallels are the Tarantism of Italy, the Tigretier of Abyssinia, the exercises of the Jumpers and Shakers.[1]

The convulsionnaires of France.—These made their first appearance in 1729. In the conflict between the Jesuits and the Jansenists, the former got the upper hand. But miracles were reported at the grave of Dean François of Paris. People crowded into the cemetery, and on approaching the grave, were seized with convulsions. In this condition, they prophesied and testified in a most edifying manner against the Jesuits and the Papal Bull (Unigenitus). These prophecies and testimonies were sealed by miraculous cures at the cemetery. In 1732, Louis XV. closed this burial-place; but the epidemic did not die out for two generations. A kindred disorder broke out in Morzines in Upper Savoy in 1857. It was noticed first among children, from whom it spread to adults. The convulsionnaires changed in character; becoming indifferent to their friends and to religion. So irritable did they become, that a word or the mere sight of a stranger was often enough to provoke a convulsion. These patients soon became quite furious. They hurled articles of furniture about, and repeated the same things endlessly. They declared that they were lost souls in hell, and believed that they were possessed of one or more evil

---

[1] The Jumpers appeared in Cornwall in 1760; came under the observation of John Wesley in Wales in 1763; patronised by William Williams, the Watts of Wales, a later date. The Shakers are the disciples of Ann Lee (1736-1784).

spirits whom they felt or heard within them. When the convulsions subsided, the patients returned to their normal condition; being sometimes quite oblivious of what had transpired during the period of their convulsions. On their physical side, these disorders were true epidemic insanities in which hysterical phenomena passed over into transient mania.

The demonolaters of India.—They are often cited as parallels to the possessed in the time of our Lord. Caldwell has given an interesting account of the same; but the description apparently applies to the phenomena generally witnessed on these occasions.[1] He tells how the circle is formed, the fire lit, and the offerings prepared. These consist of goats, fowls, rice, pulse, sugar, ghee, honey, with white chaplets of oleander and buds of jasmine. The tom-toms are beaten more loudly and more rapidly, the hum of the conversation is stilled, while a deep expectancy fills the assembly. The rickety door of the hut is dashed aside and the devil-dancer staggers out. He is tall, haggard, pensive, with sunken eyes, and matted hair. His forehead is smeared with ashes, his face is streaked with vermilion and saffron. He wears a high conical cap, which is white with a red tassel. A long robe invests him from neck to ankle, and on it are the figures of the goddesses of smallpox, cholera, and murder. On the ankles are heavy silver bangles, and in the right hand a staff or spear, also a bow, which,

[1] *Demonolatry, Contemporary Review,* Feb. 1876.

when pulled by the string, emits a dull booming sound. In the left hand is the sickle-like sacrificial knife. The dancer, with unsteady motion reels into the crowd and sits down. The assembly shows him the offerings which they intend to present; but he appears to be wholly unconscious. He croons an Indian lay in a low voice, with drooped eyelids and head sunk upon his breast. He swings slowly to and fro, his fingers twitch nervously. His head now begins to wag, his sides heave and quiver. He perspires profusely. The tom-toms are beaten faster, the pipes and reeds wail out more loudly. There is a sudden yell, a stinging ear-piercing shriek, a hideous gobble-gobble of hellish laughter. The devil-dancer has now sprung to his feet, with eyes protruding, mouth foaming, chest heaving, muscles quivering, and arms outstretched, swollen, and straining. Now and again, the quick, sharp words are jerked out, I am God, I am the true God! To him as to the present deity, sacrifices are offered up; while shrieks, vows, imprecations, and exclamations of thankful praise, blend together in one infernal hubbub. Above all, rise the ghastly laughter and the stentorian howls of the devil-dancer, I am God, I am the only true God! He cuts and hacks and hews himself, and not infrequently kills himself, there and then. Hours pass by. The crowd remains rooted to the spot. Suddenly the dancer gives a great bound into the air, and when he descends he is motionless. The fiendish look has vanished from his eyes. His demoniacal laughter is still. He speaks to this and that neighbour, quietly and reasonably. He lays aside his garb, washes his face at the nearest rivulet, and walks soberly home, a modest, well-conducted man.

Is this, then, a case of genuine demonic possession in modern times? There are very distinct difficulties in the narratives, which one would wish to have cleared up. But these complexities do not obscure the real nature of the disorder here present. It remains uncertain whether the spectators uniformly believe in "demon-possession" or "god-possession." The point is immaterial, as the line between the two is not strictly drawn by such spectators. What is to be noted is the fact that the consciousness of the devil-dancer himself is beclouded in the highest degree. The gait is also unsteady. There is twitching of the fingers, movement of the head, deepening of the respiration, rise of the temperature, drooping of the eyelids, stupor of the countenance, general muscular excitement, delirium with pleasing hallucinations. There is also partial anæsthesia and loss of self-control; evinced by self-mutilations. Evidently the devil-dancer is inspired; not by a demon, however, but by Indian hemp (bhang or ganja). The physiological effects are all in evidence here: even down to the power of partly directing the hallucinations induced. These are specially manifest in the exclamation, I am God, I am the true God! The action of the Indian hemp is heightened by the noisy music and the general excitement. There is nothing here which at all deserves the name of "supernatural." The "devil-dancer" has simply drugged himself with his favourite intoxicant.

The dervishes of Algiers.—These present a study as interesting as the previous parties. They have several points in common with them: probably they are not identical. These dervishes have been adduced as instances of genuine demonic possession in modern times. Tristram has given a vivid account of their performances as witnessed by himself.[1] The place of meeting was paved in the centre with bright tessellated tiles, on the midst of which the dervishes were squatted. Round three sides sat the musicians, beating large tambourines, and swinging their heads as they accompanied their voices in a low measured chant. Nothing could sound more monotonous than this unvaried wailing cadence, no music less capable of inspiring frenzy. The fourth side of the square was occupied by a young man, sitting cross-legged before a low table on which were a bundle of papers, and a lighted candle. Near him was a chafing dish over which the tambourines were frequently baked. One of the musicians instead of a tambourine, had a huge earthen jar, with a mouth covered by parchment. This emitted a deeper note than any of the other instruments. After a while, amid much noisy music, the dervishes "having now worked up the steam," a huge negro with a grizzly-grey moustache, plunged forward with a howl and swayed his body

[1] *The Great Sahara*, pp. 12–15.

to and fro. He was supported by the attendants stripped of his turban and outer garments, and accommodated with a loose burnous. He then danced an extempore saraband in front of the lights. Meanwhile, he had been anticipated in his excitement by a little boy in the rear, who had been working himself up for the previous twenty minutes, into an ecstasy, rolling his head and swaying on his seat, apparently unconscious and unobserved. The negro had now become outrageous, his eyeballs glowing and rolling as he grunted and growled, like a wild beast. The musicians then plied the sheepskins with redoubled energy, till the din became deafening. The negro craved aliment, and a smith's shovel red-hot, was brought him. He seized it, spat on his fingers, rubbed them across its edge, found it not sufficiently tender, blew upon it, and struck it many times with the palm of his hand. He then licked it with his tongue, found it not yet to his taste, handed it back again to the attendant with evident disgust, squatted down again, glared carnivorously, and was gratified with a live scorpion, which was eaten with evident relish, commencing carefully with the tail. Then a naked sword was handed him, which he tried to swallow but failed, as the weapon was slightly curved and a yard long. This negro then recommenced the saraband, brandishing the naked sword in a promiscuous fashion, cutting the candle to pieces, and making the musicians dive to avoid him. He then tried to bore his cheek through and to pierce himself in the abdomen; setting the hilt, now against a pillar, now against the ground. A friendly fanatic tried to help him by jumping on his shoulders, but in vain; the man evidently being a pachyderm for the nonce. Then several maniacs howled and staggered to the centre; repeating the same extravagances, including the scorpion. Three of them then knelt before the presiding chief of the dervishes, who fed them with the leaf of the prickly pear which they bit with avidity, and masticated in large mouthfuls, spines and all. Others repeated the shovel experiment; and one sturdy little fellow, naked to the waist, balanced himself on his stomach, on the edge of a drawn sword, held up by two men. Then he stood on it, supporting a tall man on his shoulders.

Are these cases, then, genuine parallels to the demoniacs of the New Testament? There is an apparent toughness and callousness of certain tissues of the body. But these features are to be correlated with the sharpness or bluntness of the swords; also with the after-effects of the red-hot shovel, the scorpion entremets, and the prickly pear. To begin with, there is an utter absence of any trace of mental derangement among those dervishes. In process of time that is developed. Intoxication by Indian hemp may be suspected but cannot be proved. But the phenomena of hypnotism are strongly in evidence and amply sufficient to account for all the occurrences described. There is clear proof of former training or experience among these performers which must not be overlooked. The whole environment is favourable to the production of auto-hypnotism. Hellwald, a high authority on this subject, also describes the dervishes of Algiers; remarking that by dancing and singing, they are able to throw themselves into a condition of ecstasy which is difficult to describe. In this state their bodies seem to be insensible to severe wounds. They are said to run pointed iron and sharp knives into their heads, eyes, necks, and breasts, without injuring themselves.[1]

The anæsthesia of the hypnotic state is well known, and has its adequate physiological explanation. It must not therefore be reckoned among things supernatural. The demoniacs of the New Testament suffer from natural insanity or idiocy; but these dervishes suffer from hypnotism, which is a transient and artificial mania, as here described. Nothing at all genuinely demonic can be discovered here.

The demoniacs of China.—They are among the recent instances adduced as parallels to the possessed of the Gospels. Nevius offers numerous examples of this alleged identity.[2] He was for forty years a missionary in China, and had no medical qualification. The case of Kwo, given at length, is a good example of the others recorded. This person was discovered by a native assistant in 1878. At the date of the first interview, he was working in the fields and was then

[1] Moll, *Hypnotism*, p. 32.
[2] Nevius, *Demon Possession and allied Themes*.

free from symptoms of mental derangement. He conversed rationally, but confessed that he had been "troubled with an evil spirit," from which he had vainly sought relief. He was advised to believe in Christ, and assured that the demon would leave him. After prayer, and certain directions, he received some Christian books. Six months later, Nevius found him in vigorous health of both body and mind. Though previously illiterate, Kwo had learned to read and had taught his young daughter to do so likewise. His age was then thirty-eight, his appearance being normal, and his disposition "bright and entertaining." He told how the spirit of the adjacent mountain had paid him a visit in 1877; but he resisted and cursed it. Then he became restless and lost control of himself; so that one day, seized with an irresistible impulse, he rushed off to a gambler's den, and there lost $16— a large sum for him. Starting home, he lost his way in the dark, but got home somehow or other; being conscious of what he was doing and saying, in a mechanical fashion, and soon forgetting what he had said. Then he lost his appetite, and again went to his gambling. On returning home, he fell down, foaming at the mouth and becoming unconscious. On recovering next day, he tried to run away, when he staggered. Everything became dark, and he rushed back to his room, where he became violent, and attacked all who came near him, even attempting to shoot his father. For five or six days, he remained in a wild raving state: and when more medicine was

Alleged Continuance of genuine Demonic Possession 245

proposed the demon said, No amount of medicine will be of any use. From the same source came the advice, Burn incense to me and submit yourself to me, and all will be well. These statements were made by Kwo when he was unconscious, and were followed by another attempt to run away. Further unconsciousness ensued, and thereafter the demon is said to have come only at intervals, sometimes of a few days, sometimes of a month or more, when "a fluttering of the heart and a sense of fear," and inability to control himself, were experienced; and the sufferer was obliged to sit or lie down; there being intervals of unconsciousness and mutterings. The demon often bade them not to fear, and promised his help in the healing of disease. The neighbours availed themselves of the promise; some being healed instantly and without medicine; "many not being under the control of the demon." He even failed with the child of Kwo; though asked to cure it. The final interview between the demon and Kwo's wife is characteristic. 'We understood that you were not to return. How is it that you have come back again? The demon replied politely: I have returned for but one visit. If your husband is determined to be a Christian, this is no place for me. But I wish to tell you that I had nothing to do with the death of your child. Then the demon was asked: What do you know of Jesus Christ? The answer was: Jesus Christ is the great Lord over all; and now I am going away and you will not see me again!'

Since that time, it is said that Kwo has not been troubled by the demon.

Is this then a case of genuine possession? There is nothing whatever inexplicable on common medical principles. It is a case of epileptic insanity; with its local colouring and its reminiscences of Christian doctrine, mingled with native delusions. The other cases of Nevius show no more critical acumen, and are all natural cases of mental disorders. This writer believed these things to be characteristic of demon-possession—

1. Automatic representation and persistent and consistent acting out of a new personality.
2. Evidence of a knowledge and intellectual power not possessed by the subject nor explicable on the pathological hypothesis.
3. Change of personality, involving complete change of moral character.

These are but the misapprehensions of an uninstructed mind and may be briefly dismissed—

1. The passage from sanity to insanity implies change of personality. The change follows a recognised pathological order.
2. There is sometimes a morbid exaltation of certain faculties; but never any real augmentation of intellectual power.
3. The dictum of Esquirol, already quoted, has in view the fact that moral deterioration is an integral part of the morbid process.

WAS GENUINE DEMONIC POSSESSION LOCAL AND TEMPORARY?

This question answers itself when the features of genuine demonic possession already discovered, are recalled—

1. Mental derangement of some sort or other, forming the natural element.
2. The confession of Jesus as Messiah, forming the supernatural element.

In the whole series of cases, cited or citable, in support of the thesis that genuine demonic possession is independent of place and time, we note—

1. The obvious persistence of the first or natural element.[1]
2. The conspicuous restriction of the latter to the ministry of Christ.

The untrained observer has in mind the physical symptoms manifested by the demoniacs of the New Testament; and when confronted by persons exhibiting analogous symptoms, he naturally calls them demoniacs also. There is an error of judgment; because the criterion of the Gospels is not in view. *Its application proves that genuine demonic possession was a unique phenomenon in the history of the world; being confined indeed to the earlier portion of the ministry of our Lord.*

---

[1] The condition of the demon dater and dervishes is essentially a temporary and artificial insanity.

WAS THE ENVIRONMENT PECULIAR IN THE TIME OF CHRIST?

The increased activity of demons at this date requires consideration. An old writer remarks that they were now forsaking the ancient oracles and taking up their abode in men. The decline of these institutions was a fact on which Thucydides and Cicero commented, and on which Plutarch composed a formal treatise. This work is referred to in proof of the foregoing statement. It is a conjecture and a fancy which need not be discussed; as neither the location of demons at the oracles nor their transference thence to men is capable of proof. More suggestive of the proper explanation of demonic activity at this time is the passage: Satan is come down to you, having great wrath, because he knoweth that he hath but a short time (Rev. xii. 12). That proposition may be taken as a general principle applicable to the present case. The kingdom of Satan has its physical and its ethical aspects. The former has not been found to be specially in evidence at this period; because it has been already shown that the Jews in the time of Christ did not materially differ from their neighbours in regard to their mental temperament and health. The physical environment did not contain any novel elements. But the other aspect of the kingdom of Satan is thrust into great prominence. The spiritual environment was wholly without a parallel. It was marked by two residual features of surpassing importance—

1. The confession of Jesus as Messiah by evil spirits.
2. The suppression of these confessions by Christ Himself.

According to the evidence of the Gospels, these demonic testimonies had their beginning and end in Him. There is but one explanation of the situation. *The incarnation initiated the establishment of the kingdom of heaven upon earth. That determined a counter-movement among the powers of darkness.* GENUINE DEMONIC POSSESSION WAS ONE OF ITS MANIFESTATIONS.

APPENDICES

APPENDIX A

Rabbinic Literature. P. 25.

Abodah Zara.	Abod. Zara.	Idolatry.
Baba Bathra.	Baba Bathra.	Municipal law.
Baba Kamma.	Baba Kamma.	Damages for injuries.
Bekhoroth.	Bekhoroth.	The Firstborn.
Berakhoth.	Ber.	Prayers and Blessings.
Bereshith Rabba.	Ber. R.	On Genesis.
Chagigah.	Chag.	The three great Feasts.
Chullin.	Chullin.	Slaughtering animals.
Debarim Rabba.	Debar. R.	On Deuteronomy.
Erubin.	Erub.	Sabbath boundaries.
Gittin.	Gittin.	Divorce.
Horayoth.	Horayoth.	Unintentional sins.
Kethuboth.	Kethuboth.	Marriage contracts.
Kiddushin.	Kidd.	Betrothal.
Nedarim.	Nedar.	Vows.
Niddah.	Nidd.	Female defilement.
Peah.	Peah.	The harvest corner.
Pesachim.	Pes.	The Passover.
Pesiqta.	Pesiqta.	The "Lessons."
Pirqe Abhoth.	Pirqe Abh.	Sayings of the Fathers.
Pirqe de R. Eliezer.	Pirqe de R. El.	The history of Israel.
Rosh-ha-Shanah.	Rosh-ha-Shanah.	The New Year Feast.
Sanhedrin.	Sanh.	The Sanhedrin.
Shabbath.	Shab.	Sabbath observance.
Shemoth Rabba.	Shemoth R.	On Exodus.
Siphre.	Siphre.	On Number. and Deuteronomy.
Sopherim.	Sopherim.	Writing of the Law.
Succah.	Succah.	The Feast of Tabernacles.

Taanith.	Taanith.	Fasting and Fast Days.
Tanchuma Mishpatim.	Tanch. Mish.	On the Pentateuch.
Yalkut Shimeoni.	Yalkut. Shim.	On the whole of the O.T.
Yebhamoth.	Yeb.	The Levirate.
Yoma.	Yoma.	The Day of Atonement.

APPENDIX B

NOMENCLATURE OF THE NEW TESTAMENT. P. 61.

The Authorised Version uses the term "devil" as the equivalent of two terms which are severely distinguished in the original—

    A. Demon (δαίμων, δαιμόνιον), one of the subordinate powers of evil.

    B. Diabolus (διάβολος), used in a specific and generic sense—

        (*a*) Denoting Satan, the great devil, *par excellence*, the head of the kingdom of evil. Matt. iv. 5. Mark i. 13. Luke iv. 3.

    (*b*) Denoting a slanderer or false accuser—

> Have not I chosen you twelve and one of you is a devil? John vi. 70.
> Their wives must not be devils. 1 Tim. iii. 11.
> In the last days men will be devils. 2 Tim. iii. 3.
> The aged women should not be devils. Tit. ii. 3.

There are also two modes of possession which are strictly differentiated—

    1. Demon-possession. This is always associated with some form of mental derangement: but no moral consequences are traced to demons.

    2. Satan-possession. This is never associated with mental derangement: but moral consequences are traced to Satanic influence.

The agents of possession are variously designated—

Demon (δαίμων). Matt. viii. 31.[1]
Spirit (πνεῦμα). Matt. viii. 16, etc.[2]
Evil spirit (πνεῦμα πονηρόν). Matt. xii. 45, etc.[3]
Filthy spirit (πνεῦμα ἀκαθαρτόν). Mark iii. 11, etc.[4]
Spirit of an unclean demon (πνεῦμα δαιμονίου ἀκαθάρτου). Luke iv. 33.

The subjects of possession are variously designated—

The demonised (δαιμονιζόμενοι). Matt. iv. 24.
Having demons (ἔχων δαιμόνια). Luke viii. 27.
Driven by a demon (ἠλαύνετο ὑπὸ τοῦ δαιμονίου). Luke viii. 29.
Whom a spirit seizes (πνεῦμα λαμβάνει). Luke ix. 39.
Whom a spirit assails (πνεῦμα καταλαμβάνει). Mark ix. 18.
Being in a foul spirit (ἐν πνεύματι ἀκαθάρτῳ). Mark i. 23.
Having a foul spirit (ἔχων πνεῦμα ἀκαθαρτόν). Mark iii. 30.
Whom a spirit enters (πνεῦμα εἰσέρχεται). Matt. xii. 45.
Annoyed by spirits (ὀχλούμενοι ὑπὸ πνευμάτων). Acts v. 16.
Harassed by spirits (ἐνοχλούμενοι ἀπὸ πνευμάτων). Luke vi. 18.
Containing a spirit (ἐν ᾧ ἦν τὸ πνεῦμα). Acts xix. 16.

The demoniacs are sometimes said "to have" or "to possess" (ἔχειν) a demon or spirit. The term "possession" has thus scriptural authority; but perhaps it owes its currency to Aristotle's discussion of the term ἔχειν (*Metaphysics*, IV. xxiii.). The fourth Gospel is not unique in its terminology; though the view of its author regarding the reality of possession may be matter of conjecture. He mentions the reproaches cast on Jesus as one possessed; but he records no healing of demoniacs. Ewald in vain tried to conjure up such an occurrence between chaps. v. and vi. The omission in itself is not surprising, as John does not attempt to exhaust the types of miracles wrought by our Lord. He has no mention of deafness, dropsy, dumbness, fever, lameness, leprosy, or paralysis. Silence, therefore, cannot be construed into dissent from the other Evangelists. Indeed, John

[1] שד. [2] רוח. [3] רוח רעה. [4] רוח טמא.

is entirely at one with Luke in regarding Judas as possessed of Satan. That is a specific point of contact which may import agreement elsewhere.

APPENDIX C

THE DUMB DEMONIAC *versus* THE BLIND-AND-DUMB DEMONIAC. P. 90.

Strauss, De Wette, and Keim here hold to a twofold narration of a single incident. That is possible, but unlikely. The critical considerations are important; but the medical are more so. Dumb demoniacs do not seem to have been numerous in Palestine in the time of our Lord. Their rarity is easily explained by the great mortality among this class of sufferers, consequent upon neglect and maltreatment. But the survival of blind-and-dumb demoniacs must have been still rarer, because of their greater proneness to death. The loss of sight, in the latter case, is not a loss to be simply added to the existing defects. That new feature implied a most serious advance in the whole course of the disease. There was therefore a very decided difference between a dumb demoniac and one who was both blind and dumb. There is no difficulty in regarding both as genuine cases of serious mental disease. The historical setting of the different narratives is in complete agreement with this view.

1. The cure of the dumb demoniac drew forth the plaudits of the unprejudiced multitudes: It was never so seen in Israel! With equal emotion the Pharisees declared: He casteth out demons in the prince of demons. The charge of conspiring with the prince of demons is as yet not much more than tentative. It is a *coup d'essai*.

2. The cure of the blind-and-dumb demoniac

astounded the unbiassed spectators, who said: May this not be the son of David? But the scornful enemies deprecated this incipient faith, saying: He has Beelzebul! Conspiracy with the prince of demons has now become possession by him. The charge is now malignant and clamant. It is a *coup de grâce*.

There is a progression of events; also an enhancement of thought and feeling and activity, in the latter case compared with the former. The whole environment of the blind-and-dumb demoniac is different from that of the dumb demoniac. Attempts at reduction of the miraculous are here unwarranted.

Which of the two cases in the first Gospel is the true parallel to that in the third? At first sight, there seems nothing to arbitrate upon; for surely the dumb demoniac of Matthew is also the dumb demoniac of Luke. Yet Meyer, Arnold, and others take the opposite view. That means then that Luke omits the mention of blindness, which ought to have been of great importance to him as a physician. Yet that is not surprising in view of the large number of similar omissions. Some of these are very notable: such as the sudden entrance of the Capernaum demoniac into the synagogue when furiously maniacal; the excessive activity, the unwearied vigilance, the ghastly mutilations, of the Gerasene demoniac; the dumbness, the deafness, the intractable disposition, the suicidal proclivities, of the epileptic idiot. This list of omissions might be greatly extended; and is highly instructive. It raises questions of authorship; for the omissions are not such as arise out of the reticence imposed by the Hippocratic oath.

In this connection also it is curious to note the omission of the miraculous element by Luke—

The respective reports on the Galilean Ministry are—

    Matt. Preaching and healing. iv. 23.
    Mark. Preaching and ejecting demons. i. 39.
    Luke. Preaching only. iv. 44.

The respective reports on the Mission of the Twelve—

    Matt. . . . .
    Mark. Preachings, ejections, anointings. vi. 12, 13.
    Luke. Preaching and healing. ix. 6.

With Luke, therefore, preaching may include healing; and healing may include the cure of the demonised. The latter point is implied again in the double form of the commission to the Twelve—

    He gave them power and authority over all demons and to cure diseases. Luke ix. 1.
    He sent them forth to preach the kingdom of God and to heal. Luke ix. 2.

These two statements are independent so far; healing being common to both. There is no withdrawal of the powers conferred in the first verse: though there is no mention of them in the second. The healing of the sick thus includes the cure of the possessed. This mannerism of Luke is of further interest in connection with the Mission of the Seventy.

APPENDIX D

FACT-BASIS OF THE EPHESIAN NARRATIVE. P. 100.

Some of the difficulties of the narrative are removable by the adoption of variant readings (B, D, etc.): others are immaterial to the study of the case as one of possession. In this respect it is of no consequence whether Sceva is a ruler (ἄρχων), or a priest (ἱερεύς), or a high priest (ἀρχιερεύς). His seven sons are exorcists who are practising abroad. Their adoption of this profession in foreign parts and their experimenting with a new Name, potent in the hands of others, are altogether in accord with the historical situation. The result of this *séance*, though very inglorious, was proof that there was power in the new Name. That determined the continuation of the practice in later times as expressly testified in Shab. 14d. The account of the experiment is eminently free from exaggeration, and bears every evidence of being thoroughly veracious. The force of the remarks of Prof. Ramsay are thus sensibly abated: "In this Ephesian description one feels the character, not of weighed and reasoned history, but of popular fancy; and I cannot explain it on the level of most of the narrative. The writer is here rather the picker-up of current gossip, like Herodotus, than a real historian" (*St. Paul the Traveller*, p. 273).

APPENDIX E

The Mission of the Seventy. P. 114.

Notwithstanding the obscurities attaching to this narrative, there are sound reasons for accepting it as founded on fact.

1. The Galilean Ministry is historical; the Peræan is equally sure (Matt. xix. 1; Mark x. 1; John x. 40). Two great divisions of Jewish territory were thus overtaken. It would have been passing strange on the part of Him whose mission was to the lost sheep of the house of Israel, had Judæa, the remaining division of the land, been neglected. The Gospel of John implies a considerable activity on the part of Jesus in Jerusalem, but no Judæan Ministry similar to that in Galilee or Peræa. According to Mark iii. 7, 8, those who followed Jesus came from—

    (*a*) Galilee.
    (*b*) Peræa.

(c) Parts about Tyre and Sidon.

(d) Judæa, including Jerusalem and Idumæa.[1]

Christ, as it were, returned the visits of those who came from Galilee, Peræa, Tyre, and Sidon. That was natural. But we find Him also visiting the outlandish region of Decapolis. It is inconceivable that while Tyre, Sidon, and Decapolis shared the beneficence of Christ, the region of Judæa should remain unvisited. The mission of the Seventy fills up the blank; and there is good reason for accepting the suggestion of Hahn, that Judæa was the objective of the Seventy.

2. The date is not quite certain. The existence of considerable opposition is assumed. The tension is similar to that existing towards the close of the Galilean Ministry. The outlook is tempered with the hope of an abundant harvest (x. 2). The injunctions closely resemble those delivered to the Twelve; proving that the conditions of the work are not greatly dissimilar. Luke seems to connect this Mission with the migration of Jesus from Galilee, through Samaria to Jerusalem. The suggestion of Hahn is that the place of appointment is Jerusalem; and the time, the Feast of Tabernacles (John vii. 2). The conjecture seems to be well founded.

3. All things indicate a certain urgency. The Seventy are appointed without the ceremony of the Twelve, who were "called" and "chosen" and "named" Apostles (Luke vi. 13); whereas Jesus simply designated (ἀνέδειξεν,—*designavit*, Vulg.) the Seventy. Greetings by the way and shifting of quarters are forbidden. Christ seems to have been under the necessity of cancelling His intention of following the Missioners; for they return to one centre to report. The whole situation is intelligible, if the time and place of appointment be as supposed. Feeling was then running very high in Jerusalem (John vii. 20).

---

[1] Idumæa, "then practically the southern Shephelah, with the Negeb." So, G. A. Smith, *Historical Geography*. But see 1 Macc. vi. 31, etc.

4. The Sanhedrim is not to be thought of in connection with the Seventy; for that body numbered not seventy but seventy-one. Nor is it possible to endorse the view of the Tübingen School, which finds here a reference to the evangelising of the world. It is true that the extra-Israelitish nations were computed at Seventy on the basis of the fanciful interpretation of Gen. xlvi. 27, and Deut. xxxii. 8. But the outlook of this Mission is strictly local and temporary. The Seventy go to the cities and places whither Jesus Himself was about to come. Now Judaea was divided into certain districts, enumerated by Josephus and Pliny. Their lists do not quite agree; but Schürer has offered a revised list, which comprises Jerusalem, Gophna, Akrabatta, Thamna, Lydda, Emmaus, Bethleptepha, Idumaea, Engaddi, Herodeion, and Jericho.[1] The first and the last of these might be omitted as otherwise provided for; so leaving nine only. If the other reading, Seventy-Two,[2] be accepted (and it is perhaps of equal worth), then there would be eight delegates to each district; so permitting the speedy completion of the Mission. The prompt action of Christ and the ample supply of labourers thus anticipated opposition and secured a surprising success.

The historicity of this Mission amply vindicates itself as the crown and consummation of the plans of Jesus for evangelising the whole land of the Jews.

The commission and the success of the Missioners deserve attention—

> Heal the sick and say to them, The kingdom of God is come nigh to you. Luke x. 9.
> Lord, even the demons are subject to us in thy name. Luke x. 17.

This remarkable juxtaposition brings into prominence a point often referred to, namely, the existence of a faith and works alleged to be in excess of the terms of

---

[1] Schürer, *The Jewish People*, II. i. p. 157 ff.
[2] So B, D, M, R, Vulg., etc.

the original commission. These statements have been made to work in two directions—

(*a*) To the credit of the Missioners as men of rare faith.

(*b*) To the discredit of the Apostles who failed with the boy.

But the inference is thoroughly indefensible. There is here no work of supererogation, nor shadow of reproach; only a threefold mannerism of the third Evangelist—

1. Ejection of demons is included in works of healing. The commission of those two parties is coextensive. The proof is a comparison of Luke ix. 2, with Luke x. 9.

2. Luke constantly manifests a tender regard for the reputation of the Twelve. Disparagement of them is here impossible. The account of Peter's fall is a monument of magnificent charity.

3. The main interest of Luke here is not the demonic element at all, but the astounding success of the Missioners. The joy of Jesus rests on a far wider basis than triumphs over evil spirits; and that feeling He shares with the delegates: Notwithstanding in this rejoice not that the spirits are subject unto you, but rather rejoice that your names are written in heaven.

APPENDIX F

Greek Demonology. P. 129.

From the time of the Christian Apologists, the Church passed deeply under "the wisdom of the Greeks." Demonology was an integral part of the same; so that it is necessary to give at least a brief outline of this branch of ancient lore. The term demon (δαίμων) connects itself with the form δαίειν—to divide;

not with δαῆναι—to know. The demons then are *the distributors of destiny*, not simply *the knowing ones*.

Homer (about 1000 B.C.) uses the term "demon," sometimes as the equivalent of deity. Thus, Minerva retires to the palace of ægis-bearing Zeus, to the "other demons" (*Il.* i. 222). Venus is described as a "demon," after her interview with Helen (*Il.* iii. 420). But the tendency is to apply the term to lesser personages. Hector threatens Diomede: I will give thee to a demon (*Il.* viii. 166). Athene assures Telemachus that he will perceive certain things in his own mind, while a demon will suggest others (*Od.* iii. 27). The sick man, pining away, is one on whom a hateful demon has gazed (*Od.* v. 396). Æolus reproaches the luckless Odysseus, after his companions had opened the bladder containing the winds: How didst thou come? What evil demon has pressed on thee (*Od.* x. 64)? The word becomes even an abstract form, as in *Il.* xvii. 98, where demon stands for "heaven's power." The Homeric demons, when not abstractions, are already good and bad.[1]

Hesiod (about 800 B.C.) divides rational beings into four classes—gods, demons, heroes (demi-gods), and men. The immortals first made a "golden race" of men, when Chronos ruled in heaven. "When doom overtook this race, by decree of mighty Zeus, demons are they, kindly, dwellers on earth, guardians of mortal men, easily observant of deeds of righteousness and works of daring, clothed in air, dwelling everywhere on earth, givers of riches" (*Works and Days*, 121–126). "Three times ten thousand are they on the bounteous earth, immortals of Zeus (*ibid.* 252, 253)." To his own brother, Perses—"the ne'er-do-well"—the poet holds

[1] Lecky, in his *History of European Morals*, says it is extremely doubtful whether the existence of evil demons was known either to the Greeks or Romans, till about the advent of Christ. "The belief was introduced with the Oriental superstitions which then poured into Rome" (i. p. 380). Homer, Empedocles, Plato, Xenocrates, Chrysippus, and others disprove this statement. It is also opposed to the teachings of anthropology.

out the hope of being one day "like a demon" (*ibid.* 314). The demons of this poet are therefore all good.

Thales (about 630-548 B.C.) held that the world was animated (ἔμψυχον), and full of demons (Diog. Laert. viii. 6). God was the intelligence of the world: demons were spiritual beings; and heroes the souls of the departed. The demons were both good and evil (Athenag., *Apol.* xxiii. Cf. Plutarch, *Plac.* I. viii. 2).

Pythagoras (about 540-510 B.C.) held that demons were stronger than men; but had not the divine part unmixed. They shared the nature of the soul and the sensation of the body; being susceptible of pain and connate passions (Plutarch, *Isis*, 25). The whole air is filled with demons or heroes, which send dreams to men and the signs of sickness or health. They also send these to sheep and other creatures, that purifications, expiations, divinations, omens, and the like, may be referred to them (Diog. Laert. viii. 19).

Empedocles (*floruit* 444 B.C.) embodied his views in his poem "On Nature," which is extant only as a fragment. Though he is often quoted by later writers of first rank, it is not easy to ascertain the details of his philosophy. According to Plutarch, he taught that demons are of a mixed and inconstant nature, and are subjected to a purgatorial process which may end in their promotion to their former abodes—

> The force of air them to the sea pursues,
> The sea again upon the land them spues,
> From land to Sol's unwearied beams they're hurled,
> Thence far into the realms of ether whirled,
> Received by each in turn, by all abhorred.

Thus chastened and purified, they again attain to that region and order suited to their nature (Plut. *Isis*, 26). Empedocles attributed to demons all the calamities, vexations, and plagues, incident to man; the gods themselves being superior to corruption, suffering, and error (Plut. *Def. Orac.* xvi.).

Socrates (about 470-399 B.C.) claimed to have a

demon within him which indicated what he was to do (Xen. *Mem.* I. ii. 4).[1] It was only an inward voice which did not at all oppose his going to death (*Apol.* xix. xxxi.). He scouted the idea that the demon was an apparition (Plut. *Demon of Soc.* xi.).

Plato (428–347 B.C.) was a poet-philosopher, whose meaning is often elusive on this subject. He does not exclude the demons from heaven; remarking that on certain occasions Zeus, the greatest sovereign of heaven, rides forth in his winged chariot, followed by a host of gods and demons (*Phædrus*, lvi.). He divided all superior beings into the uncreated God, and those produced by Him for the adornment of the heavens—the planets and the fixed stars; and demons (Athenag. *Ap.* xxiii.). The demons are inferior to stars, but act as tutelary officials to men; being themselves susceptible to pleasure and pain and hating wickedness (*Epinomis*). Plato says in another passage that a demon is intermediate between the divine and the mortal. Such a demon is Love, whose function is to interpret and to transmit to the gods petitions and sacrifices, thence bringing back commands and gifts. God does not mingle with men, but through the demons there is all intercourse and conversation (*Sympos.* 202 D, 203 A). Plato repeatedly refers to the Hesiodic demons. In the *Cratylus* (398 B.C.), "golden" means "noble and good"; and a good man would still be called golden, because "knowing or wise" ($\delta\alpha\acute{\eta}\mu\omega\nu$). When a good man dies, he has honour and a mighty portion among the dead, and becomes a demon; and every wise man who is also a good man is more than human ($\delta\alpha\iota\mu\acute{o}\nu\iota o\varsigma$), both in life and in death. Again, in the *Republic*, he quotes Hesiod; saying that those who behave nobly in war belong to "the golden age"; and at death become demons. Their sepulchres are to be afterwards revered as the shrines of such demons. In the same class and destined to the same honours, are good men who die in the course of age or otherwise. Good rulers are also

---

[1] At his trial he spoke vaguely of demons as gods or sons of gods.

admitted to this status after death (vii. 17). In regulating the lives of animals in the first ages, Plato assumes the co-operation of divine demons with the deity (*Polit.* 271 D E; 274 B.C.). In the Platonic Apocalypse, the demon assigned to each person in life conducts him to judgment, sometimes not without a struggle (*Phædo*, 130, 131). There is also a vision of "fierce and fiery men," who discharge the function of angels of punishment (*Rep.* x. 14). The majority of the Platonic demons are good.

Aristotle (384–322 B.C.) was the son of a physician and possessed no small amount of medical knowledge. His practical nature rendered him averse to speculating, like Plato, on things beyond the mundane sphere. He curtailed the realm of the spiritual. In his *Metaphysics*, he mentions four modes of being; the last being demonic (IV. viii.). He recognised the intimate relation existing between body and soul, suggesting that a change in the quality of the one might induce a corresponding change in the other. He remarks that insanity appears to attach itself to the soul; yet physicians, by appropriate remedies and dieting, free the soul from insanity. He was aware of the power of fever to cause delirium (*Dreams*, ii.). Mental derangements were referred to natural causes by this philosopher. Much passed under his name which was not his. Such are the references to demons inspiring the possessed (Eud. *Ethics*, I. i. 3); also the cure of the demonised by the use of a stone found in the Nile (*Mirab. Auscult.*).[1]

The Stoics held a somewhat variant doctrine of demons among themselves; but agreed in giving an esoteric and exoteric aspect to the same. Thus, reason is the governing power of the soul, and is part of an emanation from God. As reason is protective against evil and is conducive to good, it is the guardian spirit or demon of man. A holy spirit, therefore, dwells in us, observant of our good and evil deeds, and our guardian (Seneca, *Epist.* xli. 2). This tutelary spirit is

[1] Cf. Plutarch, *De Fluviis*.

of Jove's appointment, charged to keep ward, without sleeping and without deceit (Epict. *Dissert.* I. xiv. 12). This protector and guide is the *nous* and *logos* of each one (M. Aurel. v. 27). Seneca could also speak, in the popular sense, of each one possessing two tutelary spirits (*Epist.* cx. 1). Others of this School required demons for completing their scheme of the universe. Thus, if living things exist on the earth and in the sea, there must also be intelligent beings in the air which is so much purer. These beings are demons. In the scheme of providence, a part is assigned them by Chrysippus, who accounted for evil in the world by negligent and restless demons (Plut. *Repug.* xxxvii. 2). Some demons went about the world as public avengers of evil (Plut. *Quæst. Rom.* 51); but this was not supposed to interfere with the laws of the universe.[1]

The Neo-Platonists systematised the existing ethnic beliefs and purified the same to some extent. The virtual founder of this School is Plutarch (about 50–120 A.D.). The gods are immortal, virtuous, free from passion, and immune from sin; but demons are of a neutral or inferior nature, subject to mortal passion and necessary change, long-lived, but not immortal (*Def. Orac.* xi. xii. xvi.). He relates the death of Pan and gives the report of Demetrius who visited some of the outlying islands of Britain, called the Isles of the Demons and the Demi-gods. On the arrival of this visitor to our shores, there was a severe storm with wind and thunder; believed to denote the death of some demon (*Def. Orac.* xviii.). Plutarch held that the deity is not specially concerned with sacrifices, services, and ceremonies. These are entrusted to demons who are the spies and scouts of the gods; others avenging and punishing the wicked. Yet not all demons are good. They differ in virtue; some retaining but a slight trace of the sensuous and irrational soul; others possessing that in high degree (*Def. Orac.* xiii.). Certain

---

[1] The Epicureans rejected both the popular theology and demonology (Plutarch, *Def. Orac.* xix.; *Plac.* i. 83).

gloomy festivals, when raw flesh is eaten and the skin is torn by the nails, or others when there is fasting and beating of the breasts, with uncomely speech, head-tossings, and tumults, are for appeasing evil spirits. This is the end also of human sacrifices; certain tyrannical demons requiring for their enjoyment, some soul still incarnate, and being unable to satisfy their evil desire, incite war and sedition, till they get what they lust for. Rapes, wanderings, banishments, voluntary servitudes of the gods, are due to demons. They are concerned with oracles, which cease on their departure; but emit musical sounds on their return (*Def. Orac.* xiv. xv.). Plutarch thus ekes out his doctrine of providence, and fills up the interval between gods and men. The good demons are "hermeneutic" in the Platonic sense, carrying vows and prayers to heaven; bringing thence prophecies and gifts to men (*Isis*, xxvi.). Demons may personate the gods; assuming their name. The position of the demon is not a fixture. One might attain to divinity, while another might be entangled in a mortal body.

Plutarch does not refer his demonology to the Magi through Zoroaster, nor to Thrace, Egypt, or Phrygia.[1] Most of it bears the ethnic stamp; but somewhat clarified. Ammonius Saccas, Plotinus, Porphyry, Iamblichus, and Proclus largely elaborated the foregoing doctrines. The influence of the Neo-Platonic School on the writers of the early Church is well marked.

APPENDIX G

Greek Medicine. Pp. 129, 137.

To Greece belongs the honour of being the first to discard the barbarous practices of ignorant peoples, which connected mental disease with demonic agency.

---

[1] Keim is in error when he asserts that Plutarch was dependent on the Magi for his doctrine of demons.

This change of view belongs to that brilliant period of history which witnessed the finest artistic productions of the manifold genius of Greece. Hippocrates was the first physician to give it concise expression in his treatise on "Epilepsy," or "The Sacred Disease." He argues his case with singular felicity and shrewdness, refusing to believe that "The Sacred Disease" is more divine or sacred than any other. He attributes the common opinion to ignorance and the alleged simplicity of the cure. Men ought to know that from nothing else than the brain come joy, despondency, and lamentations, while from the same organ come also madness, delirium, the assaults of fear and terror, dreams, wanderings, anxieties, and other evils. His friend, Democritus, is made to say in a (forged) letter that he was writing on insanity, and was making dissections of animals, not in hatred of the works of the gods, but for the discovery of the nature of the gall and the bilious humour. This study of nature at first hand underlay the practice of Hippocrates. The change of medical opinion reflects itself in literature; not purely in poetry which loves to retain the archaic and the pictorial. The verb $\delta\alpha\iota\mu o\nu\tilde{\alpha}\nu$, originally applied to the state of one possessed, now comes to denote the condition of one *non compos mentis*. In the *Coephora* of Æschylus, it is said that the house "is distraught ($\delta\alpha\iota\mu o\nu\tilde{q}$) with ills." In the *Ajax* of Sophocles, the hero is seized with madness ($\mu\alpha\nu i\alpha$), jerking out words which a demon and not man has taught him. In the *Plutus* of Aristophanes, to be "ill with black bile" is to be "troubled with an evil demon." In the *Phœnissœ* of Euripides, the possessed ($\delta\alpha\iota\mu o\nu\tilde{\omega}\nu\tau\epsilon\varsigma$) are those who are "out of their senses." Herodotus relates that the Spartans thought that the madness of their king was not due to any divine influence, but to hard drinking. Plato held that there were two kinds of madness, one due to disease, the other to an inspired deviation from custom.[1]

[1] The classical $\delta\alpha\iota\mu o\nu\tilde{\alpha}\nu$ becomes the Hellenistic $\delta\alpha\iota\mu o\nu i\zeta\epsilon\sigma\theta\alpha\iota$. It is interesting to note that even Josephus applies the former to the

The Greek physicians used rational methods of treatment. Melampus cured the lycanthropy of the daughters of Proetus by the use of hellebore, with music and dancing. Hippocrates and Democritus judiciously exhibited the same drug. The Hippocratic traditions were ably continued in the School of Cos, and were carried westwards.

Asclepiades prescribed fasting in the earlier part of the day, simple liquid diet and massage in the evening. He was averse to bleeding, fomentations, mandrake, poppy, or hyoscyamus. Censorinus relates his employment of music as a remedial agent. The bad features in his treatment were the use of bonds and the allowance of gross indulgences after abstinence.

Celsus Aurelius Cornelius, a Roman physician, who flourished under Augustus and Tiberius, was rather rough in his methods. He advised hunger, chains, and stripes in the case of the more violent patients; also sudden frights. His medical treatment was drastic: but the admirable side of it was the appointment of music, recitations, sports, the excitement of cheerful hopes, massage, and regular exercise after food.

Aretæus, the Cappadocian, is sometimes cited as a believer in demonic possession. This is a mistake. Speaking of acute mania, where self-mutilations occur, he remarks that such persons cut themselves as in a holy phantasy, as if propitiating peculiar divinities. This he regarded as a madness of the apprehension and of divine origin, the victim on recovery being bright and cheerful as if introduced to the gods. He used the lancet cautiously, and followed up depletory measures with others for sustaining the strength. He made use of bathing, external applications, and cupping, also of gestation in a hammock.

Cælius Aurelianus is the most excellent of the ancient alienists. He kept his patients in a room

---

state of those frantic with excitement: Certain men persuaded the multitudes to act like madmen (δαιμονᾶν, *B. J.* II. xiii. 4). Cf. John x. 20.

properly lit and warmed. The attendant had to exclude excitement and avoid the confirmation of delusions. The latter were to be corrected by condescension or insinuation, without needless opposition. He applied warm sponges over the eyelids to relax them and act simultaneously on the coverings of the brain. Restlessness and sleeplessness were combated by gestation in a hammock. A sufficient diet was commended; excessive indulgences forbidden; also bonds and venesection. During convalescence, theatrical entertainments of the graver sort, riding, walking, the exercise of the voice, and the pursuit of former occupations, were advocated.

It would be a pleasing task to illustrate further the practice of other noted physicians, such as Galen and Alexander of Tralles. Enough has been shown to indicate how far the Greek physicians were in advance of the Jews in the treatment of mental disease. The general esteem in which scientific medicine was held by the Jews seems to be conveyed in the aphorism: The best physicians are destined for hell (*Sopherim. C.* 15. 10)!

APPENDIX H

Testimonies to the Success of Jesus. Pp. 144, 187.

It is evident that great potentialities for good must have inhered in Him Who is the Moral Miracle of the ages. Works of power must have been natural to Him. That is the testimony of the Gospels. It receives corroboration in the most unexpected quarters. The Talmud itself acknowledges so much, when it represents Jesus as a successful magician, who had learned the art in Egypt, the home of magic (*Shab.* 75a), which had received nine of the ten measures of magic allotted to the world (*Kidd.* 49b). He is said to have eluded the Egyptian officers stationed on the frontier to prevent the export of the rules and formulæ of magic; having hidden these subcutaneously (*Shab.* 104*b*). This perversion of history is, however, weighty testimony to the reality of the miraculous in the Ministry of Christ.

The Healing Ministry was a great fact. At the end of the day, the bitterest foes of Jesus confessed: HE SAVED OTHERS! That emphatic testimony cannot be gainsaid. At a later date Quadratus of Athens challenged the Roman world to examine the same point. In his Apology to the Emperor Hadrian (76–138 A.D.), he says: The deeds of our Saviour were always before you; for His miracles were real. Persons were healed and were raised from the dead, who were not only seen after they were healed or raised up; but were constantly in evidence. They remained alive a long time, not only when our Lord was on earth; but likewise after He had left it, so that some of them have survived even to our own time (Euseb. *Hist. Eccles.* iv. 3). The cure of the demoniacs was a prominent part of the Healing Ministry. Jesus dealt with the most formidable types of insanity and idiocy. His enemies again bear witness to His astounding success. They produced their theory of a conspiracy with Beelzebul to account for it. The sons of Sceva experimented with His Name, at Ephesus. A later generation continued the invocation of the same (*Shab.* 14*d*). Here is a singular persistency of belief and practice, which is undoubted confirmation of Christ's success in the cure of the demonised. With Herbert Spencer, we accept *persistency* as the test of reality.

APPENDIX I

FALLACIES. P. 155.

Any general estimate of the spiritual prospects of the insane is exceedingly hazardous. If the proposition be seriously entertained that "insanity is much nearer the kingdom of God than worldly-mindedness," then an answer must be found to these queries. Does mental derangement really effect any approximation to the kingdom of heaven? Is the door of the asylum the remote equivalent of "the strait gate"? Do institutions for the insane discharge quasi-ecclesiastical functions? Was it "quite to be expected" that those diseased in their minds, specially those whose thoughts moved in the religious sphere, should be among the first to recognise the Messiah? If so, were the sane, whose thoughts moved in the same sphere, placed at a disadvantage? Did possession, therefore, constitute part of the *præparatio evangelica*? Did restoration to mental health carry with it spiritual convalescence? To state these questions is to answer them. They disclose a fallacy, namely, insanity and worldly mindedness are not two conditions which admit of comparison with each other. The attempt to do so involves a fundamental confusion between the physical and the ethical.

It is also a serious fallacy to place the most accomplished, the most discerning, and the most suceptible, of the friends of Jesus on a lower intellectual level than the possessed. The capacity and candour of the former are in keenest contrast to the obtusity and caprice of the latter. To bracket the young with the demonised is an intolerable fallacy. Intelligence is proceeding normally in the case of the former; it has been arrested or eclipsed in the case of the latter. Children were attracted to Jesus as the most genial of friends, without being able to think of Him as the official Messiah. The possessed were in a strait betwixt two; hailing Him now as a tormentor, now as the Holy One of God. The tender mood of the docile child is the antithesis of the pugnacious demeanour of the raving demoniac.

APPENDIX J

THE USE OF POPULAR LANGUAGE BY JESUS. P. 159.

The foregoing conclusions may seem to be at variance with the records of the Evangelists—

> Jesus rebuked (the lad)[1] and the demon went out of him. Matt. xvii. 18.
> Jesus said, I charge thee, dumb and deaf spirit, come out of him. Mark ix. 25.
> Jesus rebuked the unclean spirit and healed the boy. Luke ix. 42.

Harmonists may attempt to reconcile these discrepancies by a process of amalgamation; while critics may prefer to seek the archaic and germinal matter of the real original in the first Gospel. But in neither case is the result at all momentous. The variations halt between the rebuke of the lad and the rebuke of the demon. The precise words used by our Lord on this occasion are evidently no longer recoverable. At most, it can only be said that a formula was employed which was capable of being construed into the menacing of an unclean spirit. But Jesus rebuked the fever without believing in a fever-demon. He likewise rebuked the storm without believing in a storm-demon. These things being so, the doubt as to the reality of demonic agency in this case can only be resolved by the application of the criterion of genuine possession and the examination of the symptoms manifested. The conclusion is that already expressed. This is not the only occasion on which Christ used language which was open to distortion by a crude literalism. The descriptions of the forty days' temptation, the second advent, and the doom of the wicked, have been much

---

[1] So rendered by the Vulgate, Theophylact, de Wette, Winer, Bleek, etc. That is the natural construction and otherwise justifiable. The "rebuke" is not merely a word of reproof; it is also the divine formula for the suppression of the processes of disorder. Cf. Ps. cvi. 9. Nah. i. 4. Mal. iii. 11.

misunderstood, on this wise. It may be argued, in academic fashion, that for the avoidance of all possible misconception, loose linguistic forms ought to have been eschewed in the records of revelation. But the introduction of a scientific nomenclature was plainly beyond the province of Christ as a religious teacher; even had it been feasible otherwise. Christ did all that was possible for the removal of vulgar error by showing that He had no fellowship with the unfruitful superstitions of the age. The proofs of His illumination have been already set forth. Having made His own position clear, He left the rest to the growth of intelligence; bequeathing an invaluable method: Ask, and it shall be given you; seek, and ye shall find; knock, and it shall be opened unto you.

APPENDIX K

The Demonising of the Heathen Gods. P. 161.

"Did the Apostle Paul regard the gods of the heathen as demons?" Beyschlag, followed by Dods, has answered in the negative; but the argument is very unconvincing.[1] It has been shown that the degradation of the pagan divinities to demonic rank was one of the results of the monotheistic movement in Israel. It was projected into the Septuagint and extra-canonical literature. In two notable passages, Paul distinctly signifies his adhesion to the old prophetic standpoint—

1. An idol is nothing in the world (1 Cor. viii. 4). The Hebrew "nothing" is the sarcastic designation of a heathen god, variously interpreted in the Septuagint—

Lev. xix. 4	Nothings, אלילים	Idols, εἴδωλα.
1 Chron. xvi. 26	Nothings, אלילים	Idols, εἴδωλα.
Ps. xcvi. (xcv.) 5	Nothings, אלילים	Demons, δαιμόνια.

[1] *Expositor*, March 1895.

K.—*The Demonising of the Heathen Gods* 273

2. The things which the Gentiles sacrifice, they sacrifice to demons and not to God (1 Cor. x. 20). This is a quotation from the Septuagint—

| Deut. xxxii. 17 | Shedim, שדים | Demons, δαιμόνια. |
| Deut. xxxii. 17 | No god, לא־אלה | Not God, οὐ θεός. |

Here then is a series of synonyms for the heathen gods, *demons, idols, nothings*. The series is a vanishing one; but even when called "nothings," these divinities do not shrivel up into non-existence. Over the true Israel of God they have no power at all; they are "nothings." But over their own worshippers they still exercise their baleful influence; they are "demons." The argument of Paul, "touching things offered to idols," may be thus simply construed—

In the Lord's Supper, men are the guests of Christ and hold a real spiritual fellowship with Him. In the feasts of the gods, men are the guests of the gods and hold occult fellowship with them. Behind the elements in the Lord's Supper is the presence of Christ. Behind the elements in the feasts of the gods is the presence of demons. To take part in the latter with deliberation is an act involving the Christian among the powers of darkness. "All the gods of the heathen are demons" (Ps. xcvi. 5).

The opinion of Baudissin and Everling that Paul was indebted to Alexandrian Judaism for the belief that the offerings to the heathen gods were really offerings to demons, reveals an anachronism on the part of these authorities. Paul goes behind Alexandrian Judaism to the original conception of the Hebrew Scriptures.

Another proof of Paul's adhesion to the pure religion of the Old Economy is to be found in the much disputed passage: For this cause ought the woman to have authority upon her head because of the angels (1 Cor. xi. 10). The advice was given to the "new women" of Corinth, whose zeal for a spurious emancipation had carried them beyond the bounds of propriety. The "angels" can hardly be *spies*, or *matrimonial agents*, or *presiding ministers*. Far less can they be the lawless Bene-Elohim of popular story.[1] It was uniformly understood that their invasion of the world belonged to a far-off age, and entailed penalties which prevented its repetition. Whether the "authority upon the head" ($ἐξουσία ἐπὶ τῆς κεφαλῆς$) be veil or chalebi, remains uncertain; but Paul does not think here of women being a temptation to fallen angels nor of demons lurking in the tresses of the fair. He is at the standpoint of the Psalmist when he says, Before the Elohim ($ἄγγελοι$, LXX.) will I sing praise unto Thee (Ps. cxxxviii. 1). The angels are fellow-worshippers with the saints in the services of the sanctuary.[2] It is not possible to accept here the views of Everling regarding those "angels."

APPENDIX L

JESUS OUT OF HIS SENSES? Pp. 178, 184.

Regard for the mother and brethren of our Lord has led to attempted evasion of the plain meaning of $ἐξέστη$—in Mark iii. 21. A mistaken ingenuity has suggested "exhaustion," "fainting," "ecstasy," "excitement bordering on insanity," as equivalents for a term whose significance is determined by Hippocrates (188 D), Euripides (*Bacchœ*, 850), Xenophon (*Memor.* I. iii. 12), etc. It can only mean here that the friends of Jesus considered Him insane. Hence their going forth to arrest Him ($κρατῆσαι αὐτόν$, Mark iii. 21). Their alarm was real. Possession by a common demon or conspiracy with Beelzebul, they might partly under-

---

[1] See Book of Enoch (vi.); Book of the Secrets of Enoch (xviii.); Apocalypse of Baruch (lvi.); Book of Baruch (iii. 26); Ecclus. (xvi. 7); Wisdom (xiv. 6); 3 Macc. (ii. 4); Testament of Reuben (5, 6); Yalkut Shim. Ber. 44, etc.

[2] Cf. Tobit xii. 12.

stand. *But possession by the prince of demons! What was that?* No wonder that they rushed off to lay hold of Him as one who was more than desperately insane. This hasty acceptance of the slander of the enemy was more than a mere error of judgment. It drew forth the rebuke: Who is my mother? And who are my brethren? Whosoever shall do the will of God, the same is my brother, and my sister, and my mother!

APPENDIX M

Was Jesus nicknamed Beelzebul? P. 183.

The suggestion appears on the first sending forth of the Twelve; but the passage (Matt. x. 25) does not permit an immediate settlement of the difficulty on account of a variant reading. According to the *Textus Receptus*, we read: If they have called the master of the house (οἰκοδεσπότην) Beelzebul, how much more them of his household (οἰκιακούς)! That asserts the use of a nickname. According to another version (D), we read: If they have cast up Beelzebul to the master of the house (οἰκοδεσπότῃ), how much more to them of his household (οἰκιακοῖς)! This hints at a compact with the prince of demons. Happily, we do not require to embark on the turbulent sea of variant readings; for the after-history puts the matter in clear light. The opponents of Jesus, by the very terms of their office, were experts in magic. The name of Beelzebul was held in private veneration among them. They put forth their theory, not in a jocular, but in a serious state of mind. But "possession" never meant the identification of the subject, with the agent, of possession. The personality might be swamped for a time, but not permanently effaced. To have called Jesus Beelzebul would have been such an identification; for, on the principles of the lower culture, the name is the equivalent of the personality. It was so in ancient Egypt and Babylonia. Even Greek philosophy did not entirely escape the confusion. Jesus then could not have been nicknamed Beelzebul. The latter was only "cast up" to the Master of the house.

APPENDIX N

Scene of the Healing of the Blind-and-Dumb Demoniac. P. 184.

There is a considerable hiatus in the second Gospel between the choosing of the Twelve and the simple remark, He cometh home (Mark iii. 19). That "home" is in Capernaum (cf. Mark ii. 1). Meyer notes that Mark iii. 22 "still lacks the historical information furnished by Matt. xii. 22 f." Yet the same antecedents are contemplated by the second Evangelist. On the arrival of Jesus there is a huge commotion in the town. "The multitude cometh together again so that they could not so much as eat bread." Scribes also have come down from Jerusalem,—evidently a Vigilance Committee. The bitter feud against Jesus is coming to a climax. Already voices are heard on high: "He has Beelzebul, and in the prince of demons casteth he out demons." The cure of the blind-and-dumb demoniac is, doubtless, the cause of all this stir. The friends of Jesus (οἱ παρ' αὐτοῦ, Mark iii. 21) arrive while Jesus is addressing the scribes. They "stand without"; for the dense crowd permits of no nearer approach. Whence had they come? From Nazareth, say Meyer and others. But that is more than doubtful. Nazareth was some thirty miles from Capernaum. The time to be allowed for the outgoing of the news and the incoming of the friends could not be less than two days; but the whole episode occupies but a fragment of that interval. The friends, if domiciled at

Nazareth, must have been in the immediate neighbourhood of Capernaum, when the rumour spread abroad: He has Beelzebul.

APPENDIX O

Did Jesus practise Accommodation? P. 189.

Accommodation as a therapeutic method is legitimate within certain limits, but was not practised by our Lord, even in the case of the Gerasene demoniac. Accommodation, as an ethical procedure, is altogether a different matter. Spinoza, in his *Tractatus Theologico-politicus*,[1] held that while Jesus perceived things, immediately, adequately, and truly, He yet "accommodated himself to the vulgar." So then, while He knew the truth, He did not choose to communicate it to "the vulgar." That is a charge which must go to proof.

1. It has been shown that Christ had no sympathy with the current doctrine of demons; as far as that had reference to their origin, numbers, forms, haunts, times of activity, powers, restrictions, management and redeeming features. He announced those principles which led to the rejection of these superstitions. He perceived things, immediately, adequately, and truly; and did not withhold His knowledge from "the vulgar." The mere suggestion of accommodation is here manifestly out of place.

2. It has likewise been shown that Christ had neither part nor lot in the current practices of exorcism. He never employed the common fumigations or magic formulæ. He offered no spectacular demonstration of His success in the treatment of the possessed. He held aloof from these absurdities; because He perceived things, immediately, adequately, and truly. He frankly imparted His secret to others: If I cast out demons in

[1] See "Divine Law."

the Spirit of God, then the kingdom of God has come upon you. Again therefore the suggestion of accommodation is untenable.

3. Jesus had no interest whatever in the practice of accommodation. He had no failures to hide from men. His success was as invariable as it was indisputable. He had no desire to magnify the miraculous element in His ministry, and fled repeatedly from an embarrassing popularity. The notoriety of the thaumaturge was clearly abhorrent to Him. This sinister charge of accommodation fails utterly to substantiate itself.

APPENDIX P

Ejection of Demons by Fasting. P. 193.

The textual authority for the retention of "fasting," in Mark ix. 29 (Matt. xvii. 21), is not great. It has served the turn of some persons to discredit the Apostles as guilty of some sort of prior indulgence. But the insinuation is quite unwarranted. Christ was no ascetic. He was defamed as a "glutton and a winebibber." He also defended His disciples against the charge of being lax in the observance of conventional fasts. Abstinence was never regarded by Him as possessed of any occult or dynamic virtue. So the attack on the reputation of the Twelve fails. But the "fasting" has an interest of its own.

1. Was the fasting to be done by the exorcist himself? Among primitive races in America, Africa, and India, fasting holds a recognised place in the curriculum of the sorcerer and the magician, as a means of acquiring superhuman powers through ghostly intercourse. Porphyry, as a Neo-Platonist, lauded the practice. He notes that the theologians ordered those whom they permitted to sacrifice, to abstain from the

victims and to purify themselves by fasting and abstinence from animals. Purity thus secured its possessor against the attacks and allurements of demons. It also secured the aid of friendly spirits, who indicated, through dreams and symbols and omens, what might come to pass and what might be avoided.[1] Among the various modes of ejecting demons, in the early Church, fasting on the part of the exorcist is not mentioned.

2. Was the fasting to be done by the possessed? In the Testament of Simeon, fasting with the fear of the Lord is prescribed for the conquest of the demon of envy. In the *Clementine Homilies*, abstinence and fasting and the suffering of affliction are advised as most useful for putting demons to flight. For if the demons enter the bodies of men with a view to sharing pleasures, it is clear that they are put to flight by suffering.[2] This would make the fasting a relic of superstition.

3. But the fasting may refer to the treatment of epileptic patients. That requires us to glance briefly at the treatment of epilepsy in the Greek schools of medicine. After an attack, Hippocrates ordered a restricted diet; and this practice was generally followed. Celsus prescribed abstinence from food for three days after a seizure; then a limited and intermittent diet. Aretæus reduced the allowances of epileptics, and required total abstinence from certain kinds of animal food, during convalescence. Cælius Aurelianus also enjoined fasting and the restriction of the dietary. Alexander Trallianus was also severe in this respect. If then this interpolation contemplated those methods of treating epileptic convulsions; in this combination of prayer and fasting, we have the union of means, religious and scientific.

[1] *De Abstinentia*, ii. 44, 53.   [2] IX. X.

APPENDIX Q

The popular Treatment of Epilepsy. P. 193.

The Jews employed fumigations and adjurations; also probate amulets, and bats (שרין העוף).[1] The demon had to be disgusted or terrorised. Pliny has preserved (*H. N. passim*) some popular Roman recipes which are samples of others elsewhere. Among these are several which, for sheer repulsiveness, will not bear transcription. He mentions goat's flesh grilled on a funeral pyre; goat's suet and bull's gall, boiled in equal proportions; the heart of a black ass with bread, on the first or second day of the moon; the flesh or blood of an ass, with vinegar, for forty days; the brain of an ass smoked with burning leaves, in hydromel; the hoofs of an ass, reduced to ashes, for a month; the flesh of a sucking puppy; the ashes or slough of a spotted lizard, or the animal itself; the flesh of a green lizard; the brain of a weasel. Aretaeus mentions the vulgar use of the brain of a vulture: the raw heart of the cormorant or of the domestic weasel (cat?); the blood of a gladiator; the human liver.

APPENDIX R

Witchcraft. P. 234.

The devil of the Middle Ages, while possessing a residuum of horror and repulsiveness, was mostly an object of laughter and contempt. He did not appear in witchcraft till the eight and ninth centuries. At a later date, persons were tried on this charge; but few suffered at the stake. In the tenth century, the devil began to be taken more seriously. The Seer of Patmos had spoken of the fulfilment of "the thousand years," to be followed by the loosing of Satan "for a little season" (Rev. xx. 3). The pulpits of Europe now began to resound with the announcement that the time was at hand. There were many things which apparently warranted such an expectation. Widespread calamities had engendered a deep depression among the people. Dark superstitions had invaded the Church. Gross profligacy prevailed in the highest religious circles. The infamous Theodora and her two notorious daughters constituted "the pornocracy" so called. To disasters, physical, political, moral, and religious, were added the portents of eclipses and comets. A reign of terror was inaugurated, wherein Satanic and demonic superstitions paralysed the energies of nations. The once silly devil had become the formidable enemy of mankind. The very figure of Christ, as the Good Shepherd, retreats before this king of terrors. According to Didron,[1] "Christ appears more and more melancholy, and often truly terrible. It is indeed the *rex tremendæ majestatis* of the *dies iræ*." The dread thus reflected in the realm of art, affected also the sphere of law. Satan was said to have smitten Job with boils, to have been the prince of the power of the air, and to be capable of transforming himself into an angel of light. What more probable than that his confederates, the witches, should smite with pestilence, transport themselves through the air, and work Satanic miracles? The witches were therefore the enemies of the human race, the victims of popular fury, and the objects of new legislation. Devil-possession was thus of more consequence than demon-possession.

The thousand years had concluded and the world still stood. But the expectation of the end of the age revived in the earlier part of the fourteenth century. The terror of the period increased from various causes. Constantinople fell before the Turks in 1453. The bull of Innocent VIII. (Summis desiderantes, 1484) intensified the superstition of witchcraft. Three years

[1] Lecky, *Rise and Influence of Rationalism*, p. 56.

later, Jakob Sprenger published his *Malleus Maleficarum*; settling the form of procedure against witches. Society was increasingly impressed by the ubiquity of the powers of evil. In the interval between the thirteenth and the sixteenth centuries, the epidemic insanities of the Flagellants and the Dancers had broken out. The mental balance of Europe was almost overthrown. The death-roll of the witches waxed amazingly. For them no tortures were too severe, no sympathy too scant. The Reformation made little difference in those practices which claimed the sanction of Scripture. Luther believed in the devil possessing the blind, the dumb, the deformed. "The devil has firebrands, bullets, torches, spears, and swords, with which he shoots, darts, and pierces, when God permits. Therefore, let no man doubt when a fire breaks out which consumes a village or a house, that a little devil is sitting there, blowing the fire to make it greater." Calvin was far from accepting such a view of the matter; but, when remodelling the constitution of Geneva, he left the laws relating to witchcraft untouched. James VI. and I., our British Solomon, deemed himself a *persona ingratissima* to the devil; and wrote his *Demonologie*, in three volumes. Returning from Norway with his bride in 1590, he encountered a storm which he believed the Scotch and Scandinavian witches had brewed for him. The atrocious tortures applied to Dr. Fian, as arch-conspirator, are frightfully significant of the age.

Apart from those who were the victims of malice and injustice, those who suffered for witchcraft were mostly insane. The majority were women. Many of them suffered from melancholy with its hallucinations, self-accusations, and religious fancies. Not a few suffered also from lycanthropy, and infested the country as dangerous lunatics. In the nocturnal revels of these insane creatures, the primitive cult of the devil-worshipper and the lycanthrope is evident; recalling the classical Bacchanalia and the Lupercalia. Their stews of infants' flesh, toads, frogs, etc., are survivals of ancient "hell-broths." The crimes alleged against these unfortunates were not new to history; but were punished under a novel guise. The last execution of witches in England took place in 1712; the last in Scotland, in 1722; the last in Switzerland, in 1782. It has been reckoned that in the interval elapsing between the bull of Innocent VIII. and the cessation of those prosecutions, NINE MILLIONS PERISHED.

These horrors determined a reaction against the theory of witchcraft, which is essentially pagan. John Wier, a Protestant physician, uttered the first clear note of dissent in his *De Præstigiis Dæmonum*, in 1563. He asserted that all witches were under the delusion of the devil; but had made no godless compact with him. Thomas Hobbes attacked the current superstition in his *Leviathan*, in 1651. Reginald Scot learnedly refuted the prevalent delusion, in his *Discovery of Witchcraft*, in 1657. Balthasar Bekker denied the reality of sorcery, magic, and devil-possession; even the existence of the devil, in his *Die betoverde Wereld*, in 1691. Christian Thomasius announced that the doctrine of the devil was not essential to Christianity, in 1707. Dr. Mead, one of the royal physicians, expressed the opinion that the demoniacs of the New Testament were lunatics, in his *Medica Sacra*, in 1749. A similar view was held by Lardner, *On the case of the Demoniacs*, in 1758: also by Semler, in his *Commentatio de Demoniacis*, in 1760; and by Farmer, in his *Essay on the Demons of the New Testament*, in 1775. On the other side, were writers not less learned, but more conservative; such as Jean Bodin, who answered Wier, in his *Demonomanie des Sorciers*, in 1581; and Joseph Glanvil, who combated the rising scepticism, in his *Sadducismus Triumphatus*, in 1681. By this time the witch-burning mania had well-nigh spent itself.

These writers neither destroyed nor established the authority of the Scriptures. They busied themselves with erroneous interpretations of the same. Witchcraft was not the legitimate outcome of the teachings of the Bible; but an excrescence upon it, claiming its sanction. *The whole movement was at bottom an acute paganising of Christianity, under auspices nominally Christian. The doctrines and practices of witchcraft, even part of the legislation against it, were pre-Christian. These facts dispose of the adverse comments of Huxley, in this regard.*[1]

[1] "Agnosticism," *Nineteenth Century*, Feb. 1889.

INDEX

ABRAHAM as a magician, 57.
Accommodation, 204 f., 277 f.
Ahriman. *See* Angro-Mainyu.
Akom-mano, 25.
Angro-Mainyu, 24 f., 41.
Apollonius as exorcist, 144.
Ashmedai. *See* Asmodaeus.
Asmodaeus, 24 f., 37 ff., 92, 126.
Azi-Dahaka, 25.

BAALZEBUB, a fly-god, 179 f.
Baaras, the mandrake, 127.
Bacchanalia, 282.
Barnabas, Epistle of, 219.
Baruch, Book of, 22.
Beelzebul controversy, the, 11, 174 ff.; its sequel, 190 ff.
Bel-Ea, 182 f.
Bel-Mul-lil, 182 f.
Bene-Elohim, the, 22, 42, 274.
Bidding Prayer, the, 231 f.

CAPERNAUM as focus of the Diaspora, 104.
Christ and common demonology, 50 ff.
Christ and common magic, 57 ff.
Christ's freedom from superstition, cause of, 59 f.
Christ's treatment of the possessed, 137.
Cingalese, the, 19.
Clairvoyance, 151 f.
Classification of the possessed, 157 ff.; results of, 163 ff.
Cockcrow and the demons, 46, 55.

Confession of Jesus as Messiah, significance of the, 151 ff.
Convulsionnaires, the, 236 f.
Criterion of genuine possession, 150.
Cro-Magnon race, the, 42.
Cross, sign of the, 229, 234.
Cutha, legend of, 14.

DANCING manias, the, 235 f., 282.
David's feigned dementia, 108.
Decapolis, 103 f., 120.
Degraded gods as demons, 17 f.
Demetrian, Epistle to, 229.
Demoniac of Capernaum, the, 64 ff., 122.
Demoniac of Gerasa, the, 69 ff., 123; scene of the healing of, 194 ff.
Demoniac, the blind and dumb, 89 f., 162, 174 f., 253 ff.; scene of the healing of, 276 f.
Demoniac, the dumb, 88 f., 162, 174 f., 253 ff.
Demoniacs of China, the, 243 ff.
Demoniacs, strength of, 75, 161 f.
Demoniac state, significance of the, 86.
Demonic inspiration, 156.
Demonising of heathen gods, 17 ff., 272 ff.
Demonolaters of India, 237 f.
Demonology of the Old Testament, 13 ff.; of the Septuagint, 21 f.; of the Apocryphal and Apocalyptic Books, 22 ff.; Rabbinic, 25 ff.; Ethnic, 40 ff.; Greek, 259 ff.

Demonomania of South-Eastern Europe, the, 234 f.
Demons, Rabbinic, their origin, numbers, forms, haunts, times of activity, powers, restrictions, management, redeeming features, 25 ff.; ethnic parallels, 40 ff.; attitude of Christ to, 51 ff.
Dervishes of Algiers, the, 240 ff.
Devil, use of the term, in the New Testament, 251.
Diagnosis, data of a, 61 f.; uses of a, 62.
Didache, the, 216 f.
Dilemma, the, possession real or unreal, 8.
Diognetus, Epistle to, 220 f.
Donatus, Epistle to, 135.
Double consciousness, 74 f.
Druj Nasu, the, 44, 48.

Ea, 132, 182 f.
Earring, 128.
Eleazar, the magician, 126, 128, 144.
Enoch, Book of, 23, 42.
Enoch, Book of the Secrets of, 42.
Environment peculiar in the time of Christ, 248 f.
Ephesian demoniac, the, 99 ff., 161 f.
Ephesian Letters, the, 133.
Ephesian narrative, fact-basis of the, 255 f.
Epilepsy not possession, 62 f.; popular treatment of, 280.
Epileptic idiot, the, 81 ff., 123, 158 f.
Evil and *unclean*, significance of the terms, 121 ff.

Failure of the Nine, 191 ff.
Fairy hosts, the, 14.
Fallacies, 269 f.
Fasting and ejection of demons, 278 f.
Flagellants, the, 282.
Fly-gods of the ancients, 179 f.
Folie à deux, 197 f.
Freudenschmerz, 79.

Genuine demonic possession, 147 ff.; criterion of, 150; antecedents of, 165 ff.; limits of, 171 ff.; local and temporary, 247.
Gerasene affair, the, 11; difficulties of, 194 ff.; scene of, 194 ff.; number of the demonised, 197 f.; alleged transmigration of the demons, 199 f.; data for a reconstruction, 200 ff.; stampede of the herd, 207 ff.; loss of the swine-owners, 213 f.; worth of some criticisms, 214 f.

Heilprin on the natatorial powers of swine, 214.
Hell, the sign from, 189; routes to, 201.
Hell-broths, 130, 283.
Hermas, Shepherd of, 217 f.
Hezekiah as a magician, 57.
Historicity of the Gospel narratives, 148 ff.
Huxley-Gladstone controversy, the, 11, 196 f.
Hypnotism, 173, 242 f.

Idiot boy, the. *See* Epileptic idiot.
Ignatius, Epistles of, 219 f.
Incarnation, the, and possession, 249.
Infirm woman, the, 92 ff.

Jesus nicknamed Beelzebul, 275 f.
Jesus out of His senses, 274 f.
Jews compared, with Greeks and Romans, 115 ff.; with the peoples of the British Isles, 117 ff.
Jinn, the, 15 f., 19, 43, 49.
Jubilees, Book of, 23.
Judith, Book of, 217.
Jumpers, the, 236.

Khonsu, the demon-driver, 134.

Legion, 76.
Lilin, the, 25 f., 44.
Lilith, 15, 16 f., 26 f., 44, 55.

Lord, of dung, 181; of the dwelling, 181 ff.
Luke's mannerisms, 201, 254 f., 259.
Lupercalia, the, 282.
Lycanthropes, 110 f., 115, 282.
Lycanthropy. 110 f., 115, 282.

MAGIC, black and white, 58.
Mandrake, the, 126 f.
Mary Magdalene, 90 ff., 162.
Mazziqin, the, 25.
Medicine, Greek, 129, 265 ff.
Mental health of the Hebrews, 108 ff.
Mental temperament of the Hebrews, 106 ff.
Messianic hope, the, 154 ff.
Milesian Letters, the, 133.
Moor-cock, the, 39.
Moral therapeutics, 112 ff.

NAGGAR-TURA. See Moor-cock.
Naturalness of the ethnic theory of possession, 120 ff.; of the terms "evil" and "unclean," 121 ff.
Nebuchadnezzar's lycanthropy, 110 f.
Nomenclature of the New Testament, 251 ff.
Nose-ring, the, 128.
Number of the possessed, 103 ff., 119.

OPIUM-EATERS of Bombay, 79.
Oracles, 46, 96 f., 248.

PARABLE of the last state, the, 189 f.
Passing of Pan, the, 47.
Patriarchs, Testament of the Twelve, 23, 279.
Polycarp, Epistle of, 220.
Popular language, use of, by Jesus, 271 f.
Population of Palestine, 105 f.
Possession, in sub-apostolic times, 216 ff.; in ante-Nicene and post-Nicene times, 221 ff.; in mediæval and modern times, 233 ff.; manifold, 203 f.; medical aspects of, 61 ff.; of animals, 202, 225, 227.
Power on the head, 274.
Proofs of expulsions of demons, 144 ff.
Prophetic art, the, 96 ff.
Psychological explanations of Strauss, Renan, Keim, and Matthew Arnold, 138 ff.
Pythoness of Delphi, the, 97, 115; of Philippi, 96 ff., 159.

RABBINIC literature, 256 f.
Rabbis, the, as miracle-workers, 58 f.
Rameses XII. and Konsu, 134.
Raphael and Asmodæus, 25.
Recipes for seeing demons, 26, 41.
Responsibility of the possessed, 124 f.
Ruchin and Ruchoth, 25.

SARAH and Asmodæus, 24, 126.
Satan casting out Satan, 132, 177, 185 f.
Satan-possession, 178, 251.
Satan-Sammael, 25.
Scarab-beetle, the, 179.
Sea-fight of Tarichæa, the, 213.
Seirim, the, 15, 16, 25.
Sennacherib, 105.
Septuagint, the, 21.
Seventy, the mission of the, 113 f., 256 ff.
Seventy, the, versus the Twelve, 258 f.
Shadow-figures, 13 ff.
Shakers, the, 236.
Shamir, 37 ff.
Shedim, the, 18, 25.
Shidu, 18.
Sibylline Oracles, 22.
Solomon as a magician, 37 ff., 57, 126.
Sorcery, 58 f.
Southern Semites, the, 15.
Success of Jesus, the, testimonies to, 268 f.
Suicide, 107 f., 117.
Syro-Phœnician girl, the, 86 ff., 162.

TARANTISM, 235.
Teraphim, 14, 51.
Theurgy, 58.
Thot, 131, 179.
Tigretier, 236.
Tobit, Book of, 24, 52, 126, 220.
Trade, Oriental, of the Roman Empire, 104.
Transmigration of demons, alleged, 199 f., 202.
Treatment of the insane by Greek physicians, 266 ff.
Treatment of the possessed among the Hebrews, coaxing, disgusting, and terrorising, 125 ff.; ethnic parallels to, 129 ff., 136 f.; in ante-Nicene and post-Nicene times, 221.
Treatment of the possessed by Christ, 137 ff.

UR (Mugheir), 14.

VAMPIRE, the, 17.
Ventriloquists, 161.
Vespasian, 126, 144.

WERE-WOLF, the, 42, 111.
Witchcraft, 280 ff.; death-roll of, 283; reaction against, 283.

INDEX OF NAMES

Ælian, 15.
Æschylus, 266.
Alexander Trallianus, 63, 268, 279.
Ammonius Saccas, 226, 265.
Apollonius, 144.
Apuleius, 130.
Aretæus, 63, 267, 279, 280.
Aristophanes, 161, 266.
Aristotle, 115, 252, 263.
Arnold, M., 141 ff.
Asclepiades, 267.
Athenagoras, 228.
Augustine, 197.
Augustus, 105.

Barnabas, 219.
Baudissin, 14, 180.
Baur, 113.
Bekker, 283.
Berosus, 14.
Beyschlag, 272.
Bleek, 141, 181, 198, 207, 271.
Bodin, 283.
Braun, 8.
Brecher, 130.
Browning, 110.
Bruce, 4, 62, 154, 269 f.

Cælius Aurelianus, 204, 267.
Caldwell, 237.
Calvin, 197, 282.
Celsus, C. A., 83, 116, 267, 279.
Celsus, 91.
Censorinus, 267.
Cheyne, 51.
Chrysippus, 260, 264.

Chrysostom, 197, 230, 231.
Cicero, 248.
Clement of Alexandria, 99, 13 180.
Clement of Rome, 217.
Coke, 85.
Conybeare, 8, 219.
Cornelius, 233.
Cyprian, 135, 228, 229.
Cyril, 229, 233.

D'Alviella, 202.
Darmesteter, 24.
Delitzsch, 8, 169.
Democritus, 266, 267.
Didron, 281.
Dieringer, 168.
Dods, 272.

Ebrard, 198.
Edersheim, 8, 202.
Empedocles, 260, 261.
Epictetus, 264.
Epicureans, 264.
Esquirol, 122, 246.
Euripides, 98, 115, 266, 274.
Eusebius, 233, 269.
Eustathius, 133.
Everling, 273, 274.
Ewald, 8, 80, 207.

Farmer, 8, 283.
Farrar, 3, 77, 202, 207.
Fritzsche, 24, 181.
Fuller, 24.

Galen, 63, 94, 161, 268.

Gaster, 51.
Geikie, 8.
Gesenius, 181, 280.
Gfrörer, 8, 113.
Glanvil, 283.
Gore, 8.
Gould, 7.
Gregory of Nazianzen. 179.
Gregory the Great, 233.

HAHN, 257.
Hase, 141.
Heilprin, 214.
Hellwald, 243.
Hermas, 217 ff.
Herodotus, 79, 115, 256, 266.
Hesiod, 49, 260, 262.
Hesychius, 133.
Hilarion, 166.
Hilgenfeld, 181.
Hippocrates, 94, 116, 266, 274, 279.
Hippolytus, 229.
Hitzig, 181.
Hobart, 63, 94.
Hobbes, 283.
Holtzmann, 65, 141, 198.
Homer, 133, 260.
Horace, 116.
Hort, 195.
Huxley, 194, 214, 284.

IAMBLICHUS, 265.
Ignatius, 219 f.
Innocent VIII., 281.
Irenæus, 228.

JAHN, 181.
James VI., 282.
Jerome, 166, 178, 195, 202, 230.
Josephus, 27, 52, 101, 105 ff., 110, 120, 126 ff., 144, 155, 213, 258, 266.
Justin Martyr, 101, 126, 131, 221, 228.

KEIM, 20, 65, 140 f., 195, 199, 253, 265.
Kohut, 25, 51.

LACHMANN, 195.

Lactantius, 228 f.
Laertes, 261.
Lagarde, 91.
Lange, 80, 151 f., 207.
Lardner, 8, 283.
Lecky, 260, 281.
Lee, 236.
Lenormant, 51, 58, 134, 180.
Lightfoot, 32, 91, 166, 181.
Lucian, 63, 97, 102, 128, 133.
Luther, 282.
Lutteroth, 208.

MAHAFFY, 134.
Marcus Aurelius, 264.
Martin of Tours. 230.
Maspéro, 17, 111, 179.
Mead, 8, 283.
Melampus, 267.
Meyer, 2 f., 20, 93, 99, 113, 181, 209, 276.
Michaelis, 181.
Minucius Felix, 222 f., 228.
Moll, 243.

NEANDER, 8, 141.
Neo-Platonists, 47, 226, 264.
Nevius, 145, 243 ff.

OLSHAUSEN, 78 f., 80, 125, 167 f.
Origen, 131, 195, 202, 226 ff., 229, 232 f.
Orpheus, 179.

PAPIAS, 221.
Paulus, 141, 181, 207.
Philo, 40.
Philostratus, 144, 179.
Plato, 13, 98 f., 115, 222, 260, 262 f., 266.
Plautus, 116, 160.
Pliny, 116 f., 127 f., 130, 180, 258, 280.
Plotinus, 265.
Plummer, 8.
Plutarch, 47, 115, 133, 160, 248, 261, 263 ff.
Polycarp, 220.
Porphyry, 265, 278.
Pressensé, 8, 163.
Proclus, 265.

Index of Names

Ptolemy Philadelphus, 21.
Pythagoras, 214, 261.

QUADRATUS, 269.

RAMSAY, 256.
Rashi, 34, 57.
Renan, 92, 112, 139 f.
Rosenmüller, 208.
Row, 8.

SANDAY, 8.
Sayce, 17, 51, 92.
Schenkel, 141.
Schleiermacher, 141.
Schorr, 51.
Schürer, 52, 258.
Schwartzkopff, 8.
Scot, R., 283.
Scott, Sir W., 77.
Semler, 283.
Seneca, 264.
Serenus Samonicus, 130.
Shakespeare, 127, 130.
Smith, G. A., 257.
Smith, W. R., 16.
Socrates, 222, 224, 261.
Sophocles, 115, 266.
Spencer, 40 f., 75, 269.
Spinoza, 277.
Sprenger, 282.
Stagirius, 230.
Steinmeyer, 8, 163.
Stoics, 48, 263 f.
Strauss, 113, 138 ff., 199, 214, 253.
Suetonius, 155.
Sulpitius Severus, 230.

TACITUS, 155.
Tertullian, 224 ff.
Thales, 261.
Theocritus, 22.
Theophylact, 271.
Thomasius, 283.
Thomson, 195.
Thucydides, 248.
Tischendorf, 195.
Tregelles, 195.
Trench, 8, 80, 95, 125, 169 f.
Tristram, 240.
Tylor, 129.

VIRGIL, 99.
Volkmar, 181, 207.

WAGNER, 84.
Weiss, 63, 170 f., 198, 209.
Weizsäcker, 141.
Wendt, 6 f.
Wesley, 236.
Westcott, 195.
Wetstein, 8, 213.
Wette, De, 113, 141, 181, 253, 271.
Whitehouse, 8.
Wier, 283.
Williams, 236.
Wilson, Sir C. W., 196.
Windischmann, 24.
Winer, 141, 271.
Woolston, 214.

XENOCRATES, 260.
Xenophon, 274.

ZOROASTER, 25, 49, 265.

PUBLICATIONS OF
T. & T. CLARK,
38 GEORGE STREET, EDINBURGH.
LONDON: SIMPKIN, MARSHALL, HAMILTON, KENT, & CO. LIMITED

Abbott (T. K., B.D., D.Lit.)—EPHESIANS AND COLOSSIANS. (*International Critical Commentary.*) Post 8vo, 10s. 6d.

Adam (J., D.D.)—AN EXPOSITION OF THE EPISTLE OF JAMES. 8vo, 9s.

Adamson (Rev. T., D.D.)—STUDIES OF THE MIND IN CHRIST. Post 8vo, 4s. 6d.

——— THE SPIRIT OF POWER. Second Edition, fcap. 8vo, 1s.

Ahlfeld (Dr.), etc.—THE VOICE FROM THE CROSS. Cr. 8vo, price 7s. 6d.

Alcock (Deborah)—THE SEVEN CHURCHES OF ASIA. 1s.

Alexander (Prof. W. Lindsay)—BIBLICAL THEOLOGY. Two vols. 8vo, 21s.

Allen (Prof. A. V. G., D.D.)—CHRISTIAN INSTITUTIONS. (*International Theological Library.*) Post 8vo, 12s.

Ancient Faith in Modern Light, The. 8vo, 10s. 6d.

Andrews (S. J.)—THE LIFE OF OUR LORD. Large post 8vo, 9s.

Ante-Nicene Christian Library—A COLLECTION OF ALL THE WORKS OF THE FATHERS OF THE CHRISTIAN CHURCH PRIOR TO THE COUNCIL OF NICÆA. Twenty-four vols. 8vo. Subscription price £6, 6s. Selection of Four Volumes at Subscription price of 21s. *All the Early Works containing MSS.* Usoma's.

Augustine's Works—Edited by MARCUS DODS, D.D. Fifteen vols. 8vo, Subscription price, £3, 19s. net. Selection of Four Volumes at Subscription price of 21s.

Balfour (R. G., D.D.)—CENTRAL TRUTHS AND SIDE ISSUES. Crown 8vo, 3s. 6d.

Ball (W. E., LL.D.)—ST. PAUL AND THE ROMAN LAW. Post 8vo, 4s. 6d.

Ballard (Frank, M.A., B.Sc.)—THE MIRACLES OF UNBELIEF. Third Edition. Post 8vo, 6s.

Bannerman (Prof.)—THE CHURCH OF CHRIST. Two vols. 8vo, 21s.

Bannerman (D. D., D.D.)—THE DOCTRINE OF THE CHURCH. 8vo, 12s.

Bartlet (Prof. J. Vernon, M.A.)—THE APOSTOLIC AGE: ITS LIFE, DOCTRINE, WORSHIP, AND POLITY. (*Eras of Church History.*) Crown 8vo, 6s.

Baumgarten (Professor)—APOSTOLIC HISTORY. Three vols. 8vo, 27s.

Bayne (P., LL.D.)—THE FREE CHURCH OF SCOTLAND. Post 8vo, 3s. 6d.

Beck (Dr.)—OUTLINES OF BIBLICAL PSYCHOLOGY. Crown 8vo, 4s.

——— PASTORAL THEOLOGY OF THE NEW TESTAMENT. Crown 8vo, 6s.

Bengel—GNOMON OF THE NEW TESTAMENT. With Original Notes, Explanatory and Illustrative. Five vols. 8vo, Subscription price, 31s. 6d. *Cheaper Edition,* the five volumes bound in three, 24s.

Besser's CHRIST THE LIFE OF THE WORLD. Price 6s.

Beyschlag (W., D.D.)—NEW TESTAMENT THEOLOGY. Two vols. demy 8vo, Second Edition. 18s. net.

Bible Dictionary. Edited by JAS. HASTINGS, D.D. *Special Prospectus on application.* In Four Volumes. (Vols. I., II., and III. now ready.

*** *Detailed Catalogue free on application.*

Bible-Class Handbooks. Crown 8vo. Forty-four Volumes, 1s. 3d. to 3s. each. Edited by Prof. MARCUS DODS, D.D., and ALEX. WHYTE, D.D. *Detailed List free on application.*

Bible-Class Primers. Thirty-nine now issued in the Series. Edited by Princ. S. D. F. SALMOND, D.D. Paper covers, 6d. each: free by post, 7d. In cloth, 8d.; free by post, 9d. *Detailed List free on application.*

Bigg (Prof. C., D.D.)—ST. PETER AND ST. JUDE. (*International Critical Commentary.*) Post 8vo, 10s. 6d.

Blaikie (Prof. W. G., D.D.)—THE PREACHERS OF SCOTLAND FROM THE 6TH TO THE 19TH CENTURY. Post 8vo, 7s. 6d.

Blake (Buchanan, B.D.)—HOW TO READ THE PROPHETS. Part I.—The Pre-Exilian Minor Prophets (with Joel). Second Edition, 4s. Part II.—Isaiah (ch. i.-xxxix.). Second Edition, 2s. 6d. Part III.—Jeremiah, 4s. Part IV.—Ezekiel, 4s. Part V.—Isaiah (ch. xl.-lxvi.), and the Post-Exilian Prophets. *The Series being now complete, Messrs. Clark offer the Set of Five Volumes for 15s.*

Bleek's INTRODUCTION TO THE NEW TESTAMENT. Two vols. 8vo, 21s.

Briggs (Prof. C. A., D.D.)—GENERAL INTRODUCTION TO THE STUDY OF HOLY SCRIPTURE (*Replacing the Author's 'Biblical Study,' entirely re-written and greatly enlarged*). 8vo, 12s. net.

—— THE MESSIAH OF THE APOSTLES. Post 8vo, 7s. 6d.

—— THE MESSIAH OF THE GOSPELS. Post 8vo, 6s. 6d.

—— THE BIBLE, THE CHURCH, AND THE REASON. Post 8vo, 6s. 6d.

Brockelmann (C.)—LEXICON SYRIACUM. With a Preface by Professor T. NÖLDEKE. Crown 4to, 30s. net.

Bruce (Prof. A. B., D.D.)—THE TRAINING OF THE TWELVE; exhibiting the Twelve Disciples under Discipline for the Apostleship. Fifth Edition, 8vo, 10s. 6d.

—— THE HUMILIATION OF CHRIST. 4th Ed., 8vo, 10s. 6d.

—— THE KINGDOM OF GOD; or, Christ's Teaching according to the Synoptical Gospels. New Edition, post 8vo, 7s. 6d.

—— APOLOGETICS; OR, CHRISTIANITY DEFENSIVELY STATED. (*International Theological Library.*) Third Edition, post 8vo, 10s. 6d.

—— ST. PAUL'S CONCEPTION OF CHRISTIANITY. Post 8vo, 7s. 6d.

—— THE EPISTLE TO THE HEBREWS: The First Apology for Christianity. Second Edition, post 8vo, 7s. 6d.

Bruce (W. S., D.D.)—THE ETHICS OF THE OLD TESTAMENT. Cr. 8vo, 4s.

Buchanan (Professor)—THE DOCTRINE OF JUSTIFICATION. 8vo, 10s. 6d.

—— ON COMFORT IN AFFLICTION. Crown 8vo, 2s. 6d.

—— ON IMPROVEMENT OF AFFLICTION. Crown 8vo, 2s. 6d.

Buhl (Prof. F.)—CANON AND TEXT OF THE OLD TESTAMENT. 8vo, 7s. 6d.

Bungener (Felix)—ROME AND THE COUNCIL IN 19TH CENTURY. Cr. 8vo, 5s.

Burton (Prof. E.)—SYNTAX OF THE MOODS AND TENSES IN NEW TESTAMENT GREEK. Post 8vo, 5s. 6d. net.

Calvin's INSTITUTES OF CHRISTIAN RELIGION. (Translation.) 2 vols. 8vo, 14s.

—— COMMENTARIES. Forty-five Vols. *Price on application.*

Calvini Institutio Christianæ Religionis. Curavit A. THOLUCK. Two vols. 8vo, Subscription price, 14s.

Candlish (Prof. J. S., D.D.)—THE KINGDOM OF GOD, BIBLICALLY AND HISTORICALLY CONSIDERED. 8vo, 10s. 6d.

Candlish (Prof. J. S., D.D.)—THE CHRISTIAN SALVATION. Lectures on the Work of Christ. 8vo, 7s. 6d.

Caspari (C. E.)—A CHRONOLOGICAL AND GEOGRAPHICAL INTRODUCTION TO THE LIFE OF CHRIST. 8vo, 7s. 6d.

Caspers (A.)—THE FOOTSTEPS OF CHRIST. Crown 8vo, 7s. 6d.

Cassel (Prof.)—COMMENTARY ON ESTHER. 8vo, 10s. 6d.

Cave (Principal A., D.D.)—THE SCRIPTURAL DOCTRINE OF SACRIFICE AND ATONEMENT. Second Edition, 8vo, 10s. 6d.

——— AN INTRODUCTION TO THEOLOGY. Second Edition, 8vo, 12s.

Chapman (Principal C., LL.D.)—PRE-ORGANIC EVOLUTION AND THE BIBLICAL IDEA OF GOD. Crown 8vo, 6s.

Christlieb (Prof. T., D.D.)—MODERN DOUBT AND CHRISTIAN BELIEF. 8vo, 10s. 6d.

——— HOMILETIC: Lectures on Preaching. 7s. 6d.

Clark (Professor W. R., LL.D., D.C.L.)—THE ANGLICAN REFORMATION. (*Eras of Church History.*) 6s.

——— THE PARACLETE. The Person and Work of the Holy Spirit. Crown 8vo, 3s. 6d.

——— WITNESSES TO CHRIST. A Contribution to Christian Apologetics. Crown 8vo, 4s.

Clarke (Professor W. N., D.D)—AN OUTLINE OF CHRISTIAN THEOLOGY. Ninth Edition, post 8vo, 7s. 6d.

——— WHAT SHALL WE THINK OF CHRISTIANITY? Cr. 8vo, 2s. 6d.

——— CAN I BELIEVE IN GOD THE FATHER? Crown 8vo, 3s.

Concordance to the Greek Testament—MOULTON (W. F., D.D.) and GEDEN (A. S., M.A.). Second Edition, crown 4to, 26s. net.

Crawford (J. H., M.A.)—THE BROTHERHOOD OF MANKIND. Crown 8vo, 5s.

Cremer (Professor)—BIBLICO-THEOLOGICAL LEXICON OF NEW TESTAMENT GREEK. Third Edition, with Supplement, demy 4to, 38s.

Crippen (Rev. T. G.)—A POPULAR INTRODUCTION TO THE HISTORY OF CHRISTIAN DOCTRINE. 8vo, 9s.

Cunningham (Principal)—HISTORICAL THEOLOGY. Two vols. 8vo, 21s.

Curtiss (Dr. S. I.)—THE LEVITICAL PRIESTS. Crown 8vo, 5s.

——— FRANZ DELITZSCH: A Memorial Tribute. *Portrait.* Cr. 8vo, 3s.

Dabney (Prof. R. L., D.D.)—THE SENSUALISTIC PHILOSOPHY OF THE NINETEENTH CENTURY CONSIDERED. Crown 8vo, 6s.

Dahle (Bishop)—LIFE AFTER DEATH. Demy 8vo, 10s. 6d.

Dalman (Prof. G.)—THE WORDS OF JESUS.

Davidson (Prof. A.B., D.D., LL.D.)—AN INTRODUCTORY HEBREW GRAMMAR. With Progressive Exercises in Reading and Writing. 17th Edition, 8vo, 7s. 6d.

——— A SYNTAX OF THE HEBREW LANGUAGE. 2nd Ed., 8vo, 7s. 6d.

Davidson, Dr. Samuel. Autobiography and Diary. Edited by his DAUGHTER. 8vo, 7s. 6d.

Davies (Principal D. C.)—THE ATONEMENT AND INTERCESSION OF CHRIST. Crown 8vo, 4s.

Deane (Wm., M.A.)—PSEUDEPIGRAPHA: An Account of Certain Apocryphal Writings of the Jews and Early Christians. Post 8vo, 7s. 6d.

Deissmann (Dr. G. A.)—BIBLE STUDIES. 8vo, 9s.

Delitzsch (Prof.)—SYSTEM OF BIBLICAL PSYCHOLOGY, 8vo, 12s.; NEW COMMENTARY ON GENESIS, 2 vols. 8vo, 21s.; PSALMS, 3 vols., 31s. 6d.; PROVERBS, 2 vols., 21s.; SONG OF SOLOMON AND ECCLESIASTES, 10s. 6d.; ISAIAH, Fourth Edition, rewritten, 2 vols., 21s.; HEBREWS, 2 vols., 21s.

⁎ Any Four Volumes may be had at original Subscription price of 21s. net.

Dictionary of the Bible, A. (*See page 1.*)

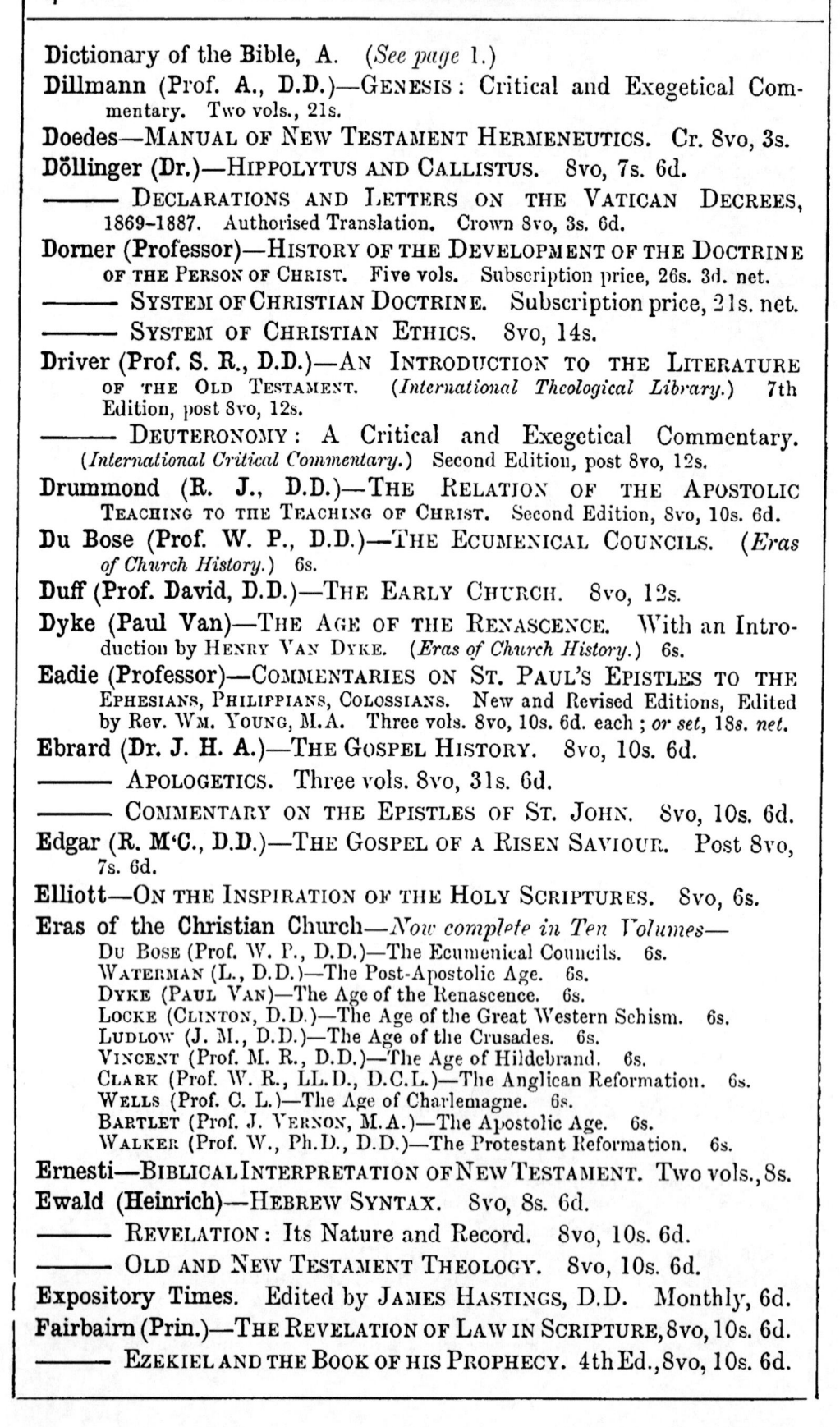

Dillmann (Prof. A., D.D.)—GENESIS: Critical and Exegetical Commentary. Two vols., 21s.

Doedes—MANUAL OF NEW TESTAMENT HERMENEUTICS. Cr. 8vo, 3s.

Döllinger (Dr.)—HIPPOLYTUS AND CALLISTUS. 8vo, 7s. 6d.

—————— DECLARATIONS AND LETTERS ON THE VATICAN DECREES, 1869–1887. Authorised Translation. Crown 8vo, 3s. 6d.

Dorner (Professor)—HISTORY OF THE DEVELOPMENT OF THE DOCTRINE OF THE PERSON OF CHRIST. Five vols. Subscription price, 26s. 3d. net.

—————— SYSTEM OF CHRISTIAN DOCTRINE. Subscription price, 21s. net.

—————— SYSTEM OF CHRISTIAN ETHICS. 8vo, 14s.

Driver (Prof. S. R., D.D.)—AN INTRODUCTION TO THE LITERATURE OF THE OLD TESTAMENT. (*International Theological Library.*) 7th Edition, post 8vo, 12s.

—————— DEUTERONOMY: A Critical and Exegetical Commentary. (*International Critical Commentary.*) Second Edition, post 8vo, 12s.

Drummond (R. J., D.D.)—THE RELATION OF THE APOSTOLIC TEACHING TO THE TEACHING OF CHRIST. Second Edition, 8vo, 10s. 6d.

Du Bose (Prof. W. P., D.D.)—THE ECUMENICAL COUNCILS. (*Eras of Church History.*) 6s.

Duff (Prof. David, D.D.)—THE EARLY CHURCH. 8vo, 12s.

Dyke (Paul Van)—THE AGE OF THE RENASCENCE. With an Introduction by HENRY VAN DYKE. (*Eras of Church History.*) 6s.

Eadie (Professor)—COMMENTARIES ON ST. PAUL'S EPISTLES TO THE EPHESIANS, PHILIPPIANS, COLOSSIANS. New and Revised Editions, Edited by Rev. WM. YOUNG, M.A. Three vols. 8vo, 10s. 6d. each; or set, 18s. net.

Ebrard (Dr. J. H. A.)—THE GOSPEL HISTORY. 8vo, 10s. 6d.

—————— APOLOGETICS. Three vols. 8vo, 31s. 6d.

—————— COMMENTARY ON THE EPISTLES OF ST. JOHN. 8vo, 10s. 6d.

Edgar (R. McC., D.D.)—THE GOSPEL OF A RISEN SAVIOUR. Post 8vo, 7s. 6d.

Elliott—ON THE INSPIRATION OF THE HOLY SCRIPTURES. 8vo, 6s.

Eras of the Christian Church—*Now complete in Ten Volumes*—
    DU BOSE (Prof. W. P., D.D.)—The Ecumenical Councils. 6s.
    WATERMAN (L., D.D.)—The Post-Apostolic Age. 6s.
    DYKE (PAUL VAN)—The Age of the Renascence. 6s.
    LOCKE (CLINTON, D.D.)—The Age of the Great Western Schism. 6s.
    LUDLOW (J. M., D.D.)—The Age of the Crusades. 6s.
    VINCENT (Prof. M. R., D.D.)—The Age of Hildebrand. 6s.
    CLARK (Prof. W. R., LL.D., D.C.L.)—The Anglican Reformation. 6s.
    WELLS (Prof. C. L.)—The Age of Charlemagne. 6s.
    BARTLET (Prof. J. VERNON, M.A.)—The Apostolic Age. 6s.
    WALKER (Prof. W., Ph.D., D.D.)—The Protestant Reformation. 6s.

Ernesti—BIBLICAL INTERPRETATION OF NEW TESTAMENT. Two vols., 8s.

Ewald (Heinrich)—HEBREW SYNTAX. 8vo, 8s. 6d.

—————— REVELATION: Its Nature and Record. 8vo, 10s. 6d.

—————— OLD AND NEW TESTAMENT THEOLOGY. 8vo, 10s. 6d.

Expository Times. Edited by JAMES HASTINGS, D.D. Monthly, 6d.

Fairbairn (Prin.)—THE REVELATION OF LAW IN SCRIPTURE, 8vo, 10s. 6d.

—————— EZEKIEL AND THE BOOK OF HIS PROPHECY. 4th Ed., 8vo, 10s. 6d.

Fairbairn (Prin.)—PROPHECY. Second Edition, 8vo, 10s. 6d.
───── PASTORAL THEOLOGY. Crown 8vo, 6s.
Fairweather (Rev. W., M.A.)—ORIGEN AND GREEK PATRISTIC THEOLOGY. 3s.
Falconer (J. W., B.D.)—FROM APOSTLE TO PRIEST. A Study of Early Church Organisation. Crown 8vo, 4s. 6d.
Fisher (Prof. G. P., D.D., LL.D.)—HISTORY OF CHRISTIAN DOCTRINE. (*International Theological Library.*) Second Edition, post 8vo, 12s.
Forbes (Prof.)—SYMMETRICAL STRUCTURE OF SCRIPTURE. 8vo, 8s. 6d.
───── ANALYTICAL COMMENTARY ON ROMANS. 8vo, 10s. 6d.
───── STUDIES IN THE BOOK OF PSALMS. 8vo, 7s. 6d.
───── THE SERVANT OF THE LORD IN ISAIAH XL.-LXVI. Cr. 8vo, 5s.
Foreign Theological Library—Four Volumes for One Guinea. *Detailed List on application.*
Forrest (D. W., D.D.)—THE CHRIST OF HISTORY AND OF EXPERIENCE. Third Edition, post 8vo, 6s.
Frank (Prof. F. H.)—SYSTEM OF CHRISTIAN CERTAINTY. 8vo, 10s. 6d.
Funcke (Otto)—THE WORLD OF FAITH AND THE EVERYDAY WORLD, As displayed in the Footsteps of Abraham. Post 8vo, 7s. 6d.
Garvie (Alex., B.D.)—THE RITSCHLIAN THEOLOGY. 8vo, 9s.
Gebhardt (H.)—THE DOCTRINE OF THE APOCALYPSE, AND ITS RELATION TO THE DOCTRINE OF THE GOSPEL AND EPISTLES OF JOHN. 8vo, 10s. 6d.
Gerlach—COMMENTARY ON THE PENTATEUCH. 8vo, 10s. 6d.
Gieseler (Dr. J. C. L.)—ECCLESIASTICAL HISTORY. Four vols. 8vo, £2, 2s.
Gifford (Canon)—VOICES OF THE PROPHETS. Crown 8vo, 3s. 6d.
Given (Rev. Prof. J. J.)—THE TRUTH OF SCRIPTURE IN CONNECTION WITH REVELATION, INSPIRATION, AND THE CANON. 8vo, 6s.
Gladden (Washington, D.D., LL.D.) THE CHRISTIAN PASTOR AND THE WORKING CHURCH. (*International Theol. Library.*) Post 8vo, 10s. 6d.
Glasgow (Prof.)—APOCALYPSE TRANSLATED AND EXPOUNDED. 8vo, 10/6.
Gloag (Paton J., D.D.)—THE MESSIANIC PROPHECIES. Cr. 8vo, 7s. 6d.
───── INTRODUCTION TO THE CATHOLIC EPISTLES. 8vo, 10s. 6d.
───── EXEGETICAL STUDIES. Crown 8vo, 5s.
───── INTRODUCTION TO THE SYNOPTIC GOSPELS. 8vo, 7s. 6d.
───── THE PRIMEVAL WORLD. Crown 8vo, 3s.
───── EVENING THOUGHTS. Crown 8vo, 4s.
Godet (Prof. F.)—AN INTRODUCTION TO THE NEW TESTAMENT—
  I. THE EPISTLES OF ST. PAUL. 8vo, 12s. 6d. net.
  II. THE GOSPEL COLLECTION, AND ST. MATTHEW'S GOSPEL. 8vo, 6s. net.
───── COMMENTARY ON ST. LUKE'S GOSPEL. Two vols. 8vo, 21s.
───── COMMENTARY ON ST. JOHN'S GOSPEL. Three vols. 8vo, 31s. 6d.
───── COMMENTARY ON EPISTLE TO THE ROMANS. Two vols. 8vo, 21s.
───── COMMENTARY ON 1ST EPISTLE TO CORINTHIANS. 2 vols. 8vo, 21s.
  ⁎ Any Four Volumes at the original Subscription price of 21s. net.
───── DEFENCE OF THE CHRISTIAN FAITH. Crown 8vo, 4s.
Goebel (Siegfried)—THE PARABLES OF JESUS. 8vo, 10s. 6d.
Gotthold's Emblems; or, INVISIBLE THINGS UNDERSTOOD BY THINGS THAT ARE MADE. Crown 8vo, 5s.

Gould (Prof. E. P., D.D.)—St. Mark. (*International Critical Commentary.*) Post 8vo, 10s. 6d.

Grimm's Greek-English Lexicon of the New Testament. Translated, Revised, and Enlarged by Joseph H. Thayer, D.D. Demy 4to, 36s.

Guyot (Arnold, LL.D.)—Creation; or, The Biblical Cosmogony in the Light of Modern Science. With Illustrations. Crown 8vo, 5s. 6d.

Hagenbach (Dr. K. R.)—History of Doctrines. 3 vols. 8vo, 31s. 6d.
—— History of the Reformation. 2 vols. 8vo, 21s.

Halcombe (Rev. J. J., M.A.)—What Think Ye of the Gospels? A Handbook of Gospel Study. 8vo, 3s. 6d.

Hall (Newman, D.D.)—The Lord's Prayer. Third Edition, crown 8vo, 4s. 6d.
—— Gethsemane; or, Leaves of Healing from the Garden of Grief. Second Edition, crown 8vo, 4s.
—— Divine Brotherhood. Third Edition, crown 8vo, 4s.

Hamilton (T., D.D.)—Beyond the Stars; or, Heaven, its Inhabitants, Occupations, and Life. Third Edition, crown 8vo, 3s. 6d.

Harless (Dr. C. A.)—System of Christian Ethics. 8vo, 10s. 6d.

Harris (S., D.D.)—God the Creator and Lord of All. Two vols. post 8vo, 16s.

Haupt (Erich)—The First Epistle of St. John. 8vo, 10s. 6d.

Hävernick (H. A. Ch.)—Introduction to Old Testament. 10s. 6d.

Heard (Rev. J. B., M.A.)—The Tripartite Nature of Man—Spirit, Soul, and Body. Fifth Edition, crown 8vo, 6s.
—— Old and New Theology. A Constructive Critique. Cr. 8vo, 6s.
—— Alexandrian and Carthaginian Theology contrasted. The Hulsean Lectures, 1892-93. Crown 8vo, 6s.

Hefele (Bishop)—A History of the Councils of the Church. Vol. I., to A.D. 325. Vol. II., A.D. 326 to 429. Vol. III., A.D. 431 to the close of the Council of Chalcedon, 451. Vol. IV., A.D. 451 to 680. Vol. V., A.D. 626 to 787. 8vo, 12s. each.

Hengstenberg (Professor)—Commentary on Psalms, 3 vols. 8vo, 33s.; Ecclesiastes, etc., 8vo, 9s.; Ezekiel, 8vo, 10s. 6d.; The Genuineness of Daniel, etc., 8vo, 12s.; History of the Kingdom of God, 2 vols. 8vo, 21s.; Christology of the Old Testament, 4 vols. 21s. net; St. John's Gospel, 2 vols. 8vo, 21s.

⁎ Any Four Volumes at the original Subscription price of 21s. net.

Herkless (Prof. J., D.D.)—Francis and Dominic. Crown 8vo, 3s.

Herzog—Encyclopædia of Living Divines, etc., of all Denominations in Europe and America. (*Supplement to Herzog's Encyclopædia.*) Imp. 8vo, 8s.

Hill (Rev. J. Hamlyn, D.D.)—The Earliest Life of Christ ever Compiled from the Four Gospels: Being 'The Diatessaron of Tatian' Literally Translated from the Arabic Version, and containing the Four Gospels woven into one Story. With an Historical and Critical Introduction, Notes, and Appendix. 8vo, 10s. 6d.
—— St. Ephraem the Syrian. 8vo, 7s. 6d.

Hodgson (Principal J. M., M.A., D.Sc., D.D.)—Theologia Pectoris: Outlines of Religious Faith and Doctrine. Crown 8vo, 3s. 6d.

Hutchison (John, D.D.)—Commentary on Thessalonians. 8vo, 9s.
—— Commentary on Philippians. 8vo, 7s. 6d.
—— Our Lord's Signs in St. John's Gospel. Demy 8vo, 7s. 6d.

Innes (A. D., M.A.)—CRANMER AND THE ENGLISH REFORMATION. Crown 8vo, 3s.

Innes (A. Taylor)—THE TRIAL OF JESUS CHRIST. In its Legal Aspect. Post 8vo, 2s. 6d.

International Critical Commentary.
- DRIVER (Prof. S. R., D.D.)—Deuteronomy. 12s.
- MOORE (Prof. G. F., D.D.)—Judges. 12s.
- SMITH (Prof. H. P., D.D.)—Samuel. 12s.
- TOY (Prof. C. H., D.D.)—Proverbs. 12s.
- GOULD (Prof. E. P., D.D.)—St. Mark. 10s. 6d.
- PLUMMER (ALFRED, D.D.)—St. Luke. 12s.
- SANDAY (Prof. W., D.D.) and HEADLAM (A. C., B.D.)—Romans. 12s.
- ABBOTT (Prof. T. K., B.D., D.Lit.)—Ephesians and Colossians. 10s. 6d.
- VINCENT (Prof. M. R., D.D.)—Philippians and Philemon. 8s. 6d.
- BIGG Prof. C., D.D.)—St. Peter and St. Jude. 10s. 6d.

For List of future Volumes see p. 15.

International Theological Library.
- DRIVER (Prof. S. R., D.D.)—An Introduction to the Literature of the Old Testament. 12s.
- SMYTH (NEWMAN, D.D.)—Christian Ethics. 10s. 6d.
- BRUCE (Prof. A. B., D.D.)—Apologetics. 10s. 6d.
- FISHER (Prof. G. P., D.D., LL.D.)—History of Christian Doctrine. 12s.
- ALLEN (Prof. A. V. G., D.D.)—Christian Institutions. 12s.
- McGIFFERT (Prof. A. C., Ph.D.)—The Apostolic Age. 12s.
- GLADDEN (Washington, D.D.)—The Christian Pastor. 10s. 6d.
- STEVENS (Prof. G. B., D.D.)—The Theology of the New Testament. 12s.
- RAINY (Prin. R.)—The Ancient Catholic Church. 12s.

For List of future Volumes see p. 14.

Janet (Paul)—FINAL CAUSES. Second Edition, demy 8vo, 12s.
——— THE THEORY OF MORALS. Demy 8vo, 10s. 6d.

Johnstone (P. De Lacy, M.A.)—MUHAMMAD AND HIS POWER. 3s.

Johnstone (Prof. R., D.D.)—COMMENTARY ON 1ST PETER. 8vo, 10s. 6d.

Jones (E. E. C.)—ELEMENTS OF LOGIC. 8vo, 7s. 6d.

Jouffroy—PHILOSOPHICAL ESSAYS. Fcap. 8vo, 5s.

Kaftan (Prof. J., D.D.)—THE TRUTH OF THE CHRISTIAN RELIGION. *Authorised Translation.* 2 vols. 8vo, 16s. net.

Kant—THE METAPHYSIC OF ETHICS. Crown 8vo, 6s.
——— PHILOSOPHY OF LAW. Trans. by W. HASTIE, D.D. Cr. 8vo, 5s.
——— PRINCIPLES OF POLITICS, ETC. Crown 8vo, 2s. 6d.

Keil (Prof.)—PENTATEUCH, 3 vols. 8vo, 31s. 6d.; JOSHUA, JUDGES, AND RUTH, 8vo, 10s. 6d.; SAMUEL, 8vo, 10s. 6d.; KINGS, 8vo, 10s. 6d.; CHRONICLES, 8vo, 10s. 6d.; EZRA, NEHEMIAH, ESTHER, 8vo, 10s. 6d.; JEREMIAH, 2 vols. 8vo, 21s.; EZEKIEL, 2 vols. 8vo, 21s.; DANIEL, 8vo, 10s. 6d.; MINOR PROPHETS, 2 vols. 8vo, 21s.; INTRODUCTION TO THE CANONICAL SCRIPTURES OF THE OLD TESTAMENT, 2 vols. 8vo, 21s.; HANDBOOK OF BIBLICAL ARCHÆOLOGY, 2 vols. 8vo, 21s.

*** Any Four Volumes at the original Subscription price of 21s. net.

Keymer (Rev. N., M.A.)—NOTES ON GENESIS. Crown 8vo, 1s. 6d.

Kidd (James, D.D.)—MORALITY AND RELIGION. 8vo, 10s. 6d.

Killen (Prof.)—THE FRAMEWORK OF THE CHURCH. 8vo, 9s.
——— THE OLD CATHOLIC CHURCH. 8vo, 9s.
——— THE IGNATIAN EPISTLES ENTIRELY SPURIOUS. Cr. 8vo, 2s. 6d.

Kilpatrick (Prof. T. B., D.D.)—CHRISTIAN CHARACTER. 2s. 6d.

König (Dr. Ed.)—The Exiles' Book of Consolation (Deutero-Isaiah). Crown 8vo, 3s. 6d.
König (Dr. F. E.)—The Religious History of Israel. Cr. 8vo, 3s. 6d.
Krause (F. C. F.)—The Ideal of Humanity. Crown 8vo, 3s.
Krummacher (Dr. F. W.)—The Suffering Saviour; or, Meditations on the Last Days of the Sufferings of Christ. Eighth Edition, crown 8vo, 6s.
—— David, the King of Israel. Second Edition, cr. 8vo, 6s.
—— Autobiography. Crown 8vo, 6s.
Kurtz (Prof.)—Handbook of Church History (from 1517). 8vo, 7s. 6d.
—— History of the Old Covenant. Three vols. 8vo, 31s. 6d.
Ladd (Prof. G. T.)—The Doctrine of Sacred Scripture: A Critical, Historical, and Dogmatic Inquiry into the Origin and Nature of the Old and New Testaments. Two vols. 8vo, 1600 pp., 24s.
Laidlaw (Prof. J., D.D.)—The Bible Doctrine of Man; or, The Anthropology and Psychology of Scripture. New Edition Revised and Rearranged, post 8vo, 7s. 6d.
Lane (Laura M.)—Life of Alexander Vinet. Crown 8vo, 7s. 6d.
Lange (J. P., D.D.)—The Life of our Lord Jesus Christ. Edited by Marcus Dods, D.D. 2nd Ed., in 4 vols. 8vo, price 28s. net.
—— Commentaries on the Old and New Testaments. Edited by Philip Schaff, D.D. Old Testament, 14 vols.; New Testament, 10 vols.; Apocrypha, 1 vol. Subscription price, net, 15s. each.
—— St. Matthew and St. Mark, 3 vols. 8vo, 31s. 6d.; St. Luke, 2 vols. 8vo, 18s.; St. John, 2 vols. 8vo, 21s.
*** Any Four Volumes at the original Subscription price of 21s. net.
Le Camus (É., Bishop of La Rochelle)—The Children of Nazareth. Fcap. 4to. 4s.
Lechler (Prof. G. V., D.D.)—The Apostolic and Post-Apostolic Times. Their Diversity and Unity in Life and Doctrine. 2 vols. cr. 8vo, 16s.
Lehmann (Pastor)—Scenes from the Life of Jesus. Cr. 8vo, 3s. 6d.
Lewis (Tayler, LL.D.)—The Six Days of Creation. Cr. 8vo, 7s. 6d.
Lilley (J. P., M.A.)—The Lord's Supper: Its Origin, Nature, and Use. Crown 8vo, 5s.
—— The Pastoral Epistles. 2s. 6d.
—— Principles of Protestantism. 2s. 6d.
Lillie (Arthur, M.A.)—Buddha and Buddhism. Crown 8vo, 3s.
Lindsay (Prof. T. M., D.D.)—Luther and the German Reformation. Crown 8vo, 3s.
Lisco (F. G.)—Parables of Jesus Explained. Fcap. 8vo, 5s.
Locke (Clinton, D.D.)—The Age of the Great Western Schism. (*Eras of Church History.*) 6s.
Lotze (Hermann)—Microcosmus: An Essay concerning Man and his relation to the World. Cheaper Edition, 2 vols. 8vo (1450 pp.), 24s.
Ludlow (J. M., D.D.)—The Age of the Crusades. (*Eras of Church History.*) 6s.
Luthardt, Kahnis, and Brückner—The Church. Crown 8vo, 5s.
Luthardt (Prof.)—St. John the Author of the Fourth Gospel. 7s. 6d.
—— Commentary on St. John's Gospel. 3 vols. 8vo, 31s. 6d.
—— History of Christian Ethics. 8vo, 10s. 6d.
—— Apologetic Lectures on the Fundamental (7 *Ed.*), Saving (5 *Ed.*), Moral Truths of Christianity (4 *Ed.*). 3 vols. cr. 8vo, 6s. each.

Macdonald—INTRODUCTION TO PENTATEUCH. Two vols. 8vo, 21s.
———— THE CREATION AND FALL. 8vo, 12s.
Macgregor (Rev. Jas., D.D.)—THE APOLOGY OF THE CHRISTIAN RELIGION. 8vo, 10s. 6d.
———— THE REVELATION AND THE RECORD: Essays on Matters of Previous Question in the Proof of Christianity. 8vo, 7s. 6d.
———— STUDIES IN THE HISTORY OF NEW TESTAMENT APOLOGETICS. 8vo, 7s. 6d.
Macgregor (Rev. G. H. C., M.A.)—SO GREAT SALVATION. Cr. 32mo, 1s.
Macpherson (Rev. John, M.A.)—COMMENTARY ON THE EPISTLE TO THE EPHESIANS. 8vo, 10s. 6d.
———— CHRISTIAN DOGMATICS. Post 8vo, 9s.
McCosh (James), Life of. 8vo, 9s.
McGiffert (Prof. A. C., Ph.D.)—HISTORY OF CHRISTIANITY IN THE APOSTOLIC AGE. (*International Theological Library.*) Post 8vo, 12s.
M'Hardy (G. D.D.)—SAVONAROLA. Crown 8vo, 3s.
M'Intosh (Rev. Hugh, M.A.)—IS CHRIST INFALLIBLE AND THE BIBLE TRUE? Second Edition, post 8vo, 9s.
M'Realsham (E. D.)—ROMANS DISSECTED. A Critical Analysis of the Epistle to the Romans. Crown 8vo, 2s.
Mair (A., D.D.)—STUDIES IN THE CHRISTIAN EVIDENCES. Third Edition, Revised and Enlarged, crown 8vo, 6s.
Martensen (Bishop)—CHRISTIAN DOGMATICS. 8vo, 10s. 6d.
———— CHRISTIAN ETHICS. (GENERAL — INDIVIDUAL — SOCIAL.) Three vols. 8vo, 10s. 6d. each.
Matheson (Geo., D.D.)—GROWTH OF THE SPIRIT OF CHRISTIANITY, from the First Century to the Dawn of the Lutheran Era. Two vols. 8vo, 21s.
Meyer (Dr.)—CRITICAL AND EXEGETICAL COMMENTARIES ON THE NEW TESTAMENT. Twenty vols. 8vo. *Subscription price,* £5, 5s. *net; selection of Four Volumes at Subscription price of* 21s.; *Non-Subscription price,* 10s. 6d. *each volume.*
ST. MATTHEW, 2 vols.; MARK AND LUKE, 2 vols.; ST. JOHN, 2 vols.; ACTS, 2 vols.; ROMANS, 2 vols.; CORINTHIANS, 2 vols.; GALATIANS, one vol.; EPHESIANS AND PHILEMON, one vol.; PHILIPPIANS AND COLOSSIANS, one vol.; THESSALONIANS (*Dr. Lünemann*), one vol.; THE PASTORAL EPISTLES (*Dr. Huther*), one vol.; HEBREWS (*Dr. Lünemann*), one vol.; ST. JAMES AND ST. JOHN'S EPISTLES (*Huther*), one vol.; PETER AND JUDE (*Dr. Huther*), one vol.
Michie (Charles, M.A.)—BIBLE WORDS AND PHRASES. 18mo, 1s.
Milligan (George, B.D.)—THE THEOLOGY OF THE EPISTLE TO THE HEBREWS. Post 8vo, 6s.
Milligan (Prof. W., D.D.)—THE RESURRECTION OF THE DEAD. Second Edition, crown 8vo, 4s. 6d.
Milligan (Prof. W., D.D.) and Moulton (W. F., D.D.)—COMMENTARY ON THE GOSPEL OF ST. JOHN. Imp. 8vo, 9s.
Moffatt (James, B.D.)—THE HISTORICAL NEW TESTAMENT. Second Edition, demy 8vo, 16s.
Monrad (Dr. D. G.)—THE WORLD OF PRAYER. Crown 8vo, 4s. 6d.
Moore (Prof. G. F., D.D.)—JUDGES. (*International Critical Commentary.*) Second Edition, post 8vo, 12s.
Morgan (J., D.D.)—SCRIPTURE TESTIMONY TO THE HOLY SPIRIT. 7s. 6d.
———— EXPOSITION OF THE FIRST EPISTLE OF JOHN. 8vo, 7s. 6d.

Moulton (W. F., D.D.) and Geden (A. S., M.A.)—A Concordance to the Greek Testament. Crown 4to, 26s. net, and 31s. 6d. net.

Muir (Sir W.)—Mohammedan Controversy, Etc. 8vo, 7s. 6d.

Müller (Dr. Julius)—The Christian Doctrine of Sin. 2 vols. 8vo, 21s.

Murphy (Professor)—Commentary on the Psalms. 8vo, 12s.

——— A Critical and Exegetical Commentary on Exodus. 9s.

Naville (Ernest)—The Problem of Evil. Crown 8vo, 4s. 6d.

——— The Christ. Translated by Rev. T. J. Després. Cr. 8vo, 4s. 6d.

——— Modern Physics. Crown 8vo, 5s.

Neander (Dr.)—Church History. Eight vols. 8vo, £2, 2s. net.

Nicoll (W. Robertson, M.A., LL.D.)—The Incarnate Saviour. Cheap Edition, price 3s. 6d.

Novalis—Hymns and Thoughts on Religion. Crown 8vo, 4s.

Oehler (Prof.)—Theology of the Old Testament. 2 vols. 8vo, 21s.

Olshausen (Dr. H.)—Biblical Commentary on the Gospels and Acts. Four vols., 21s. net. Crown 8vo Edition, four vols., 24s.

——— Romans, one vol. 8vo, 10s. 6d.; Corinthians, one vol. 8vo, 9s.; Philippians, Titus, and First Timothy, one vol. 8vo, 10s. 6d.

Oosterzee (Dr. Van)—The Year of Salvation. 2 vols. 8vo, 6s. each.

——— Moses: A Biblical Study. Crown 8vo, 6s.

Orelli (Dr. C. von)—Old Testament Prophecy; Commentary on Isaiah; Jeremiah; The Twelve Minor Prophets. 4 vols. Subscription price, 21s. net; separate vols., 10s. 6d. each.

Owen (Dr. John)—Works. *Best and only Complete Edition.* Edited by Rev. Dr. Goold. Twenty-four vols. 8vo, Subscription price, £4, 4s. The '*Hebrews*' may be had separately, in seven vols., £2, 2s. net.

Palestine, Map of. Edited by J. G. Bartholomew, F.R.G.S., and Prof. G. A. Smith, M.D., D.D. With complete Index. Scale—4 Miles to an Inch.

Philippi (F. A.)—Commentary on the Romans. Two vols. 8vo, 21s.

Piper—Lives of Leaders of Church Universal. Two vols. 8vo, 21s.

Popular Commentary on the New Testament. Edited by Philip Schaff, D.D. With Illustrations and Maps. Vol. I.—The Synoptical Gospels. Vol. II.—St. John's Gospel, and the Acts of the Apostles. Vol. III.—Romans to Philemon. Vol. IV.—Hebrews to Revelation. In four vols. imperial 8vo, 12s. 6d. each.

Plummer (Alfred, D.D.)—St. Luke. (*International Critical Commentary.*) Second Edition, post 8vo, 12s.

Pressensé (Edward de)—The Redeemer: Discourses. Crown 8vo, 6s.

Pünjer (Bernhard)—History of the Christian Philosophy of Religion from the Reformation to Kant. 8vo, 16s.

Räbiger (Prof.)—Encyclopædia of Theology. Two vols. 8vo, 21s.

Rainy (Principal)—Delivery and Development of Christian Doctrine. 8vo, 10s. 6d.

——— The Ancient Catholic Church. (*International Theological Library.*) Post 8vo, 12s.

Reusch (Prof.)—Nature and the Bible: Lectures on the Mosaic History of Creation in relation to Natural Science. Two vols. 8vo, 21s.

Reuss (Professor)—History of the Sacred Scriptures of the New Testament. 640 pp. 8vo, 15s.

Riehm (Dr. E.)—MESSIANIC PROPHECY. New Edition. Post 8vo, 7s. 6d.
Ritschl (Albrecht, D.D.)—THE CHRISTIAN DOCTRINE OF JUSTIFICATION AND RECONCILIATION. 8vo, 14s.
Ritter (Carl)—COMPARATIVE GEOGRAPHY OF PALESTINE. 4 vols. 8vo, 21s.
Robinson (Rev. S., D.D.)—DISCOURSES ON REDEMPTION. 8vo, 7s. 6d.
Robinson (E., D.D.)—GREEK AND ENG. LEXICON OF THE N. TEST. 8vo, 9s.
Rooke (T. G., B.A.)—INSPIRATION, and other Lectures. 8vo, 7s. 6d.
Ross (C.)—OUR FATHER'S KINGDOM. Crown 8vo, 2s. 6d.
Rothe (Prof.)—SERMONS FOR THE CHRISTIAN YEAR. Cr. 8vo, 4s. 6d.
Saisset—MANUAL OF MODERN PANTHEISM. Two vols. 8vo, 10s. 6d.
Salmond (Princ. S. D. F., D.D.)—THE CHRISTIAN DOCTRINE OF IMMORTALITY. New Edition, post 8vo, 9s.
Sanday (Prof. W., D.D.) and Headlam (A. C., B.D.)—ROMANS. (*International Critical Commentary.*) Third Edition, post 8vo, 12s.
Sartorius (Dr. E.)—DOCTRINE OF DIVINE LOVE. 8vo, 10s. 6d.
Schaff (Professor)—HISTORY OF THE CHRISTIAN CHURCH. (New Edition, thoroughly Revised and Enlarged.) Six 'Divisions,' in 2 vols. each, extra 8vo.
  1. APOSTOLIC CHRISTIANITY, A.D. 1–100, 2 vols. 21s. 2. ANTE-NICENE, A.D. 100–325, 2 vols., 21s. 3. NICENE AND POST-NICENE, A.D. 325–600, 2 vols., 21s. 4. MEDIÆVAL, A.D. 590–1073, 2 vols., 21s. (*Completion of this Period, 1073-1517, in preparation*). 5. THE SWISS REFORMATION, 2 vols., extra demy 8vo, 21s. 6. THE GERMAN REFORMATION, 2 vols., extra demy 8vo, 21s.
Schleiermacher's CHRISTMAS EVE. Crown 8vo, 2s.
Schubert (Prof. H. Von., D.D.)—THE GOSPEL OF ST. PETER. Synoptical Tables. With Translation and Critical Apparatus. 8vo, 1s. 6d. net.
Schultz (Hermann)—OLD TESTAMENT THEOLOGY. Two vols. 18s. net.
Schürer (Prof.)—HISTORY OF THE JEWISH PEOPLE. 5 vols. Subscription price, 26s. 3d. net.
  ** Index. In separate Volume. 2s. 6d. net.
Schwartzkopff (Dr. P.)—THE PROPHECIES OF JESUS CHRIST. Crown 8vo, 5s.
Scott (Jas., M.A., D.D.)—PRINCIPLES OF NEW TESTAMENT QUOTATION ESTABLISHED AND APPLIED TO BIBLICAL CRITICISM. Cr. 8vo, 2nd Edit., 4s.
Sell (K., D.D.)—THE CHURCH IN THE MIRROR OF HISTORY. Cr. 8vo, 3/6.
Shedd—HISTORY OF CHRISTIAN DOCTRINE. Two vols. 8vo, 21s.
—— SERMONS TO THE NATURAL MAN. 8vo, 7s. 6d.
—— SERMONS TO THE SPIRITUAL MAN. 8vo, 7s. 6d.
—— DOGMATIC THEOLOGY. Three vols. ex. 8vo, 37s. 6d.
Sime (James, M.A.)—WILLIAM HERSCHEL AND HIS WORK. Cr. 8vo, 3s.
Simon (Prof.)—THE BIBLE; An Outgrowth of Theocratic Life. Cr. 8vo, 4/6.
—— RECONCILIATION BY INCARNATION. Post 8vo, 7s. 6d.
Skene-Bickell—THE LORD'S SUPPER & THE PASSOVER RITUAL. 8vo, 5s.
Smeaton (Oliphant, M.A.)—THE MEDICI AND THE ITALIAN RENAISSANCE. 3s.
Smeaton (Professor)—DOCTRINE OF THE HOLY SPIRIT. 2nd Ed., 8vo, 9s.
Smith (Prof. H. P., D.D.)—I. AND II. SAMUEL. (*International Critical Commentary.*) Post 8vo, 12s.

Smith (Professor Thos., D.D.)—MEDIÆVAL MISSIONS. Cr. 8vo, 4s. 6d.

Smyth (John, M.A., D.Ph.)—TRUTH AND REALITY. Crown 8vo, 4s.

Smyth (Newman, D.D.)—CHRISTIAN ETHICS. (*International Theological Library.*) Third Edition, post 8vo, 10s. 6d.

Snell (F. J., M.A.)—WESLEY AND METHODISM. Crown 8vo, 3s.

Somerville (Rev. D., D.D.)—ST. PAUL'S CONCEPTION OF CHRIST. 9s.

Stählin (Leonh.)—KANT, LOTZE, AND RITSCHL. 8vo, 9s.

Stalker (Jas., D.D.)—LIFE OF CHRIST. Large Type Ed., cr. 8vo, 3s. 6d.

—— LIFE OF ST. PAUL. Large Type Edition, crown 8vo, 3s. 6d.

Stanton (V. H., D.D.)—THE JEWISH AND THE CHRISTIAN MESSIAH. A Study in the Earliest History of Christianity. 8vo, 10s. 6d.

Stead (F. H.)—THE KINGDOM OF GOD. 1s. 6d.

Steinmeyer (Dr. F. L.)—THE MIRACLES OF OUR LORD. 8vo, 7s. 6d.

—— THE HISTORY OF THE PASSION AND RESURRECTION OF OUR LORD, considered in the Light of Modern Criticism. 8vo, 10s. 6d.

Stevens (Prof. G. B., D.D.)—THE THEOLOGY OF THE NEW TESTAMENT. (*International Theological Library.*) Post 8vo, 12s.

Stevenson (Mrs.)—THE SYMBOLIC PARABLES. Crown 8vo, 3s. 6d.

Steward (Rev. G.)—MEDIATORIAL SOVEREIGNTY. Two vols. 8vo, 21s.

—— THE ARGUMENT OF THE EPISTLE TO THE HEBREWS. 8vo, 10s. 6d.

Stier (Dr. Rudolph)—ON THE WORDS OF THE LORD JESUS. Eight vols. 8vo, Subscription price of £2, 2s. Separate volumes, price 10s. 6d.

—— THE WORDS OF THE RISEN SAVIOUR, AND COMMENTARY ON THE EPISTLE OF ST. JAMES. 8vo, 10s. 6d.

—— THE WORDS OF THE APOSTLES EXPOUNDED. 8vo, 10s. 6d.

Stirling (Dr. J. Hutchison)—PHILOSOPHY AND THEOLOGY. Post 8vo, 9s.

—— DARWINIANISM: Workmen and Work. Post 8vo, 10s. 6d.

—— WHAT *IS* THOUGHT? 8vo, 10s. 6d.

Tholuck (Prof.)—THE EPISTLE TO THE ROMANS. Two vols. fcap. 8vo, 8s.

Thomson (J. E. H., D.D.)—BOOKS WHICH INFLUENCED OUR LORD AND HIS APOSTLES. 8vo, 10s. 6d.

Thomson (Rev. E. A.)—MEMORIALS OF A MINISTRY. Crown 8vo, 5s.

Tophel (Pastor G.)—THE WORK OF THE HOLY SPIRIT. Cr. 8vo, 2s. 6d.

Toy (Prof. C. H., D.D.)—PROVERBS. (*International Critical Commentary.*) Post 8vo, 12s.

Troup (Rev. G. Elmslie, M.A.)—WORDS TO YOUNG CHRISTIANS: Being Addresses to Young Communicants. On antique laid paper, chaste binding, fcap. 8vo, 4s. 6d.

Uhlhorn (G.)—CHRISTIAN CHARITY IN THE ANCIENT CHURCH. Cr. 8vo, 6s.

Ullmann (Dr. Carl)—REFORMERS BEFORE THE REFORMATION, principally in Germany and the Netherlands. Two vols. 8vo, 21s.

Urwick (W., M.A.)—THE SERVANT OF JEHOVAH: A Commentary upon Isaiah lii. 13-liii. 12; with Dissertations upon Isaiah xl.-lxvi. 8vo, 3s.

Vinet (Life and Writings of). By L. M. LANE. Crown 8vo, 7s. 6d.

Vincent (Prof. M. R., D.D.)—THE AGE OF HILDEBRAND. (*Eras of Church History.*) 6s.

—— PHILIPPIANS AND PHILEMON. (*International Critical Commentary.*) Post 8vo, 8s. 6d.

Walker (James, of Carnwath)—ESSAYS, PAPERS, AND SERMONS. Post 8vo, 6s.

Walker (J., D.D.)—THEOLOGY AND THEOLOGIANS OF SCOTLAND. New Edition, crown 8vo, 3s. 6d.

Walker (Prof. W., D.D.)—THE PROTESTANT REFORMATION. (*Eras of Church History.*) 6s.

Walker (Rev. W. L.)—THE SPIRIT AND THE INCARNATION. Second Edition, 8vo, 9s.

Warfield (B. B., D.D.)—THE RIGHT OF SYSTEMATIC THEOLOGY. Crown 8vo, 2s.

Waterman (L., D.D.)—THE POST-APOSTOLIC AGE. (*Eras of Church History.*) 6s.

Watt (W. A., M.A., D.Ph.)—THE THEORY OF CONTRACT IN ITS SOCIAL LIGHT. 8vo, 3s.

—— A STUDY OF SOCIAL MORALITY. Post 8vo, 6s.

Watts (Professor)—THE NEWER CRITICISM AND THE ANALOGY OF THE FAITH. Third Edition, crown 8vo, 5s.

—— THE REIGN OF CAUSALITY: A Vindication of the Scientific Principle of Telic Causal Efficiency. Crown 8vo, 6s.

—— THE NEW APOLOGETIC. Crown 8vo, 6s.

Weir (J. F., M.A.)—THE WAY: THE NATURE AND MEANS OF SALVATION. Ex. crown 8vo, 6s. 6d.

Weiss (Prof.)—BIBLICAL THEOLOGY OF NEW TESTAMENT. 2 vols. 8vo, 21s.

—— LIFE OF CHRIST. Three vols. 8vo, 31s. 6d.

Welch (Rev. A. C., B.D.)—ANSELM AND HIS WORK. 3s.

Wells (Prof. C. L.)—THE AGE OF CHARLEMAGNE. (*Eras of the Christian Church.*) 6s.

Wendt (H. H., D.D.)—THE TEACHING OF JESUS. 2 vols. 8vo, 21s.

Wenley (R. M.)—CONTEMPORARY THEOLOGY AND THEISM. Crown 8vo, 4s. 6d.

White (Rev. M.)—SYMBOLICAL NUMBERS OF SCRIPTURE. Cr. 8vo, 4s.

Williams (E. F., D.D.)—CHRISTIAN LIFE IN GERMANY. Crown 8vo, 5s.

Wilson (S. Law, D.D.)—THE THEOLOGY OF MODERN LITERATURE. Post 8vo, 7s. 6d.

Winer (Dr. G. B.)—A TREATISE ON THE GRAMMAR OF NEW TESTAMENT GREEK, regarded as the Basis of New Testament Exegesis. Third Edition, edited by W. F. MOULTON, D.D. Ninth English Edition, 8vo, 15s.

Witherow (Prof. T., D.D.)—THE FORM OF THE CHRISTIAN TEMPLE. 8vo, 10/6.

Woods (F. H., B.D.)—THE HOPE OF ISRAEL. Crown 8vo, 3s. 6d.

Workman (Prof. G. C.)—THE TEXT OF JEREMIAH; or, A Critical Investigation of the Greek and Hebrew, etc. Post 8vo, 9s.

Wright (C. H., D.D.)—BIBLICAL ESSAYS. Crown 8vo, 5s.

THE INTERNATIONAL THEOLOGICAL LIBRARY.

The following eminent Scholars have contributed, or are engaged upon, the Volumes named:—

An Introduction to the Literature of the Old Testament.	By S. R. Driver, D.D., Regius Professor of Hebrew, and Canon of Christ Church, Oxford. [*Seventh Edition.* 12s.
Christian Ethics.	By Newman Smyth, D.D., Pastor of the First Congregational Church, New Haven, Conn. [*Third Edition.* 10s. 6d.
Apologetics.	By the late A. B. Bruce, D.D., Professor of New Testament Exegesis, Free Church College, Glasgow. [*Third Edition.* 10s. 6d.
History of Christian Doctrine.	By G. P. Fisher, D.D., LL.D., Professor of Ecclesiastical History, Yale University, New Haven, Conn. [*Second Edition.* 12s.
A History of Christianity in the Apostolic Age.	By Arthur Cushman McGiffert, Ph.D., D.D., Professor of Church History, Union Theological Seminary, New York. [12s.
Christian Institutions.	By A. V. G. Allen, D.D., Professor of Ecclesiastical History, Episcopal Theological School, Cambridge, Mass. [12s.
The Christian Pastor.	By Washington Gladden, D.D., Pastor of Congregational Church, Columbus, Ohio. [10s. 6d.
Theology of the New Testament.	By George B. Stevens, Ph.D., D.D., Professor of Systematic Theology in Yale University, U.S.A. [12s.
The Ancient Catholic Church.	By Robert Rainy, D.D., Principal of The New College, Edinburgh. 12s.
Theology of the Old Testament.	By A. B. Davidson, D.D., LL.D., Professor of Hebrew, The New College, Edinburgh.
The Literature of the New Testament.	By S. D. F. Salmond, D.D., Principal, and Professor of Systematic Theology and New Testament Exegesis, United Free Church College, Aberdeen.
Old Testament History.	By H. P. Smith, D.D., late Professor of Biblical History and Interpretation, Amherst College, U.S.A.
Canon and Text of the New Testament.	By Caspar René Gregory, Ph.D., Professor in the University of Leipzig.
The Latin Church.	By Archibald Robertson, D.D., Principal of King's College, London.
Encyclopædia.	By C. A. Briggs, D.D., Professor of Biblical Theology, Union Theological Seminary, New York.
Contemporary History of the Old Testament.	By Francis Brown, D.D., Professor of Hebrew and Cognate Languages, Union Theological Seminary, New York.
Contemporary History of the New Testament.	By Frank C. Porter, Ph.D., Yale University, New Haven, Conn.
Philosophy of Religion.	By Robert Flint, D.D., LL.D., Professor of Divinity in the University of Edinburgh.
The Study of the Old Testament.	By the Right Rev. H. E. Ryle, D.D., Lord Bishop of Exeter.
Rabbinical Literature.	By S. Schechter, M.A., Reader in Talmudic in the University of Cambridge.
The Life of Christ.	By William Sanday, D.D., LL.D., Lady Margaret Professor of Divinity, and Canon of Christ Church, Oxford.
The Christian Preacher.	By John Watson, D.D. ('Ian Maclaren'), Sefton Park Presbyterian Church of England, Liverpool.

THE INTERNATIONAL CRITICAL COMMENTARY.

TEN VOLUMES NOW READY, VIZ.:—

Deuteronomy, Judges, I. and II. Samuel, Proverbs, S. Mark, S. Luke, Romans, Ephesians and Colossians, Philippians and Philemon, S. Peter and S. Jude.

The following other Volumes are in course of preparation:—

THE OLD TESTAMENT.

Genesis.	T. K. CHEYNE, D.D., Oriel Professor of the Interpretation of Holy Scripture, Oxford, and Canon of Rochester.
Exodus.	A. R. S. KENNEDY, D.D., Professor of Hebrew, University of Edinburgh.
Leviticus.	J. F. STENNING, M.A., Fellow of Wadham College, Oxford; and the Rev. H. A. White, M.A., Fellow of New College, Oxford.
Numbers.	G. BUCHANAN GRAY, M.A., Lecturer in Hebrew, Mansfield College, Oxford.
Joshua.	GEORGE ADAM SMITH, D.D., Professor of Hebrew, United Free Church College, Glasgow.
Kings.	FRANCIS BROWN, D.D., Professor of Hebrew and Cognate Languages, Union Theological Seminary, New York.
Isaiah.	A. B. DAVIDSON, D.D., LL.D., Professor of Hebrew, New College, Edinburgh.
Jeremiah.	A. F. KIRKPATRICK, D.D., Regius Professor of Hebrew, and Fellow of Trinity College, Cambridge.
Minor Prophets.	W. R. HARPER, Ph.D., President of Chicago University.
Psalms.	C. A. BRIGGS, D.D., Edward Robinson Professor of Biblical Theology, Union Theological Seminary, New York.
Job.	S. R. DRIVER, D.D., Regius Professor of Hebrew, Oxford.
Daniel.	Rev. JOHN P. PETERS, Ph.D., late Professor of Hebrew, P. E. Divinity School, Philadelphia, now Rector of St. Michael's Church, New York City.
Ezra and Nehemiah.	Rev. L. W. BATTEN, Ph.D., Professor of Hebrew, P. E. Divinity School, Philadelphia.
Chronicles.	EDWARD L. CURTIS, D.D., Professor of Hebrew, Yale University, New Haven, Conn.

THE NEW TESTAMENT.

Synopsis of the Four Gospels.	W. SANDAY, D.D., LL.D., Lady Margaret Professor of Divinity, Oxford; and Rev. W. C. ALLEN, M.A., Exeter College, Oxford.
Matthew.	Rev. WILLOUGHBY C. ALLEN, M.A., Exeter College, Fellow, and Lecturer in Theology and Hebrew, Exeter College, Oxford.
Acts.	FREDERICK H. CHASE, D.D., Christ's College, Cambridge.
Corinthians.	ARCH. ROBERTSON, D.D., Principal of King's College, London.
Galatians.	Rev. ERNEST D. BURTON, A.B., Professor of New Testament Literature, University of Chicago.
The Pastoral Epistles.	WALTER LOCK, D.D., Dean Ireland Professor of Exegesis, Oxford.
Hebrews.	E. C. S. GIBSON, M.A., Professor, Hawarden College, Chester.
James.	Rev. JAMES H. ROPES, A.B., Instructor in New Testament Criticism in Harvard University.
The Johannine Epistles.	S. D. F. SALMOND, D.D., Principal, United Free Church College, Aberdeen.
Revelation.	Rev. H. CALDWELL, D.D., Trinity College, Dublin.

Other engagements will be announced shortly.

The World's Epoch-Makers

Edited by OLIPHANT SMEATON.

Messrs. T. & T. Clark have much pleasure in announcing that they have commenced the publication of an important new Series, under the above title.

The following Volumes have now been issued:—

Buddha and Buddhism. By Arthur Lillie, M.A.

Luther and the German Reformation. By Professor T. M. Lindsay, D.D.

Wesley and Methodism. By F. J. Snell, M.A.

Cranmer and the English Reformation. By A. D. Innes, M.A.

William Herschel and his Work. By James Sime, M.A.

Francis and Dominic. By Professor J. Herkless, D.D.

Savonarola. By G. M'Hardy, D.D.

Anselm and his Work. By Rev. A. C. Welch, B.D.

The Medici and the Italian Renaissance. By Oliphant Smeaton, M.A., Edinburgh.

Origen and Greek Patristic Theology. By Rev. W. Fairweather, M.A.

Muhammad and his Power. By P. De Lacy Johnstone, M.A.(Oxon.).

The following have also been arranged for:—

Socrates. By Rev. J. T. Forbes, M.A., Glasgow.

Plato. By Professor D. G. Ritchie, M.A., University of St. Andrews.

Marcus Aurelius and the Later Stoics. By F. W. Bussell, D.D., Vice-Principal of Brasenose College, Oxford.

Augustine and Latin Patristic Theology. By Professor B. B. Warfield, D.D., Princeton.

Scotus Erigena and his Epoch. By Professor R. Latta, Ph.D., D.Sc., University of Aberdeen.

Wyclif and the Lollards. By Rev. J. C. Carrick, B.D.

The Two Bacons and Experimental Science. By Rev. W. J. Couper, M.A.

Calvin and the Reformed Theology. By Principal Salmond, D.D., U.F.C. College, Aberdeen.

Pascal and the Port Royalists. By Professor W. Clark, LL.D., D.C.L., Trinity College, Toronto.

Descartes, Spinoza, and the New Philosophy. By Professor J. Iverach, D.D., U.F.C. College, Aberdeen.

Lessing and the New Humanism. By Rev. A. P. Davidson, M.A.

Hume and his Influence on Philosophy and Theology. By Professor J. Orr, D.D., Glasgow.

Rousseau and Naturalism in Life and Thought. By Professor W. H. Hudson, M.A., Leland Stanford Junior University, California.

Kant and his Philosophical Revolution. By Professor R. M. Wenley, D.Sc., Ph.D., University of Michigan.

Schleiermacher and the Rejuvenescence of Theology. By Professor A. Martin, D.D., New College, Edinburgh.

Hegel and Hegelianism. By Professor R. Mackintosh, D.D., Lancashire Independent College, Manchester.

Newman and his Influence. By C. Sarolea, Ph.D., Litt. Doc., University of Edinburgh.

Published Price, THREE SHILLINGS per Volume.

Date Due

JAN 1 '50			
MAY 21 '57	DEC 9 '69		
MAY			
MAY 26			
MAY 26			
AUG 7			

L. B. Cat. No. 1137

3 5002 00075 7497

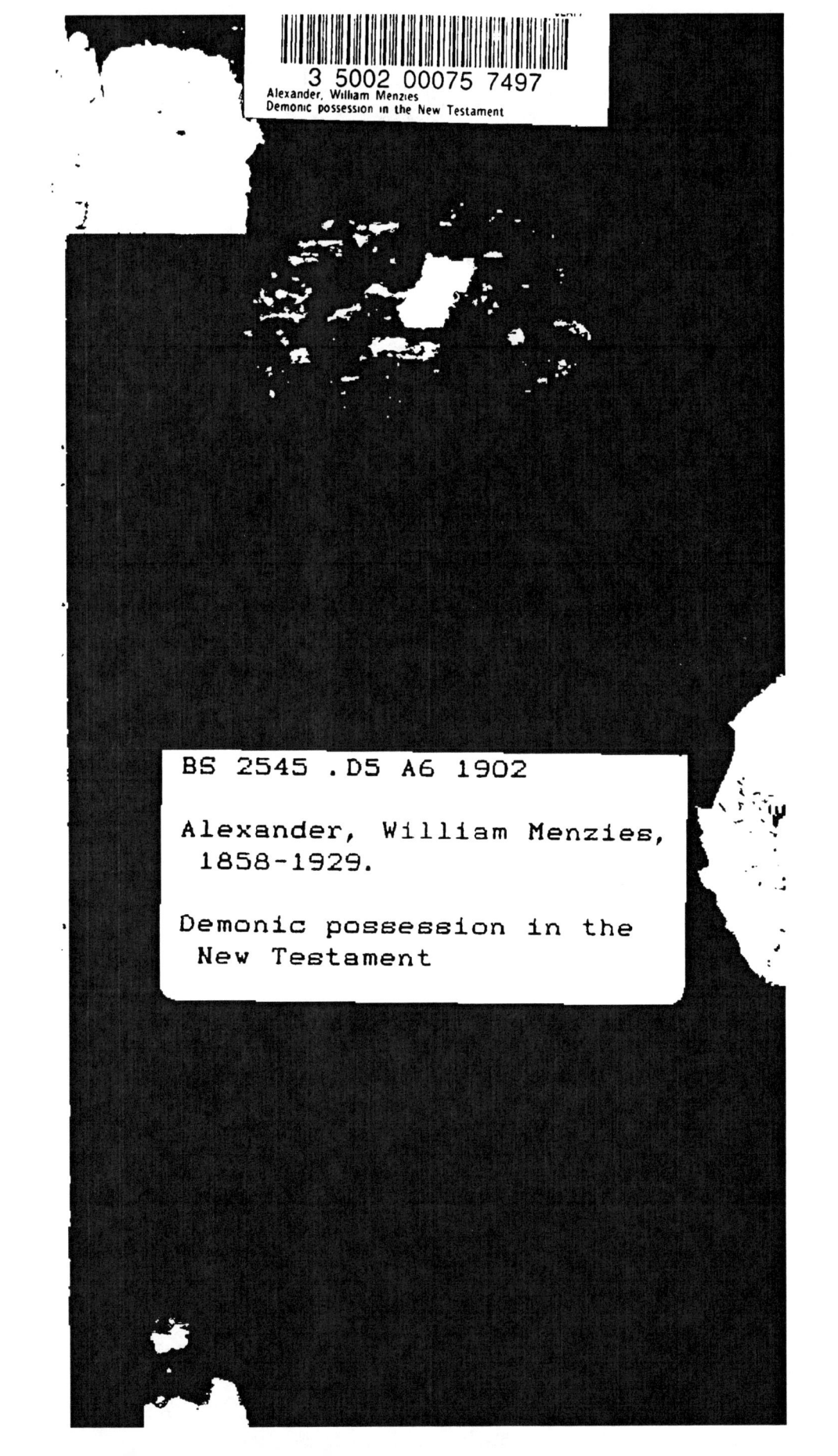

Alexander, William Menzies
Demonic possession in the New Testament

BS 2545 .D5 A6 1902

Alexander, William Menzies,
1858-1929.

Demonic possession in the
New Testament

CPSIA information can be obtained at www.ICGtesting.com
Printed in the USA
BVOW04s1720230415

397471BV00005B/51/P

9 781294 975458